God Bless You,
Buffalo Bill

God Bless You, Buffalo Bill

A Layman's Guide to History and the Western Film

Wayne Michael Sarf

Rutherford ● *Madison* ● *Teaneck*
Fairleigh Dickinson University Press
New York ● *Cornwall Books* ● *London*

Associated University Presses and Cornwall Books
4 Cornwall Drive
East Brunswick, N.J. 08816

Cornwall Books
27 Chancery Lane
London WC2A 1NF, England

Cornwall Books
Toronto M5E 1A7, Canada

Library of Congress Cataloging in Publication Data

Sarf, Wayne, 1957–
    God bless you, Buffalo Bill.

    Bibliography: p.
    Includes index.
    1. Western films—History and criticism.   I. Title.
PN1995.9.W4S27   791.43′09′093278   80-71118
ISBN 0-8453-4732-2 (Cornwall)   AACR2
ISBN 0-8386-3089-8 (F.D.)

Frontispiece: An example of "Pan-Indian" clothing at work. The caption accompanying this photo reads: "A native American applauds the action in Warner Bros 'Sergeant York' which had its premiere at the Astor Theatre. His Supreme Highness Prince Gusi Manco Huyana Supreme Inti Augui, last of the Incas, in full regalia." The regalia is that of a North American Plains tribesman. *(Movie Star News)*

Printed in the United States of America

. . . Yet to understand the West as somehow a joke comes a little closer to getting it straight.

—Leslie Fiedler, *The Return of the Vanishing American*

Contents

7

Preface

Though short films on recognizably "Western" subjects first appeared during the mid-1890s, the Western film proper, termed by Jack Nachbar "the single most important American story form of the twentieth century," might be said to have been born in 1903 with *The Great Train Robbery*, one of the earliest motion pictures to tell its story using basic cinematic editing techniques. What follows here is neither a history of the Western nor a comprehensive analysis of this oldest American genre as either art form or social document. It is instead an informal look at some of the ways in which the Old West differed from the West of film, and at some of the reasons behind them.

Such a work must of necessity be incomplete. As the most popular American setting for "historical" fiction, drama, and film, it is only natural that the Old West also become the most thoroughly distorted, and one cannot hope to deal adequately with everything that might merit inclusion. Indeed, whatever the degree of apparent "realism" involved or the intentions behind it—whether a film attempts to dramatize some past event, reflect current social concerns, provide a political or religious allegory, explore character relationships, or simply tell a good story—the Western must always distort "reality" simply because it is the product of artists and entertainers.

One may easily speak of a mythic West, but not, with any precision, of a single, rigidly defined "Western myth." The longing for a hero benefiting society through righteous violence brings forth lawmen-civilizers such as Bill Hickok and Wyatt Earp—and glorifies outlaws such as the James brothers. The untutored Indian serves as a hostile force to be overcome by courageous pioneers—and rides side by side with the wronged Noble Savage. The settlement of the West is a source of pride—and threatens to replace the natural virtues of the wilderness with civilized degeneracy. In emphasizing specifics of error and misrepresentation, I have made what I feel to be adequate references to the particular mythic influences at work; those seeking

9

more detailed studies may consult a variety of interesting books, for the Western can no longer be characterized as a critically neglected genre.

The Old West's value for those seeking entertainment and a refuge from the day-to-day world has never been limited to Americans; its appeal is universal. Yet with its violence, incredible achievements, anarchic individualism, and endurance in the face of adversity, this part of our history has given Americans more than simply an adventurous dream world or dramatic backdrop. It has also provided what has been termed our national epic, a substitute for an *Iliad* or *Aeneid* that serves as a young nation's heroic age and a reflection of that nation's values. "We need it," says historian C. L. Sonnichsen, and we probably do. But knowing something about the Old West will not destroy its mythic value, for as Sonnichsen also points out, many of us can live in both the "West That Was" and the "West That Wasn't" without apparent discomfort, even as we follow the insistent urge to reject unreality and seek out what truth we can.

Anyone who makes a habit of pointing out other writers' mistakes should be all the more aware of his own fallibility; therefore, all readers detecting errors of fact in this book are urged to report them to the author, who will do his best to find a scapegoat. At this point I would like to express my thanks to all who offered information, comments, and other assistance, including Dr. Robert Ready of Drew University for suggesting revisions in the first two chapters, Justin Griffin for advising me on the length of the manuscript and inspiring a footnote, George Babcock for providing research materials, Paul Herzfeld for arranging screenings, Marc Gaetani for an anecdote not used, Jo Bolt, Tom Williams, and especially Robin Mitchell for their casual comments on *Butch Cassidy and the Sundance Kid*, Howard French of *Guns and Ammo* magazine for his response to my queries, and last but not least my parents.

This book is dedicated to the late "Long-Haired" Steve Curtis, of Bristol, England, Western fan and author of the Western Gunfight wargame rules, who helped spark my obsession with the glorious Old West.

Wayne Michael Sarf
Riverdale, New Jersey

God Bless You,
Buffalo Bill

1
Blessed Are the Peacemakers
or What's Wrong with This Picture?

Telephone? This is 1870! The telephone hasn't been invented
yet!
                                            —GROUCHO MARX in *Go West* (1940)

Whatever you put there, they'll believe that's how it is.
                                            —IRVING THALBERG

Western films do not, of course, have a monopoly on anachronisms. But they are unique among period films in their sloppiness of historical reconstruction and almost universal failure to ensure any accuracy of physical detail. The phenomenon goes back to Edwin S. Porter's *The Great Train Robbery* (filmed in the wilds of New Jersey) and has persisted for over three quarters of a century, with the result that the physical appearance of any Western, whether the cheapest of "B" hoss operas or a lavishly budgeted Cinerama "epic" such as *How the West Was Won* (1962), will generally bear only an approximate resemblance to that of the historical period allegedly being simulated—and sometimes not even that. The same easily avoidable errors recur in film after film, ultimately impressing themselves on the public—not to mention the people who actually make such films—as bits of bona fide Western Americana.

There can be little doubt that the average moviegoer is willing to credit the physical realism of the West that appears on the screen, if not its other features. In the popular culture, the Hollywood visual image is that which dominates, and which has come to influence many other representations.

Children's toys, comic books, political cartoons, book-jacket illustrations—all mirror a Hollywood West seemingly regarded by its creators and perpetrators as authentic. Sometimes they appear almost smug about it, as in the 1973 science-fiction film *Westworld*. Early on we are informed that Westworld, an amusement park peopled by robots, is an "exact reproduction" of an 1880 frontier town. What it turns out to be is an exact reproduction of a typical backlot set, its fantasy-fulfilling automatons (including Yul Brynner dressed in his *Magnificent Seven* costume) issued familiar Western-movie props and clothes.

Westworld's self-confidence aside, it is clear that even many of those who direct such films merely assume that such trappings are authentic. This is made especially obvious by the way in which the same errors often occur even in films specifically intended to give a "realistic," as opposed to a mythological, view of the West, or those for which certain definite steps have been taken to further authenticity.

Let us consider John Ford's 1924 silent film *The Iron Horse*. Surely Ford, one of our greatest directors, cannot be dismissed as an uncaring hack—particularly not with respect to this film, which at the time of its production was the most ambitious and expensive project he had ever executed. And certainly it was not intended as a mere Wild West romance, for despite its somewhat melodramatic revenge plot *The Iron Horse* had epic ambitions and an inspiration rooted in a great historical event: the linking by rail of East and West. At times the primitive conditions of location filming resembled those endured in the railway's original construction, and though the two trains used in the final sequence were not, as the publicists claimed, those actually present at the driving of the golden spike in 1869, a serious effort was made to give the film an authentic appearance and atmosphere. But apparently Ford never bothered to find out whether the revolver in star George O'Brien's holster was historically correct or not.

It wasn't.

O'Brien's gun, which makes as good a starting point as any for the discussion of anachronisms, was a Colt single-action Army revolver, Model 1873—the fabled Colt "Peacemaker," usually produced in .45 caliber and possibly the most famous single handgun on earth. Now often known as "the Gun That Won the West," it achieved a popularity on the frontier never approached by that of any other handgun, and its legend endures to this day.

Unfortunately the legend has gotten so big that the Colt .45 Peacemaker, as the gun automatically associated with the Old West, is nearly always the one used in a Western whether or not that particular film is set during or after 1875, when the gun first became readily available to the general public. Seemingly indestructible, the Peacemaker can survive and triumph even in a pre-1875 story on which some research *has* been done.

For his 1937 epic *The Plainsman*, master showman Cecil B. De Mille, who prided himself on the extensive research undertaken for even the most fanciful of his historical sagas ("The compilation of research done for my latest work, *The Ten Commandments*, was honored by being published in book form by the University of Southern California under the title *Moses and Egypt*"), employed a team of six researchers who worked for months. Despite their efforts, almost everybody in the picture, which opens in the year 1865, carries a Peacemaker—all eighty-six pistols used supposedly having come from the director's own collection. The same thing happened in De Mille's 1939 railway saga *Union Pacific*, which, like Ford's *Iron Horse*, concluded in 1869 and for which considerable research data had been compiled. Since anyone interested might have gone to a public library and discovered the history and usage of the Peacemaker, it is possible that De Mille was aware of the mistake but reluctant to break with tradition.

Before 1836 there were, despite experiments made along this line for many years, no revolvers at all on the commercial market, except for several models of the unreliable and inaccurate "pepperbox," which featured a cluster of complete pistol barrels revolving around a central axis. Most people of that day rejected such newfangled contraptions altogether and stuck to their single- or double-barreled pistols or the shorter-ranged but more reliable fighting knife, which, unlike the quirky firearms of the age, never misfired and was a necessity of dress for many Southern gentlemen and frontiersmen (not to mention certain members of Congress, cautious of debates getting out of hand).

But, in that ill-fated year of the Alamo, young Samuel Colt produced in Paterson, New Jersey, the first clumsy specimens of his patented "revolving pistol," offering a cylinder with five (later six) loaded chambers rather than multiple barrels. These early pistols were of the cap-and-ball type: rather than slipping in self-contained brass cartridges, one had to fiddle with a loose charge of black powder, a lead ball or conical bullet, and a metal percussion cap for each chamber.

So Colt marketed his new pistol, the world did not beat a path to his door, and he did not become rich and famous. For some reason, hardly anyone seemed to lust after this marvelous device, which enabled its owner to kill five (later six) people all at once and from a safe distance. The army bought a few of Colt's pistols and some rifles built on the same principle[1] and emptied them into Florida's Seminole Indians, while the Texas Rangers got hold of some pistols and used them with spectacular success against the Comanche. But Colt still went broke in 1842, while the less expensive pepperbox became, for a time, the preferred arm of those desiring a multishot weapon. Only the Mexican War put him back in business, and he began production of an improved weapon in 1847. As public demand grew, other firms joined Colt in manufacturing revolvers. All of their guns were cap-and-ball until 1857, when a small, new firm called Smith and Wesson brought out a tiny .22 seven-shooter using brass cartridges loaded from the rear of the cylinder. Mark Twain would crack that "it took all seven to make a dose for an adult," but the

Clint Eastwood, as an ex-Confederate guerrilla in *The Outlaw Josey Wales*, displays a few of his cap-and-ball revolvers. In his hands are two 1847 Walker Colts, caliber .44, while the revolver stuck in his belt looks like a Colt 1860 Army .44. *(Movie Star News)*

firm was soon bringing out models in heavier calibers, their monopoly on this type of revolver being protected by patent until 1867. Cap-and-ball revolvers remained predominant, however, until the 1870s.

Such cap-and-ball guns are rarely seen in the Westerns where they would be appropriate, normally being replaced by the near-ubiquitous Peacemaker. Sometimes this makes no major difference. When, in Ford's *The Searchers* (1956), John Wayne shoots out a dead Indian's eyes, it really doesn't matter whether he uses a correct 1860 Army Colt or an anachronistic Peacemaker, since the end result would be the same in either case.[2] More annoying is a character who unleashes a hail of lead when by rights he should be able to fire only once before slowly reloading. This occurs with distressing frequency in such films as *The Comancheros* (1961) and *Lone Star* (1952), both set in pre-Annexation Texas, where any sort of revolver was extremely scarce, much less the Peacemakers John Wayne and Clark Gable handle so adroitly in their respective hero roles. This is the more serious type of anachronism, directly influencing the action of the film and not simply its decorative aspects.

Howard Hawks apparently believed that he was making such an error deliberately for his famous cattle-drive spectacular *Red River* (1948), which he shot in monochrome rather than the "garish" color then available in order to give it "a feeling of the period"; evidently convinced that revolvers were not in common use by the early 1850s (when his story begins), he nevertheless supplied them to his players. "I got a bunch of letters about using six-shooters," he explained in response to later criticism by *Red River* screenwriter Borden Chase, "but I didn't want to stop a scene to have a guy reload his gun before he could fire." There were actually more revolvers in use by that time than either Hawks or Chase seemed to believe, so perhaps the "six-shooters" of which the letters supposedly complained were really just the Peacemakers everyone was using.

One of the most serious cases of improper armament can be found in Tom *(Billy Jack)* Laughlin's 1975 *The Master Gunfighter*. This one ostensibly unfolds in an 1836 Mexican-ruled California, where there were, of course, no gunfighters—master, apprentice, or otherwise—simply because the revolvers which made such men possible hadn't been around long enough even for the lucky man who owned one to become very good at killing with it. Thus Laughlin (whose custom-made pistols carry *twelve* shots apiece) succeeded in inserting into his "lavish historical epic" not only anachronistic weaponry, but also an anachronistic hero who would have had no purpose in the film's supposed setting.

The *Los Angeles Times* called *The Master Gunfighter* "a splendid period re-creation."

The Winchester repeating rifle, which by some strange coincidence is often referred to as "the Gun That Won the West," has annoyingly enough also become a legend, with predictable results. The first model was produced in 1866, although it was preceded by a number of other multishot rifles and carbines (including its direct ancestor the Henry, which closely resembled it) as well as by single-shot breechloaders such as the immensely popular 1848 Sharps; until after the Civil War many Western riflemen were still making do with muzzle-loading guns, which might take half a minute or more to reload after each shot. Often Peacemaker and Winchester go wrongly, if somehow appropriately, together, as in *The Comancheros*, but not always; the Colt-armed Texans in *Lone Star*, for instance, all carry proper muzzle-loading long arms.

A similar lack of discrimination extends to most other Western guns, down to the small "stingy" pistols carried by gamblers, "soiled doves," and others in sleeve, pocket, or bosom. When the plot requires such a weapon a two-shot .41 Remington Double Derringer—a standard hideout gun well into the twentieth century and therefore, I imagine, somewhat "legendary" also—is usually provided. In one Civil War Western, the 1940 *Virginia City*, we find hero Errol Flynn staring down the barrels of a Remington Double held on him by a desperado who had previously tried to pass himself off as a gun salesman.

The unflappable Flynn coolly remarks that he'd *thought* that derringer looked a little too well-worn to be a display model. But when and how it could have received such hard usage is unknown, as production didn't begin until 1871, some six years after the stated time of the story.

The Gatling gun, originally intended as a humanitarian device (its inventor fancying that if weapons became sufficiently destructive warfare would be abolished), has come in for more than its share of hard misuse. Considering the number of films in which it plays a part, there must be something irresistibly attractive in the idea of mowing down expendable extras with this nineteenth-century machine gun—perhaps because it seems so much more "modern" than its setting, rather like the superscientific Victorian inventions of a Jules Verne story. In both *Red Tomahawk* (1967) and *The Gatling Gun* (1972), the screenwriters even prove they've done a bit of research by calling time out and having a soldier give, for no particular reason, a little sales talk detailing the history of the gun to us and to members of the cast. But in virtually all films the wrong type of gun (one of the later and more streamlined models) is employed, and there is a strong tendency to place the gun in the wrong place at the wrong time. There were, for instance, only a dozen Gatlings actually used in combat by the entire Union Army during the Civil War, all seeing action near Petersburg, Virginia; the gun was not *officially* adopted until 1866. So it seems rather extravagant for Sergio Leone, in his 1966 *The Good, the Bad and the Ugly (Il buono, il brutto e il cattivo)* to give his Yankees two or three of the weapons for a sideshow fight in New Mexico.

Due to the nearly universal adoption of standard West-winning guns, other weapons are rarely employed unless specifically called for in the script, such as the 1848 Colt Dragoon revolver lugged about by Kim Darby in *True Grit* (1969). But even when a particular weapon is called for, the right one doesn't always show up on screen: in Arthur Penn's fairly authentic-looking *The Missouri Breaks* (1976), Thomas McGuane's screenplay has rustler Jack Nicholson order someone to "hand over that bird's-head Colt." What he is supposed to have handed to him is a double-action revolver (capable of being fired simply by squeezing the trigger without first thumb-cocking the hammer) of a type which derived its nickname from the shape of its grips. What he gets instead is a single-action "hog-leg" Colt, specifically the same old boring Peacemaker.

More often a script calls for weapons which are totally unwarranted, as does Budd Boetticher's scenario for Don Siegel's *Two Mules for Sister Sara* (1971). This Mexican-based adventure had Clint Eastwood using much dynamite to blow up things and people, especially French troops propping up the regime of the Austrian emperor Maximilian—troops who had all withdrawn from Mexico by 1867, the same year the Swedish inventor Alfred Nobel patented the stuff and succeeded in selling eleven tons of it. In real life Clint would have used bulky black powder or volatile nitroglycerin to disintegrate his foes.

The low-slung, quick-draw holsters in which the average movie gunfighter wears his Peacemakers—they began showing up in Westerns with some frequency during the 1930s and became the favored style during the 1950s— owe their existence to Hollywood and were never used during what we would consider the heyday of the "gunfighter's West." They evolved from the authentically Western buscadero rig, in which the holster is not worn directly over the belt, but instead hangs from a strip of leather fitting into a slot cut into the belt. The original form of this rig came into use only around the turn of the century, and in any case resembled only vaguely the Hollywood gunbelts, which often employ a strip of leather so long that the revolver hangs almost to the knee from a fat, ugly swelling on the belt; this necessitates a leather thong tying the holster to the leg so it won't ride up when the gun is drawn. (Such a tie-down device was used very rarely in frontier days.)

Naturally the use of such holsters, sometimes steel-lined for additional smoothness of draw, has persisted largely because Westerns continue to copy one another more often than they copy the West. It is readily accepted partly because, as the most efficient holsters for a "fast draw, " they seem so right for the professional—so much so that in some films their use appears restricted to the more skilled *pistoleros*, leaving the nonprofessionals with standard belt holsters. One day I chanced to hear an actor on a television talk show exulting over the fact that for his he-man part in a made-in-Spain Western he had been "wearin' my holster down to my *knees!*" He clearly thought that this signified deadliness with one's artillery. But in fact the typical Western gun-wearer, who had to consider the most convenient method of packing a pistol that might be on his hip all day, appears to have worn his holster roughly at waist level or slightly lower. Anyone who needed a gun hanging anywhere around his knees would be instantly marked as inept.

In the early years of the revolver era even the man who *wanted* to wear his guns extremely low would have had some difficulty, since there were no gunbelts. The first real evidence for any mass use of belt holsters seems to be an order for 1,000 to equip some U.S. mounted troops in 1855; from the 1840s until roughly the end of the Civil War most civilians just stuck their pistols into ordinary belts or waist sashes, or in pommel holsters on their horses' saddles. Most of the early civilian holsters of the later 1860s and early 1870s resembled the original military rigs in having the gun butt facing forward for a twist-draw, the most convenient way of going for a gun worn under a coat (though the original idea seems to have been enabling a trooper to reach over and draw the revolver with his left hand, if necessary). Many also copied the Army's models in having protective flaps. Most people, unless they went in for shoulder holsters, leather-lined pockets, or some more exotic rig, eventually came to wear their guns with butts to the rear in open-topped holsters, usually tight sheaths enclosing all but the handle of the gun, though the leather might be cut to expose the trigger guard. In addition to protecting the metal, this enclosure reduced the chance that the gun might be worked loose and fall out of the holster.

Any reasonably intelligent adult who has seen the comic-opera regalia worn by such gaudy old-time juvenile and/or musical Western stars as Roy Rogers is perfectly aware that their outfits have little basis in the reality of the Old West. Conscious of the false glitter, the viewer retains no illusion of reality. In more "realistic" Westerns the costumes are less flashy, more credible, generally dirtier, and clearly intended to be accepted as authentic. But in fact most Westerns have employed a let's-dress-up-like-cowboys approach with the result that almost anything looking vaguely frontierish can be, and is, worn.

Although the white hat–black hat dichotomy of good guys and bad has been obsolete for some thirty-odd years (not that it was ever completely or even largely the rule except among certain "B" series players and singing cowboys), Western millinery still leaves much to be desired. Ordinarily the would-be film frontiersman merely jams onto his head any piece of headgear with a brim large enough to warrant being called a "cowboy hat." But usually the brims of such tend to be too highly curved upward for the time and place, often resembling more the headgear worn by modern cowboys and their fans than the picturesque and often battered scalpwarmer of the cowman or frontiersman. Of course, different styles of hat were favored at various times and in various regions of the Old West—wider brims, for example, were usually preferred by cowboys in the sunnier Southwestern climes—but perhaps it would be too much to ask that such differences be painstakingly illustrated.

Sometimes items of clothing that don't really belong in *any* part of the Old West show up. Such evidence as Ike-style jackets in Henry King's *The Gunfighter* (1950) might lead one to assume not only a lack of research, but also an unfamiliarity with genuine Western costume as portrayed in contemporary photographs, or in the paintings and sketches of such well-known Western artists as Frederic Remington and Charles M. Russell. But this isn't always the case. *The Gunfighter* itself seems intended to suggest nineteenth-century photography in its harsh, unadorned black-and-white style, and Howard Hawks, who boasted a large collection of works by Remington and Russell, claimed that he attempted to work some of their "color and atmosphere" into his last two Westerns. But the people in *El Dorado* (1967) and *Rio Lobo* (1970) somehow lack the "look" of Remington and Russell figures, dressed as they are in standard, though by no means overly glamorous, Hollywood-style costumes. For an earlier film, the famous *Rio Bravo* (1959), Hawks had, he later recalled, simply let Dean Martin pick out his own costume in let's-dress-up fashion, though in this case Hawks promptly rejected it as too "pretty" for the drunk role Martin was playing and issued him instead the common collarless work shirt which in the Western has usually been reserved for barflies, comic-relief types, assorted riffraff, and old prospectors.

Some films have made a conscious effort to show Western clothing, if not always certain accoutrements, as it was, or at the very least to capture the basic "look" of such clothing as it appeared in contemporary graphic materials. These include *The Missouri Breaks* and Dick Richards' cattle-drive

Unglamorized members of *The Culpepper Cattle Company*. (Museum of Modern Art/Film Stills Archive)

picture *The Culpepper Cattle Company* (1972), which in fact begins with an under-the-credits sequence of sepia-tinted photographs, seemingly from a nineteenth-century studio but actually depicting members of the cast dressed in their cowboy costumes. Unfortunately Richard's drovers still carried their Peacemakers in buscadero holsters, but it's nice to know that somebody's been paying a bit of attention to the old pictures.

Turning from the civilian to the military, we find that Hollywood, while patriotically financing scores of films celebrating the post–Civil War, Indian-fighting Army, has for the most part failed to provide its troopers with the proper uniforms or equipment, though they are sometimes provided with better weapons than were ever issued by the War Department. That the basic uniform of dark-blue blouse, light-blue trousers, and boots actually changed in various ways over a period of several decades is a fact usually ignored, as is the fact that different styles of headgear were employed. The leather-brimmed, French-style kepi usually worn during the Civil War was eventually superseded by government-issue black campaign hats or privately purchased headgear;[3] the khaki-colored campaign hat seen in so many films, such as Ford's 1949 *She Wore a Yellow Ribbon* (set in 1876), was not issued until 1885, the same year in which the swallowtailed, gilt-starred Stars and Stripes troops guidons, first adopted in 1863, were abandoned for red-over-white pennants.[4]

It is this red-and-white pattern that appears in nearly all cavalry films, the Stars and Stripes model visible in only a few pictures, such as *Duel at Diablo* (1966) and *Tonka* (1958), though in these films they lack golden stars and bear the standard white ones. Sometimes one may see guidons created out of whole cloth, as it were, rather than inspired by any historical research, like the guidon of the Seventh Cavalry in the Custer's Last Stand epic *They Died with Their Boots On* (1941). Bearing a large regimental 7 under a pair of crossed sabers, this distinctive ensign reappeared eight years later as the "bloody guidon of the immortal Seventh Cavalry" seen at the beginning of *She Wore a Yellow Ribbon*. Such a flag was never used,* and neither were the crossed-sabers-over-company-letters guidons which pop up in this and other Ford films—not to mention the full-sized American flags under which the cavalry gallantly charges in so many movies. These were not issued to cavalry regiments until 1895.

Far worse than the unwarranted proliferation of Old Glory (patriotism aside, it makes a great image) is the dread Yellow Neckerchief, which has adorned the throats of our brave troopers in innumerable films ever since the first Technicolor bluebellies made their rather brief appearance in *Western Union* (1940), and is evidently assumed to have been part of the regulation uniform. While on the campaign trail, dusty and sweaty as it often was, officers and men did habitually wear neckerchiefs, but these were individually purchased and usually any color but yellow; some cavalry officers did wear it because it was their branch color (as was blue for infantry and red for artillery), so perhaps that's how this particular error arose.

A far more common anachronism, and one that shows no sign of ever passing from the scene, is the carbine boot, a short open-toed scabbard, attached to the saddle, in which the cinema trooper almost invariably carries his weapon. It didn't come into use until the final campaigns against the Apache in the 1880s, and even then the soldier nearly always retained his

---

*I did recently see a Seventh Cavalry guidon somewhat resembling it while visiting the First Cavalry Division Museum at Fort Hood, Texas: however, it also included the battalion number and company letter. I was informed by one of the museum employees that this pattern had no real official standing and only came into use well into the twentieth century, which would explain why I was unfamiliar with it.

Two cavalrymen of the Civil War or late 1860s, both carrying Spencer repeating carbines. The private on the left wears the piped shell jacket that was supposed to be worn (with metal shoulder scales) at all times but was usually reserved for dress occasions, while the sergeant wears the unpiped sack coat usually worn by members of volunteer regiments and Regulars alike. On his light-blue pants the sergeant wears a cavalry-yellow stripe befitting his rank.

Two Indian fighters of the Regular army, both pictured without carbine slings. On the left is a private as he might have looked around 1876, in the official-issue black campaign hat of 1874 and the regulation sack coat with yellow trim. (Several other patterns, not then regulation, were also worn.) On the right is a trooper from the 1880s who wears only a blue flannel shirt on campaign rather than the plain five-buttoned blouse prescribed, along with a colored kerchief at the throat and a light-colored slouch hat, brim upturned. His light-blue pants are reinforced at the seat and inner legs with canvas, and at his canvas cartridge belt he wears the 1880-issue utility knife in a beaded Indian scabbard. Both men carry single-shot 1873 Springfield carbines, but they have left their sabers behind either at the fort or on their horses.

thick leather carbine sling, worn over the left shoulder and attached to the gun with a snap hook. One can see such slings in almost every cavalry painting or drawing by Frederic Remington, but although John Ford had tried to make *She Wore a Yellow Ribbon* look "as Remington as possible," the carbine sling is not employed in this or indeed in any other Ford cavalry picture except the 1950 *Rio Grande*.* Here they are worn buckles to the front, which was rarely if ever done (though there doesn't appear to have been any formal regulation against it). Other films in which slings are worn more conventionally include *The Plainsman, They Died with Their Boots On*, and *The Bravos*, a 1972 TV movie.

The Bravos also happens to be one of the relatively few films to give its cavalrymen cap-and-ball revolvers. Usually, regardless of the period, troopers are armed with .45 Colts (the first shipment didn't reach the Army until 1874) as well as single-shot 1873 Model Springfield carbines or, less often, Winchester repeaters, which, although purchased by some soldiers with their own funds, were never at any time issued to the U. S. Army despite the evidence of such films as *Only the Valiant* (1951). Habitually ignored are the Sharps breechloaders, Henry lever-action rifles and Spencer seven-shot repeaters which, along with other Civil War surplus weapons and conversions, were used prior to 1873.[5]

The carelessness plaguing the Western film often spills over into non-Westerns related to the genre in one way or another. Thus Raoul Walsh's 1953 *Distant Drums*, set in 1830s Florida and connected to the Western by its Indian-fighting aspects, has Gary Cooper shooting Seminoles with a Peacemaker and commanding soldiers armed and equipped for a post-Appomattox scrimmage with the Sioux. More typical is the anachronistic Civil War film, and most of these have in fact been Westerns or contained heavy Western-like elements. In movies such as *Virginia City* everyone goes dressed in the usual horse-opera costume, carries the usual horse-opera weapons, and does the usual horse-opera things, such as fighting Indians or bandits, chasing or being chased on horseback, and shooting it out with sixguns—the background of the Rebellion providing at least partial plot motivation as well as the occasional full-fledged battle. We therefore find Civil War soldiers equipped with Peacemakers, Winchester repeaters, and Springfield carbines, wearing incorrect uniforms, and carrying the wrong guidons and flags. (Any battle reenactment group of Civil War enthusiasts would be put to shame if its members committed such amateurish mistakes.)

Sometimes Western-style anachronisms will spill over into the comparatively rare "mainstream" Civil War film such as *Shenandoah* (1965), in which

---

*Ford was of course referring primarily to "color and atmosphere" and visual composition rather than to costume details; but he would have been ill-advised to seek uniform information in Remington's works anyway since that artist often drew largely on his own observations for such details and didn't get out west until 1885. When painting scenes from an earlier period Remington often fell into anachronism, as did other Western artists such as Charles *(Attack at Dawn)* Schreyvogel.

Virginia farmer Jimmy Stewart totes a Winchester, or Ford's *The Horse Soldiers* (1959), which had John Wayne's troopers outfitted in much the same inaccurate manner as in *Rio Lobo*—a film which itself starts off with Blue-Gray hostilities but eventually has a demobilized Duke sitting in an 1865 Western saloon with those swinging doors not common until the 1880s. This sort of tie-in might even account for certain errors—such as Colt revolvers used during the 1831 Nat Turner slave revolt—in TV's immensely popular slavery-days miniseries *Roots* (1977), which, although mostly set in antebellum times, is nevertheless connected to the Civil War film and thus to the Civil War Western and its civilian counterpart.

Hollywood's carelessness and false confidence in its own accuracy seem to affect most strongly those films set at some point in that period of Old West history during which men carried six-shooters—or, as in the case of *The Master Gunfighter*, what is imagined to be that period. This is the literally timeless Western of our dreams, usually existing some time after the Civil War but often reaching back long before. Those films, comparatively few in number, which deal with the musket-toting, revolverless pioneers of an earlier day—they have been termed "coonskin Westerns" or "pre-Westerns"—seem somewhat less prone to outrageous anachronism.

But let six-shooters, warranted or not, enter the picture and we are faced with the Classic West, in which all dress and go armed in obeisance to a certain standard basically the same whether the movie is set during the Mexican War or the turn of the century. Indeed, if a film were to be made about the life of a Texas frontiersman who reached maturity in the 1840s and survived until New Year's Day of 1905, there might logically be no change whatsoever in clothing styles or anything else over the story's sixty-year span. I do not, of course, believe that this would happen—*somebody* would probably realize that something was wrong—but in fact each decade embraced by this span has been portrayed as almost exactly resembling all the others. Most Westerns, of course, do not bother to identify the exact year in which they are set, and often precise knowledge of *where* a story is taking place is not important either. It is enough to know that we are in the Old West.

It is not always possible to say just why errors in a film occur. But the "legendary" nature of this setting is obviously a prime cause of anachronism. The Old West exists not so much as a part of American history (no matter how heroic) bounded by geography and time, but as something harder to pin down—"a country of the mind," as Archibald MacLeish observed, "and so eternal." Such "legendary" periods as the vaguely defined Age of Chivalry often share this misty timelessness and a consequent tendency toward anachronism. In his *Visions of Yesterday*, Jeffrey Richard claims that most films dealing with British India (some of them made by Americans), no matter what their ostensible setting in time, belong "spiritually to the 1890s. It is as if the myth has frozen into that decade, which is seen to epitomize and summarize British rule in the subcontinent. The uniforms, the attitudes, the political situation, all belong to the latter part of the nineteenth century."[6] Whatever research is evident with regard to a particular film is likely to be confined precisely to those facets of the story which lie farthest *outside* the familiar, standardized setting. The French troops in Sam Peckinpah's *Major Dundee* (1965), *The Undefeated* (1969), *Vera Cruz* (1954), and *Two Mules for Sister Sara* are more accurately provided for than the American characters in these Mexican-based Westerns.

The frontier's nearness in time to the production of the first Western films may also have contributed to the chronological vagueness of the classic West. One should remember that the "wild," six-shooter West was far from completely dead when the Western film's primitive era began (the Arizona Rangers, for example, were not formed to suppress increasing horseback outlawry until 1901, being disbanded only in 1909), and in some cases was treated less as a historical period than as part of the immediate, nostalgia inducing past, or even as just a current regional phenomenon.* With respect to certain features of the West, history may have been best served in films of the silent period (after the filmmakers had moved out West rather than relying on the East Coast locations of the *very* earliest days). Value was sometimes derived from the knowledge and experience of men like ex-lawman and cowboy Charlie Siringo, who once acted as a technical advisor to film star William S. Hart and had a small part in Hart's last film, *Tumbleweeds* (1925). John Ford employed for some of his silents and for the classic *Stagecoach* (1939) one Ed Garrett, alias Pardner Jones, another ex-lawman (and relative of the famous Pat Garrett) who did trick shooting for films and who gave Ford advice on certain period details. As a result, said Ford, "nobody wore flashy clothes and we didn't have dance hall scenes with the girls in short dresses. As Pardner said, 'In Tombstone, we never saw anything like that.'" For *Stagecoach* Ford, who didn't like his Westerners "all dolled up," even had a beltless John Wayne wear *suspenders* in his role as the Ringo Kid—causing, we are told, quite a negative reaction among the juvenile fans of the time.

Whatever the origins of the no-research tradition, it endures. But the very mistakes become part of an unwritten code, since the Western film, like any other form of art or entertainment, builds on the foundation of what has been done before. The effect of film upon film is particularly obvious in non-American Westerns, and is perhaps appropriate for movies rooted in the conventions of an established genre rather than in any domestic historical tradition. The notorious "spaghetti Westerns" of Sergio Leone and other Italian directors reproduce in near-exact detail not the appearance of some specific time and place in the American West, but that of the American Western. Much the same can be said of other foreign-made Westerns such as

---

*Adding to the confusion are later films treating the Old West as part of the contemporary scene even when it indisputably wasn't; oddest of all were some more or less child-oriented spectacles of the forties and fifties mixing badmen and Injun raids with Nazi or Commie villains and jet rockets. Perhaps the comfortable familiarity of the classic West was responsible for this; the Western is the period film for people who don't like period films.

Mountain men **Robert Redford,** carrying a muzzle-loading Hawken rifle, and **Will Geer** in *Jeremiah Johnson,* a prerevolver Western set in the 1840s. (Museum of Modern Art / Film Stills Archive)

the Spanish and German, save that the latter often seem less successful in their goal. This is partly due to an apparent inability to find on location in Germany (or Yugoslavia) scenery that can approximate the more desolate and arid regions of the West (despite scenes filmed on beaches and rocky plateaus), and these films may sometimes fail to convince through an overabundance of lush rolling plains, picturesque forests, and postcard-perfect mountain streams. This is not to say that the industrious Germans do not attempt *some* feeling of verisimilitude; in one Teutonic hayburner I even saw some rather oddly garbed "Apaches" ride past a black cactus apparently crafted from wooden beams and erected to add authenticity.

One may reasonably ask just why anyone should care about recreating the Old West as it actually looked, simply to satisfy a tiny minority of people such as myself—why the cinematic West should not remain a valuable mythic setting, with illusion its only indispensable characteristic. Even the plea of "historical reality" may not always seem convincing, for on history's scales the question of what sort of gun Trooper Smith used to shoot the Indian will surely not weigh heavily. I suppose that it all comes down to the feeling that films which are, ultimately, rooted in a certain past era should look something like what they pretend to be.

But at the same time even I (who, on first learning of the inexcusable errors rampant in the Western, reacted with extreme displeasure toward any film in which I detected what I thought a serious error) recognize that such details are almost always of secondary concern, and that "the play's the thing." The cavalrymen in *The Bravos* may be outfitted perfectly and wear their carbine slings correctly, but this can't change the fact that *Rio Grande* is a much better film. So now I can just sit back and, like the ignorant seventeenth-century groundling listening to the chiming clock in *Julius Caesar*, enjoy it all, almost unmindful of the errors in such films as *The Texas Rangers, Rocky Mountain, Comanche Station, Rancho Notorious, Johnny Guitar, The Tall T, Butch Cassidy and the Sundance Kid, Ulzana's Raid, A Fistful of Dollars, For a Few Dollars More, Little Big Man, The Left-Handed Gun, Sergeant Rutledge, The Legend of Nigger Charley, Decision at Sundown, The Man Who Shot Liberty Valance, Broken Arrow, The Magnificent Seven, The Return of the Seven, The Man from Laramie, Buffalo Bill and the Indians. . . .*

Still, I wish things would improve a bit. All it takes is effort—if anyone is interested.

NOTES

1. The revolving rifle, sometimes equipped with as many as eight barrels, was manufactured well into the Civil War but never really caught on, partly because, like the pepperbox, it tended to discharge more than one chamber at once, blowing off the user's left hand as it gripped the forestock.

2. I had originally intended to include a note saying that a somewhat more serious error in this film (though one which did not really affect the course of the action) was the use of the Texas Rangers in scenes set in 1868. This was three years after the Rangers had (according to most historians) been disbanded due to their wartime service as Confederate cavalrymen, only to be reorganized in 1875. However, I have recently learned from Bern Keating's *An Illustrated History of the Texas Rangers* (Chicago: Rand McNally, 1975) that this was not the case. In any event a band of civilian volunteers would have served much the same function in the script, the "error" basically amounting to some incorrect references in the dialogue. (The unofficial founding date of the Rangers, who go back before the days of the Texas Republic to the early American settlements in what was then part of Mexico, might be considered to be May 23, 1823.)

3. It should be remembered that, while strict dress regulations were normally enforced while in garrison, they were often very relaxed while in the field. Officers seem to have been particularly fond of wearing nonregulation items of clothing or simply dressing in civilian frontier style.

4. A somewhat different red-white design was used prior to 1863, but as the Confederates also used them in the initial stages of the war a more distinctive ensign was felt necessary.

5. By 1863 over a hundred different types of rifles and carbines were regarded by the Federal government as being official Army-issue weapons. This does not of course include still other models of weapons unofficially bought and carried by individual Union soldiers.

6. Certain similarities between the epic of westward expansion and the epic of empire, which we needn't go into here, may have been behind the remaking of certain Indian Army films as Westerns: George Stevens's classic 1939 adventure *Gunga Din* became the weak Frank Sinatra vehicle *Sergeants 3*, while the 1935 *Lives of a Bengal Lancer*—allegedly described by its director, Henry Hathaway, as "just another horse opera, set in India" and starring Gary Cooper as a "Scotch-Canadian" officer of the Raj—was partly cannibalized in 1939 for *Geronimo*.

2
Trail of the Fighting Pimps
or Why Earp?

This is the West, sir. When the legend becomes fact, print
the legend!

—John Ford's
The Man Who Shot Liberty Valance (1962)

The Old West cannot be understood unless Wyatt Earp is
also understood.

Stuart N. Lake

Few indeed of the Old West's countless peace officers have been honored with
·celluloid immortality, and only these have names familiar to the general
public. In treating of this handful of demigods, I shall begin with the first to be
properly deified by Hollywood: James Butler Hickok, better known as Wild
Bill.

This hero's first full-length screen biography, a 1923 silent film forthrightly
entitled *Wild Bill Hickok*, starred and was directed by William S. Hart. In an
opening title Hart apologized to his fans for not looking like Hickok and
expressed the hope that his "friends".(most of whom doubtless neither knew
nor cared what Hickok had looked like) would accept him as he was. Hart did
not bother to apologize for the fact that Hickok's life had been dramatized in a
decidedly unauthentic manner, with Hart—a man with a great love for
Western "realism" but too much the romantic sentimentalist to let it tie him
down—suppressing or prettifying the less appealing aspects of his subject's
life.

Not, one might say, unlike Hickok himself.

James Butler Hickok first became a national celebrity after an 1865 interview with Colonel George Ward Nichols, a dude journalist out West in search of "local color," was published in the February 1867 issue of *Harper's New Monthly Magazine* under the title "Wild Bill." The article was, to say the least, colorful, particularly when quoting what was alleged to be Bill's own description of a battle he'd had at the outset of the Civil War with some vicious "secesh" (secessionists) at Rock Creek Station, Nebraska. At first, wrote Nichols, Hickok was reluctant to talk about the affair. But talk he finally did, recounting the story in all its bloodcurdling detail. It went like this:

Trapped at a lonely cabin by ten members of the M'Kandlas gang ("desperadoes, horsethieves, murderers, regular cut-throats, who were the terror of everybody on the border"), and realizing that he has only five rounds in his cap-and-ball revolver, Wild Bill spies a powder horn and some small bars of lead lying on a table. He uses one of these bars as a bullet, hammering it home into the chamber after a suitable dose of powder—and not a moment too soon, for now the "reckless, bloodthirsty devils" are upon him.

He grabs up a trusty rifle, and, when the dreaded Dave M'Kandlas bursts in, shoots him squarely through the heart, leaving our hero, in his own memorable phrase, with "only six shots and nine men to kill."

> There was a few seconds of that awful stillness, and then the ruffians came rushing in at both doors. How wild they looked with their red, drunken faces and inflamed eyes, shouting and cussing! But I never aimed more deliberately in my life.
>
> One—two—three—four; and four men fell dead.
>
> That didn't stop the rest. Two of them fired their birdguns at me. And then I felt a sting run all over me. The room was full of smoke. Two got in close to me, their eyes glaring out of the clouds. One I knocked down with my fist. "You are out of the way for awhile," I thought. The second I shot dead. The other three clutched me and crowded me onto the bed. I fought hard. I broke with my hands one man's arm. He had his fingers round my throat. Before I could get to my feet I was struck across the breast with the stock of a rifle, and I felt the blood rushing out of my nose and mouth. Then I got ugly, and I remember that I got hold of a knife, and then it was all cloudy like, and I was wild, and I struck savage blows, following the devils up from one side to the other of the room and into the corners, striking and slashing until I knew that everyone was dead. . . . There were eleven buckshot in me. I carry some of them now. I was cut in thirteen places. All of them bled enough to have let the life out of a man.

This vivid battle report, supplemented by Nichols's comments on the hero's other notable deeds and a terrifying engraving of Wild Bill in action against the M'Kandlases, thrilled countless readers who managed to swallow every word, even though the colonel's little local-color story differed somewhat from the less publicized facts brought forward by later writers. On July 12, 1861, Dave McCanles (not "M'Kandlas") was indeed killed by someone—most

James Butler Hickok, with ivory-handled revolvers carried in his usual fashion and an improbably sheathless fighting knife at his belt. (Kansas State Historical Society)

probably Hickok himself, though there remains the possibility that one of his friends was responsible. Whoever it was hid behind a curtain and shot Dave through the heart with his trusty rifle as McCanles stood in front of the Rock Creek stage station, where Hickok worked as an attendant. McCanles's two companions were then wounded by Hickok with a pistol and pursued by several of Wild Bill's associates, who slew them without mercy, James Gordon being shotgunned to death and James Wood having his skull crushed by a hoe as he lay helpless. Only McCanles's twelve-year-old son Monroe escaped the carnage, possibly through an oversight. Since it seemed unlikely, though not impossible, that a man intent on starting a fight would have taken his young son along to view the action, and since all three victims were alleged to have been unarmed, Hickok and his companions were arraigned for murder; their plea of self-defense was accepted at the preliminary hearing and the case went no further. The original dispute had apparently been over some money owed McCanles by the stage company.

Hickok, to his discredit, had inflated this incident into an epic combat during conversations with others. But Nichols, a fairly common type among chroniclers of Wild West derring-do, undoubtedly added at least a few touches of his own to the narrative, in addition to imposing upon Mr. "Hitchcock," as he mistakenly called him, a crude frontier dialect quite foreign to the real Wild Bill (more local color) and crediting his hero with having personally dispatched hundreds of Confederates during his Civil War scouting days. Frontier newspapers ridiculed the absurdities of Nichols's article and his condescendingly inaccurate descriptions of Missouri's citizenry (still more local color), but fortunately their circulation—unlike that of the nationally read *Harper's*—was extremely limited, and so Wild Bill's conquest of the M'Kandlas gang passed into Wild West history.

In view of the true and somewhat sordid circumstances behind the Rock Creek "shoot-out," it was understandable that McCanles's relatives should have protested against the use of the family name in Bill Hart's film, which featured a battle somewhat resembling that of Nichols's account. Being a gentleman, Hart obligingly changed the name—and retained the fight.

Had it not been for the Nichols interview, it is quite likely that Hickok might forever have remained a relatively obscure figure in Western history, for his pre-*Harper's* career, though reasonably exciting, was no more so than that of many another hardy but now forgotten plainsman. Born in Illinois in 1837, Hickok first found employment as a peace officer in 1858, when he was elected village constable of Monticello Township in Nebraska—an uneventful job. The following year he became a driver of freight wagons, and in 1861 disposed of Dave McCanles in what was basically just another violent and, save for its enigmatic aspects, uninteresting frontier brawl.

Since Dave McCanles had not been, as Hickok (or Nichols) was so cunningly to claim, an open Southern sympathizer, Bill's first real contribution toward saving the Union was made as a civilian scout. He then served some time as a wagonmaster and later switched back to being a scout; he was an efficient, daring one whose services apparently proved most valuable. In 1865, while pursuing his chosen postwar profession of gambler, Hickok, who had picked up the sobriquet "Wild Bill" somehow or other, killed in a prearranged duel in the public square of Springfield, Missouri, a man named Dave Tutt, with whom Hickok had quarreled over a card game and/or a woman. This street fight horrified many citizens and Hickok was tried for manslaughter; he was acquitted even though the judge had carefully charged the jury to convict should the duel prove to have been "in any way premeditated by the defendant."

Pausing in Springfield to have his little conversation with Colonel Nichols, Bill went on to do some more gambling, serve as a deputy U.S. marshal chasing army deserters and horse thieves, and perform creditably as an army scout; chief among his exploits in the last position was a running fight with Cheyenne warriors, one of whom got close enough to thrust a lance deep into Hickok's thigh. In August of 1869, fame already spread by *Harper's*, he was elected sheriff of Ellis County, Kansas, with his headquarters at the wide-open town of Hays City. Here he killed two men, both having tried to kill or injure Bill first. Standing for reelection that November, Hickok was defeated by his own deputy, Peter Lanihan, and left town some time after his term of office expired.

Roaming around a bit as was his wont, Bill finally drifted back into Hays, where he got into a self-defensive shooting scrape with some rowdy troopers of the famed Seventh Cavalry, killing one and seriously wounding another; legend says that General George Custer's brother Tom was involved, but he wasn't. In 1871 Bill was appointed marshal of a larger and more famous Western community, the cowtown of Abilene, which had been booming ever since the railway to the Eastern cattle markets had come through in 1867 (and not, as stated in *Red River*, 1865; the cattle arrive in town two years too early in that film).

Contrary to the myths spread by the more moonstruck of his biographers, Wild Bill did not "tame" Abilene, mainly because it had already been tamed by one Thomas James "Bear River Tom" Smith, who had been appointed town marshal on July 4, 1870, and had at once proceeded to enforce the town's no-gun ordinance. When faced with resistance from the rowdy Texas cowboys who came into town to whoop it up, he used his fists—puzzling the Texans, who (movie saloon brawls to the contrary) generally used their cherished guns to settle disputes and were unable to think up a defense against this new menace. A veritable Boy Scout in his nondrinking, nonsmoking, and noncussing, Smith kept Abilene in good order, and there were no gun killings during his reign. On August 9 a grateful citizenry responded by raising his monthly salary from $150 to $225, retroactive to the Fourth of July. But it was all too good to last. On November 2 Smith was shot outside Abilene by a homesteader whom he had attempted to arrest; an accomplice then all but decapitated the fallen marshal with an ax. Despite his accomplishments, Tom Smith never became a folk hero or a favorite of the Western storytellers, possibly because little is known of his earlier life (though this could be an advantage for some legend makers, a void left to be filled by the imagination), possibly because he never killed anyone while marshal.

After their experience with Smith, some residents were of the opinion that hiring a gambler-gunman such as Hickok was taking a step backward. (After all, would you want a policeman named Wild Bill on *your* block?) There were complaints that Hickok didn't enforce the town gun ordinance and other laws as had Smith and was not doing enough to earn his salary—which, by the way, had been lowered back to $150 per month and was not subsequently raised in recognition of Wild Bill's superior qualifications.

Hickok in fact seems to have done very little while in office aside from dressing up in fancy Prince Albert coats and red sashes, playing cards at his

"Bear River Tom." (Kansas State Historical Society)

headquarters in the Alamo Saloon, and cavorting with the belles of the red-light district. The irksome duty of patrolling the streets he left for the most part to his deputies, and when he did venture forth Hickok always kept to the middle of the street (the so-called gunman's sidewalk) while avoiding dark alleyways and the direct glare of streetlamps. But, in all fairness, it should be pointed out that he served a valuable purpose simply by taking the job and was primarily an instrument of psychological warfare, albeit one well equipped to take action should the need arise. Bill's fully justified reputation as a pistol expert and man-killer—the chief reason for hiring him in the first place—had preceded him, and his personal appearance reinforced the mystique of Hickok's deadliness. "When I came along the street," reminisced one ex-cowboy, "he was standing there with his back to the wall and his thumbs hooked in his red sash. He stood there and rolled his head from side to side looking at everything and everybody from under his eyebrows—just like a mad old bull. I decided then and there I didn't want any part of him." Most potential troublemakers felt likewise, and the Hickok legend could even serve to preserve the family peace, mothers invoking the name of "Wild Bill" as a bogeyman to terrorize recalcitrant youngsters.

The prudent Hickok's sole "adventure" in Abilene during his eight months' service as marshal resulted in the shooting of two men. Hearing shots one fine night, he rushed to the scene to confront the Texas gambler Phil Coe and some rowdy companions in the street. Coe, who was not fond of Hickok (people disagree about the reason), held a pistol which he claimed to have fired at a dog and which he then, depending on whose version you care to believe, did or didn't aim at Hickok, who either way shot Coe twice in the belly as a pair of the gambler's bullets cut through his coat. While this was going on, Mike Williams, a fellow lawman and friend of Hickok intent on aiding him, dashed into the line of fire, so Bill ended up putting two slugs into him too. The death of Williams grieved him considerably.

The local paper supported Bill's efforts, but they went unappreciated by the town council; as soon as the hectic cattle season ended they dismissed him without so much as a thank-you, the reason curtly given in the minute book being that Abilene was "no longer in need of his services." Perhaps this meant simply that such an expensive and quick-shooting lawman would now be a useless frill, since the city fathers, upset by the evils of the trade, had decided to tell the Texans to take their cows elsewhere—which decision naturally put an end to the town's boom days.

Luckily Bill still had a bankable name, and he consequently went into show business as master of ceremonies for a Niagara Falls frontier show and Indian buffalo hunt (with three buffalo). It was a financial disaster, so Hickok reverted to gambling until his fellow scout Buffalo Bill Cody offered him a role in a blood-and-thunder Western drama back east—a distinctly secondary role, by the way, since Hickok's allegedly girlish and certainly uneager voice jibed ill with his "naturally theatrical appearance." The hero finally quit in disgust after an embarrassing stint of shyly mouthing outrageous dime-novel dialogue ("Fear not, fair maid; by heaven you are safe at last with Wild Bill, who is ever ready to risk his life and die if need be in defense of weak and defenseless womanhood") and getting chewed out by boss Cody for boozing, shooting blanks at the extras' legs to powder-burn them, and an overall lack of zeal.

Following this footlight interlude, Hickok spent much of his time in Cheyenne, Wyoming, gambling and plotting a mining expedition to the Black Hills of South Dakota; he was later described, with what justice we cannot say, by the *Cheyenne Leader* as having been a "very tame and worthless loafer and bummer" during his stay there. (The *Cheyenne Daily News*, on the other hand, had termed him "a noble specimen of Western manhood.") Hickok was eventually charged with vagrancy—a charge probably made against a drifter perceived as a potential source of trouble rather than as a man lacking "visible means of support"—but had left town by the date set for his trial and later returned without being molested. On March 5, 1876, he married comely widow circus owner Agnes Lake Thatcher.

From Cheyenne came Bill a-riding, to Deadwood in the Dakotas, hoping to earn enough money to support both his wife and himself while worrying about his failing eyesight and wondering if he could still protect himself in a gunfight. On August 2, as he sat playing cards in Deadwood's No. 10 Saloon, he was shot in the back of the head by a cross-eyed stumblebum named Jack McCall—who, when later asked why he had not chosen to face Hickok in a fair-and-square gunfight, allegedly replied, "I didn't want to commit suicide." McCall claimed that Hickok had killed his brother, but as this person was found never to have existed the murder has commonly been ascribed to a pathetic desire to kill a famous gunman, although there is also evidence that McCall was angry at Hickok for having bested him in a card game, and that some other person may have paid him to pull the trigger. The cards held by Hickok in his last poker game—aces and eights—became known as the Dead Man's Hand and were subsequently to be found mounted behind the bar of many a frontier watering hole, thoughtful cowboys pondering whatever spiritual significance the cards might have as they imbibed.

There you have it, folks: the life and adventures of the great Wild Bill Hickok, "Prince of Pistoleers"—a brave and certainly intriguing individual but, perhaps, less deserving of national idolatry than other, less heralded plainsmen. If a "hero," in the best sense of that word, he was no more so than innumerable others who roamed the West during the same period; if a villain, as might be the case if his actions at Rock Creek came under the heading of murder rather than of self-defense (or something in between), his villainy was neither spectacular nor particularly important. Very probably he was neither saint nor fiend, though with his striking physical appearance, impressive personality, and remarkable aptitude in the use of weapons, he surely stood apart from the crowd. Judging from contemporary accounts, it would seem to me that Hickok often impressed observers (some doubtless influenced in their opinion of him by what they'd already heard or read) more through these personal qualities—by simply *being* Wild Bill Hickok—than by any of his deeds.

But what Hickok had actually been and done didn't matter: to the rescue of the legend, which had begun during Wild Bill's own lifetime with assorted tall tales and lies, rode worthy successors to Colonel Nichols—starry-eyed hero-worshipers and hard-eyed exploiters and just-plain-sloppy writers who would turn out for popular consumption a more meaningful version of the Hickok story, an epic saga of unequaled, selfless gallantry. They would triple and quadruple his body count (though their usual wholehearted acceptance of the "M'Kandlas" story rendered this service almost unnecessary), ignore or veil his amorous indiscretions when not comparing them to those of Lancelot or David, prudishly downplay his drinking, and—most important of all—give him a crusader's moral purpose. Others would in turn succeed them as they had succeeded Nichols, often adding whatever they could think up themselves to the gory fables they'd heard or read of in order to create in Hickok the *beau idéal* of the plainsman and Indian fighter, who slays but to civilize and make the West a better place in which to live. Hickok would cease to be a human being and become a symbol—the type of figure to whom generic hero stories are attached, and who epitomizes a certain class of man. Those who disagreed were prone to reach for the opposite extreme and present him as a bloodthirsty devil, but these were in a minority.

In the meantime conscientious historians, disdaining for the most part to examine such "childish" subjects as the "Wild West" and its man-killers of note, left the field comparatively clear for the easily fooled, the careless, the adventure-story scribblers, dime novelists, hack journalists—and, last but not least, Hollywood.

On New Year's Day, 1937, Paramount Pictures released *The Plainsman*, produced and directed by Cecil B. De Mille, with a screenplay by Waldemar Young, Harold Lamb, and Lynn Riggs based on an unpublished original screen story by Courtney Riley Cooper, the book *Wild Bill Hickok: The Prince of Pistoleers* by Frank J. Wilstach, and additional material compiled by Jeanie Macpherson. Nine days later Idwal Jones wrote in the *New York Times*, concerning the film's historical background, that "Harold Lamb, versed in writing history, spent a year in checking over the facts and working the true feeling of the times into the script. That ought to make it as much 'history' as any historical film has any right to be. 'The picture will be history to those who look for that,' says De Mille, 'and a Western to those who don't.'"

Being greedy, I looked for both and found, alas! only the Western—as had Frank S. Nugent, who in reviewing *The Plainsman* for the *Times* a few days later, contradicted his more credulous colleague Mr. Jones by terming it a film in which "small details are faithfully reproduced and established historical facts scrupulously rewritten. . . . Mr. DeMille has no conscience about these things, which probably is one reason why his pictures are so much fun.

"It is one of his foibles to pretend that he only makes sagas or epics, never anything so elementary as a splashing adventure film."

Noting that the foreword to *The Plainsman* explained that "the story which follows compresses many years, many lives and widely separated events into one narrative in an attempt to do justice to the courage of the Plainsmen of the West," Nugent commented simply: "That may have been his idea originally, but things seem to have got out of hand."

Nugent was not about to sound very surprised at this turn of events, since *The Plainsman* did fit in fairly neatly with the other "historical" works of the De Mille oeuvre. In his cavalier attitude toward the facts, De Mille was an adequate representative of the film industry as a whole; however, he also had a few rather distinctive eccentricities. For one thing, he would go to elaborate lengths to insure that the physical detail of each picture (much harder for a layman or critic to check up on than the historical narrative) was correct in every detail, compiling volumes of research material and sending his minions poring through old records as though in mortal fear that an army of nitpickers would descend on Southern California in blind fury at the cut of King

Richard's chain mail or Gary Cooper's revolver (which he managed to get wrong anyway). Research might also uncover picturesque bits of fact which could be worked into the narrative or at least inspire his writers, and De Mille would sometimes adhere to odd bits of history adding little to a picture's authenticity; after deciding to include the phrase "Go west, young man" in *The Plainsman,* he insisted that it be attributed correctly to John B. Soule of the *Terre Haute Express* rather than to its more famous misquotee Horace Greeley.

But, insists De Mille biographer Charles Higham, "it did not matter: De Mille was aiming at a legendary abstraction of events, informed with the very spirit of the West [whatever he took that to be]. In this he triumphantly succeeded: the film had a blazing energy and drive, its skirmishes, battles . . . and vigorous central romance showing the director at his best."

This "vigorous central romance" between Gary Cooper's[1] rather folksy, clean-shaven Bill and that famous frontier virago Calamity Jane invites some scrutiny, especially as it was the only element of his epic which De Mille himself admitted (in his posthumously published *Autobiography*) to have been somewhat antihistorical. "I confess to taking some liberties in [the] casting: pictures I have seen of the real Calamity Jane were far removed indeed from the piquant loveliness of Jean Arthur. But, if I may say so, it was good casting nonetheless."

Calamity Jane's appearance was indeed "far removed" from that of the blonde Miss Arthur, for Martha Jane Cannary was a female only in the narrowest technical sense, and during her suspected service as a "painted cat" must have appealed only to the most hardened of those rough-and-ready frontiersmen who chanced to cross her path. Her manners were as unattractive to most contemporaries as her appearance, for as one acquaintance apologetically put it: "She swore, she drank, she wore men's clothing. Where can you find a woman today who doesn't do such things? She was just fifty years ahead of her time." She also chewed tobacco, a large gob of which this frail *nymph du prairie* once expectorated with commendable accuracy upon the dress of an actress whose antics on stage had displeased her. ("That's for your damn dress," cried the big-hearted Jane, tossing a gold piece onto the stage.) Although she was quite popular among the saloon crowd, it is not difficult to understand why most of this century's pro-Hickok writers (including Frank Wilstach, whose book served as a source for *The Plainsman*) indignantly rejected the theory that their hero would have had anything to do with the likes of Miss Cannary—a theory which, by the time of De Mille's film, was advanced largely by anti-Hickok writers wishing to portray their nonhero as a man with deviant sexual tastes as well as a murdering bushwhacker.

The romantic legend of Jane's love affair with Bill seems to have had its origin in her alleged membership in the entourage that had ridden with Hickok into Deadwood, Jane subsequently, according to one writer, following him about "as a dog follows its master," the better to bathe in his reflected glory. Working in Calamity's favor after Bill's death were her catchy and

The good-hearted but rough-mannered Calamity Jane, dressed to kill. (Library of Congress)

expressive nickname (and the importance of The Name can never be underestimated when considering any Wild West legend), her supposed association with the great scout, and the fact that heroines of Amazonian mold were not unpopular in the trashy Western literature of the day. She therefore became a figure of romance and the subject of such dime novels as 1882's *Calamity Jane*, which featured tender love scenes between Jane and Bill amid the usual helpings of gore.

She was a living legend, all right—but that didn't help her alcoholism, which dominated her life as she roamed her dissipated way through the West, growing old and haggard before her time. In 1896 she was exhibited by an enterprising showman as a carnival attraction, much like Jo-Jo the Dog-faced Boy or the Original Siamese Twins; her drunkenness interfering with the show, she was fired and reduced to cadging drinks with copies of her ghostwritten, fictitious "autobiography," which had been published in a cheap paperback edition. She died in 1903, approximate age fifty, although she looked twenty years older.

Nope, she wasn't much like Jean Arthur at all.

The Plainsman remains to this day the most famous and most popular of all the films deifying Wild Bill Hickok, a splendid adventure movie hard to resist even for English historian and Western enthusiast Joseph G. Rosa, who dedicated his myth-busting 1964 biography of Hickok, *They Called Him Wild Bill*, to Gary Cooper for his portrayal of the hero. Contemporary critics loved it, and to hell with historical accuracy: it was superb hokum, an animated dime novel on a grand scale—and in any case the history being distorted was only Western history and so did not count.

Moments after Abe Lincoln, finished with his minispeech on the necessity of making the West safe and told by his wife that "we'll be late for the theater," hurries off to meet his destiny, we find ourselves looking in on a group of evil businessmen sitting around and wondering what they can do with all those nice shiny repeating rifles, which, says the script, have become a drug on the market with the ending of the Civil War. Inevitably, they decide to sell them to the Plains Indians for "hunting purposes."

Meanwhile Wild Bill Hickok, mustered out of the Union Army, encounters his old pal Buffalo Bill Cody (James Ellison) in Saint Louis and heads for the nearest bar, where he faces down a crooked gambler while barflies talk about how Wild Bill killed the whole "McDaniels" gang singlehanded. (So much for research, if not tact.) Hickok also runs into old flame Calamity Jane, whom he still loves but whose kisses he keeps wiping off as he maintains an it's-all-over-between-us attitude; when Jane is kidnapped, Bill shows his true colors by catching up with the Injuns responsible and offering to trade even his stag-handled .45s in exchange for her. Despite this, both end as prisoners in the camp of the Cheyenne chief Yellow Hand, who's also an old pal of Bill's and who tortures him over a bonfire until Calamity reveals the route of a cavalry supply train carrying, as the chief puts it, "many bullets."

Both are released, and while Calamity rides for help, Hickok runs through a hail of bullets to join Buffalo Bill and the now-besieged supply detachment in what looks suspiciously like the 1868 Battle of Beecher's Island, at which neither of these two noted frontiersmen were actually present. After six days of siege, the troopers are about to go off their collective rocker, but Hickok calms them down by telling them a rather pointless fable about a tame catfish that fell off a bridge into a river and drowned, and then dashes out among hundreds of charging braves to recover his pocketwatch and sixguns from a Cheyenne he has just shot.

Just as the survivors are going nuts again and preparing to charge out to join their fallen comrades ("It's the dead calling!" cries one, hearing a distant bugle) the battle is resolved by the nick-of-time arrival of the Seventh Cavalry under Custer, who by a singular coincidence was never at this particular fight either. Wild Bill then heads for Hays City, where Calamity is about to be run out of town on a rail for spilling her guts and causing all those soldiers to be killed. Smartly clad in tight leather pants, she manages to fend off the citizenry with her trusty whip* until Bill arrives to put a stop to things and to hunt for the evil Lattimore (Charles Bickford), who on behalf of the businessmen at the beginning of the film is supplying guns to the aborigines. After killing three soldiers paid by the gunrunner to destroy him, incurring the enmity of General Custer, and getting lectured to by Mrs. Cody on how nasty it is to kill people, Hickok sensibly flees, pursued by his good friend Cody, who has orders from Custer to bring Hickok back. Just as the two Bills are about to kill one another (reluctantly, of course), word comes of more Indian troubles and Cody goes for help while Hickok rides for Deadwood.

There he encounters not only Calamity Jane tending bar but also the evil Lattimore conducting business as usual. By this time Hickok has begun thinking and, after meeting Lattimore minion Jack McCall (a plump Porter Hall in dude clothes and bowler hat, who keeps showing up all through the movie), lets him go instead of killing him. "Maybe Mrs. Cody was right," he broods aloud. "Who am I to decide whether a man lives or dies?"

"You feelin' all right, Bill?" asks Calamity.

Fortunately this attack of sentiment is only temporary, and Hickok soon recovers sufficiently to kill Lattimore and round up all his henchmen. But as he plays a game of cards with his captives while waiting for Buffalo Bill and the cavalry to arrive, the harmless-looking McCall gets hold of the six-shooter in that open drawer behind the bar and plugs him, and Calamity Jane gives him a kiss that he'll never be able to wipe off.[2] In the final shot we see the heroic Hickok and the previouly martyred General Custer, evidently in Valhalla, galloping triumphantly forward at the head of a troop of massed cavalrymen riding behind Old Glory.

During 1976's Bicentennial Week, one New York television station broadcast *The Plainsman* as part of a series of late-night films dealing with our nation's past under the title "America! America!" I naturally considered De Mille's slice of frontier life a terrible choice to represent the era of westward expansion, and tried to think of a better one, dealing with real events and figures of Western history in an entertaining and yet reasonably factual manner. Unfortunately, nothing sprang to mind at the time. *The Plainsman* is a more or less typical Wild West biography.

But now back to the ever-continuing saga of Wild Bill, hyped-up Western hero. By the time of De Mille's saga the fearless lawman was well on the way to becoming merely an exploitable name which could be tied up with standard Western antics in order to raise box-office receipts. Calling your average six-gun hero Wild Bill presumably aroused among the masses a strong desire to plunk down hard cash and relive the apocryphal exploits of this great frontiersman. Besides such "star" vehicles as Columbia's low-budget serial *The Great Adventures of Wild Bill Hickok* (1938), Bill was always good for a

---

*Jean practiced on De Mille's wrist with a ten-foot-long bullwhip until she got it right. "I insist upon authenticity," wrote the director later.

The death of a hero. Gun undrawn, Wild Bill Hickok (Gary Cooper) lies dead, treacherously gunned down by the bowler-hatted Porter Hall in *The Plainsman*. Jean Arthur, as Calamity Jane, looks on in dismay.

cameo appearance in such films as Ford's *Iron Horse* and 1950's *Dallas*, in which ex-Bill Gary Cooper was helped out by Reed Hadley's new Bill, who then rides off to abandon his marshal's job and become an actor, boasting that "they'll pay plenty to see the hairy article!" The distaff side of the legend was given its due in 1949's *Calamity Jane and Sam Bass*,[3] which had the glamorous Jane (Yvonne De Carlo) enjoying a fictional romance with the noted Texas desperado, though the beauteous Jane Russell had played Calamity strictly for laughs in the Bob Hope spoof *The Paleface* only the year before. Also on the nondramatic front was the Doris Day musical *Calamity Jane*, co-starring Howard Keel as Wild Bill and released in 1953—a particularly fruitful year for the Hickok legend, boosted as it was not only by two more epic Westerns and a national television series, but by no less a Western fan than the president of the United States. During a televised address in which he condemned unfair political tactics, Dwight D. Eisenhower reminisced:

> I was raised in a little town of which most of you have never heard. But in the West it is a famous place. It is called Abilene, Kansas. We had as our marshal for a long time [sic] a man named Wild Bill Hickok. If you don't know anything about him, read your Westerns more. Now that town had a code, and I was raised as a boy to prize that code.

It was: meet anyone face to face with whom you disagree. You could not sneak up on him from behind, or do any damage to him, without suffering the penalty of an outraged citizenry. If you met him face to face and took the same risks he did, you could get away with almost anything, as long as the bullet was in front.

Well, nobody ever claimed that Hickok had shot Dave McCanles in the back. And, whatever happened, he *did* get away with it.

This holding up of Hickok as an example for us all upset a few historians, Western buffs and others aware that Hickok was possessed of some minor imperfections, but disturbed not the blissfully ignorant average citizen, who if in any doubt at all of Hickok's virtue could always go to his *Encyclopedia Americana* and discover for himself the irrefutable fact that Wild Bill "never killed but in self-defense or line of duty" and was an all-around champion of law and trailblazer of civilization besides. Unfortunately the people who compiled such encyclopedias often found themselves consulting the same adulatory biographies as did the average reader, although the situation has vastly improved since Ike made his speech with the growth of accurate research and popular writing on the Wild West and its man-killers of note. Too bad Ike hadn't worshiped Bear River Tom.

Of the two major Hickokian dramas released that year, one was in the traditional heroic mold, and the other in radical departure from that tradition. *Pony Express* featured Charlton Heston and Forrest Tucker as Cody and Hickok fighting to get the mail through despite enemies both white and red. But Sidney Salkow's *Jack McCall, Desperado* portrayed Hickok as a villainous white renegade who sells guns to the Indians (shades of Charles Bickford) only to wind up dead in a fair-and-square fight at the hands of righteous title character George Montgomery, whose parents he has murdered. Montgomery goes unpunished by the law—and indeed, the real McCall was acquitted at his trial (a rather odd verdict considering that Hickok had been shot in the back of the head); what the film fails to show is that the verdict, having been rendered by a miners' lynch court, was null and void and that McCall was subsequently rearrested by federal authorities, who stretched his neck for him good and legal-like. This one didn't even have the sad excuse of "legend" to justify its obscenity.

TV's contribution for 1953 was the series "Will Bill Hickok"—a name chosen, no doubt, only after much heated debate among network executives. The late Andy Devine served as comic sidekick and Guy Madison was the youthful and heroic marshal, who averaged better than one killing a week as he strode through adventures having no basis in fact but serving to sell millions of boxes of Sugar Corn Pops, make considerable money (far more important than mere history), and perpetuate the godlike stature of Wild Bill far better than any mere presidential address could have done.

Not that the movies ever forgot him; in 1966 Universal even remade Paramount's *The Plainsman*, with Don Murray and Guy Stockwell as Hickok and Cody. It used the same basic plot but lacked the gloss and entertainment value of the De Mille epic, being a drab, low-budget piece originally made for CBS-TV; its only significance, if any, lay in its indication of Hollywood's decline and continuing adherence to nonhistory.

The cynical seventies produced two films featuring a rather unromantic Hickok. Arthur Penn's *Little Big Man* (1970) had one of the few screen Bills who looked something like the moustached, long-haired, long-nosed original, although even here actor Jeff Corey bowed to Hollywood convention and wore his anachronistic Peacemakers in a Western-movie buscadero. (In the comic novel from which the film was adapted Hickok tells the hero, "I never have held by a holster," and, as in real life, carries his Navys stuck into his waistband.) Since book and film were both satirical in nature, Hickok is played as an awe-inspiring but paranoid *pistolero*, reaching for his gun at every suspicious move or sound until his overcaution infects the runty hero and would-be gunfighter Jack Crabb (Dustin Hoffman), who complains, "Now you got *me* doing it!" as a noise makes both men reach for their iron. Shortly thereafter we see the reason for Bill's prudence when he shoots an aspiring assassin, who, bleeding quite freely, instantly cures Crabb of any desire to be a gunman. Sometime before the movie's "Custer's Last Stand" sequence (although Hickok actually died *after* that event and his murder is not depicted in the novel), Wild Bill is shot in the back by a young boy who, dragged away by onlookers, screams, "He killed my father! He killed my father!"—which is, I suppose, an attempt at deep meaning and significance: those who live by the sword, etc.

Little Big Man's caricature of Hickok was, however, infinitely preferable to that palmed off as factual in the NBC-TV movie *This Is the West That Was* (1974), a supposedly comic stripping away of old myths which set its own tone with the opening titles, superimposed over old photos showing such things as clownish-looking frontier types pointing unloaded guns at each other. Things went rapidly downhill from there: according to this rabid debunker's fantasy, Hickok (Ben Murphy) was an inept oaf who won his inflated rep through a misunderstanding and literally couldn't shoot to save his life, though surely none of his victims would have concurred in this assessment. This dreary little film was apparently made to cash in on a trend toward debunking (whether justifiably or not) well-known national heroes, but rather than reveal the neglected truth about the man, it merely abandoned one lie to foster another, more obvious one.

But from antimyth we swing, almost inevitably it seems, back to myth again. The latest Hickok movie, made in 1978, has been Dino De Laurentiis's production of Richard Sale's novel *The White Buffalo*. Charles Bronson and Will Sampson played, respectively, Wild Bill and the Sioux war leader Crazy Horse, two famous Western figures who, of course, never had anything to do with each other. Tom Custer also put in an appearance. De Mille lives on in spirit, it would seem, though nowadays the results are apt to be less entertaining than they used to be.

An unromantic vision. Jack Crabb (Dustin Hoffman), in overwrought gunman's costume, contracts the paranoia of Jeff Corey's Wild Bill in *Little Big Man*. Note buscadero holsters. (Museum of Modern Art/Film Stills Archive)

Such overblown legends as that of Wild Bill were usually stitched and patched together by many hands before they were ever touched by a single screenwriter, the typical early chronicler of the pistoleer's West being, if not himself a liar or reckless romantic, an innocent victim likely to fall prey to others' falsehoods. The chief culprit was not so much any single individual as the unspoken, collective need for a hero to represent the taming of a lawless region during an age of great achievement. But there was one such legend which sprang practically full-blown from the mind and pen of one brilliant scribe, a man to whom all true fans of the Wild West should pay silent homage. The man was Stuart N. Lake, and the legend that of Wyatt Earp.

This is not to say that Mr. Earp had previously been unknown to students of Western violence, or even the Hollywood community. Living out his sunset years in Los Angeles, he played a bit part in Allan Dwan's 1915 *The Half-Breed*, and at one point urged William S. Hart to make a *Wild Bill Hickok*-style film based on the modest Earp's own career in law enforcement. Hart and Tom Mix served as pallbearers at his funeral, and among the other Hollywood personalities who knew him was director Raoul Walsh, who in his memoirs describes not only the hero himself but also a dinner Walsh once had with

Earp and Jack London. "The legendary Earp," he wrote, "was tall and a little stooped, but I could still see in him the marshal of Tombstone. . . . Neither man wanted to talk about himself, but I did manage to get a few good details from Earp about the Clanton family and the famous shoot-out at the OK Corral." Soon after Wyatt wound up his description of this bygone event, who should come over to the table but Charlie Chaplin? According to Walsh, the Little Tramp "viewed Earp with evident awe."

"You're the bloke from Arizona, aren't you?" asked Chaplin. "Tamed the baddies, huh?"

Despite such consorting with the great, Wyatt had to molder in his grave for two years before really achieving national (soon to be worldwide) glory. For it wasn't until 1931 that Stuart Lake's biography *Wyatt Earp, Frontier Marshal* appeared in the bookshops after having been serialized in *The Saturday Evening Post*. Although a few other works, of varying stature, had treated of Wyatt before this, *Frontier Marshal* was *the* book which established the colossal Earp legend; a stirring, action-packed account of one man's struggle against Old West lawlessness, it was honored with rave reviews even from such staid publications as the *New York Times*, which praised both its style and its hard-bitten authenticity. But this same work, as Western writer Harry Sinclair Drago expressed it, also "did more to distort and confuse Western history than any book published before or since," and its incredible falsehoods have, through its acceptance as a standard reference work, been incorporated as historical truth into many otherwise reputable books. Even the honest and cynical James D. Horan and Paul Sann, who thought nothing of savaging the Wild Bill Hickok myth, swallowed Lake whole and summarized his fictions as fact in a section of their 1954 *Pictorial History of the Wild West* entitled, with unwitting irony, "The Story-book Marshal." No one can blame them: the book *sounds* authentic enough, and who could have guessed what Lake was really up to? I should confess at this point that I used to believe in him myself.

It is altogether fitting and proper that Hollywood base (albeit loosely) so many films on this particular book, for Lake reworked the raw fact of his hero's life and career so completely and skillfully as to rival the most ambitious of screenwriters, so completely and so skillfully that Earp the Frontier Marshal has become, through his media incarnations, the most famous lawman in the history not only of the West, but very possibly of the entire Western world. In the UN General Assembly, a British diplomat calls an American colleague a "Wyatt Earp looking for a showdown at the OK Corral" due to his aggressive stand against an anti-Zionist resolution. Pat Caddell, pollster for 1976 presidential contender Jimmy Carter, refers to the Pennsylvania Democratic primary as "the OK Corral of the campaign between [Sen. Henry] Jackson and us." A German pulp Western magazine advertises an entire series of cheap novelettes dealing with Earp, confirming that he was indeed "der beruehmtes-ten Marshal im wilden Westen," the most famous of all frontier lawmen. The most significant phrase in the ad makes the claim which, though sometimes left unspoken, is the key to all such exploitation of Western figures: "ER HAT WIRKLICH GELEBT"—"He really lived."

Though a complete fraud, Lake's dramatic chronicle was a very profitable one, and one which he attempted successfully to protect from all would-be revisionists. When, in his book *The Colorado*, Frank Waters published some facts gleaned from Virgil Earp's widow, Allie, and corroborated by research, Lake threatened legal action if retraction were not made. Waters refused, standing on his documented truths; one of Lake's attorneys subsequently went to the files of the Arizona Pioneers' Historical Society in Tucson and dropped the threatened suit after consulting Waters's manuscript containing Allie Earp's reminiscenses, published in 1960 as *The Earp Brothers of Tombstone*.

Of Lake's "pack and passel of lies," as Mrs. Virgil Earp called it, one of the more outrageous and widely accepted was *Frontier Marshal*'s account of how former wagon driver and buffalo hunter Wyatt Berry Stapp Earp became deputy marshal and chief lawbringer of wild and woolly Wichita, Kansas, in 1874, cleaning up the town in short order. Lake's story showed just how much a fella could get away with when writin' about such small (if notorious) Western towns, for as it happens Wyatt was never marshal in Wichita. He was instead, in 1875, a mere city policeman who did nothing of importance during his term of office and was generally referred to as "Policeman Erp" whenever he rated a mention in the local paper. (Also active in Wichita at this time were at least five women listed in municipal records as bearing the Earp name, one of them the wife of Wyatt's brother James. All were whores.) Fined $30 and costs for assaulting an opposition candidate for marshal (Wyatt apparently favored the incumbent because he hoped to have him hire two of Earp's brothers as lawmen), he was relieved of his badge, and there appears to have arisen some doubt as to whether he had turned in all the money collected in fines on behalf of the community. Soon the "two Erps," Wyatt and one of his brothers, had the vagrancy act invoked against them and were run out of town.

In 1955 Jacques Tourneur directed for Allied Artists an "epic" Western starring Joel McCrea as Wyatt Earp. Based very, very loosely on material from Stuart Lake's biography, it told a tale of the immortal Wyatt ridding a lawless cowtown of those who would disturb the peace.

The film, shot in glorious Technicolor and breathtaking Cinemascope, was entitled *Wichita*.

"You have cleaned up Wichita. Come over and clean up Dodge." Thus ran the urgent telegram from an anxious mayor, a telegram burning a hole in the pocket of the fictional Wyatt as he saddled up and rode in to save yet another Kansas cowtown coming apart at the seams: Dodge City. Here he would, for a well-deserved salary of $250 a month, fight to preserve order against the rowdy Texas cowboys, tumbling them into the calaboose by the score and making, in his own (?) words, "quite a dent in cowboy conceit."

Averting our eyes from this deity and looking at the records, we find that the real Wyatt managed to serve two terms in Dodge as a deputy marshal at $75

A group of lawmen and/or gamblers pose for a group shot in 1883 after the conclusion of the Dodge City "War," a bloodless dispute largely having to do with the city's harassment of sporting man Luke Short *(standing, second from left)*, who charged discrimination. Also included are Wyatt Earp *(seated, second from left)* and the derbied Bat Masterson, who once wrote truthfully that in Dodge gambling "was not only the principal and best-paying industry . . . but was also reckoned among its most respectable." (Kansas State Historical Society)

per month plus $2.00 for each arrest, of which he made only thirty-five in 1878 and twelve during 1879. Said one critic of Wyatt's breed: "They were called Tinhorn Gamblers, Cappers and Rounders for gambling games, bartenders and dealers. They were forever on the lookout for someone just come to town who had money, and forever trying to get to be deputy sheriff, or constable, or deputy anything, so that they could have the authority to carry a six-shooter and swagger around among the people and be on the lookout for tips as to when money was coming in or being sent out." In addition to such opportunities for wealth, a badge secured for its wearer the privilege of wearing a gun in towns where ordinary citizens were forbidden to do so. A Colt .45 in conspicuous evidence not only massaged the wearer's ego (a service Mr. Earp required frequently), but also gave him a distinct psychological advantage in any dispute over a game of cards—and Wyatt, formerly a professional gambler who, according to one acquaintance, was "up to some dishonest trick every time he played," continued to earn much of his income gambling even after becoming a peace officer, a common practice and one quite acceptable to Western mores.

Tiring of Dodge, Wyatt resigned from the force and, as every lisping infant knows, eventually arrived with his brethren in Tombstone, Arizona, where the Earps destroyed their enemies, the Clantons, in the gunfight at the OK Corral, that most legendary showdown of the legendary West. The standard Stuart Lake version of the story, followed in varying degrees by Hollywood, has Earp finding Tombstone a wild and wooly frontier town badly in need of the usual dose of law and order; opposed by corrupt county sheriff Johnny Behan, and aided by the enigmatic, consumptive dentist-gambler-gunman "Doc" Holliday, the Earp brothers finally wipe out the outlaw Clanton clan at the OK Corral to the joyful hosannas of the good townspeople. Then Wyatt, tall in the saddle and firm in his dedication to law, rides on to rid most of Arizona of its outlaw menace, a U.S. marshal's tin badge shining as gold over his stout heart.

On December 1, 1879, Wyatt, three of his brothers, and assorted wives arrived in the silver-mining town of Tombstone, where Wyatt got a job as a "shotgun messenger" on the Wells, Fargo stagecoach line, later becoming a civil deputy sheriff. He soon resigned and was replaced in this latter position by John H. Behan, who soon beat Wyatt out for an appointment as sheriff of Cochise County. Not one to remain idle long, Wyatt soon obtained an interest in the unsavory Oriental Saloon and Gambling House, where he installed brother Morg as a faro dealer; in the meantime brother Virgil ran for city marshal and lost. At this stage of the game the Earps were financially hard-pressed, and their gambling earnings had to be supplemented by their wives' sewing at a penny a yard. Wyatt's wife, Mattie, did her bit, but Wyatt chose to show his gratitude by openly cheating on her in collaboration with an actress named Sadie, ultimately taking her from the man who had first charmed her into leaving her traveling show troupe—Sheriff John Behan.

On March 15, 1881, a stagecoach was ambushed near Tombstone, the driver and a passenger being killed. A posse including the Earps and some of their friends but led by the thrice-hated Behan eventually nabbed an accomplice of the outlaws, but he soon escaped. The Earps, blaming Behan for this and implying publicly that he was in league with the robbers, waxed wroth when they heard the current rumors implicating their pal Doc Holliday (spotted galloping away from the vicinity moments after the double slaying). But the available evidence not only indicates that Holliday himself fired the fatal shots, but also seems to hint that Wyatt himself was the head of a stagecoach-robbery gang and was regularly tipped off to good pickings by a cooperative Wells, Fargo agent. (Virgil Earp's widow confirms as much, although she suspected that the introverted James Earp did the actual planning for the outfit since Wyatt "was bossy but didn't have much sense.") The killing of the driver was apparently a botched attempt by Doc on the life of a Fargo operative sent to investigate the rash of robberies, who had changed seats with the driver just before the ambush.

The three outlaws sought in connection with the stagecoach ambush were apparently quite annoyed at Doc Holliday for bungling the holdup by shooting two people rather than one of the lead horses, which action would have stopped the stagecoach very effectively; if captured by Behan's men, they might conceivably tell what they knew, as might the Clanton and McLaury brothers—the former petty rustlers connected with the Earp stage-robbery gang, the latter small-scale ranchers and friends of both the Clantons and the three wanted men. With suspicion centering on the "Earp Gang," Wyatt decided to kill two birds with one stone: he would offer the full $6,000 reward to the Clantons and McLaurys if they would betray the three outlaws into an ambush so that the Earps could kill them, thus removing three potential witnesses, paying off others, and transforming Wyatt Earp and Co. into guardians of the law. But when Wyatt told Ike Clanton of this clever scheme, Ike spurned his offer.

This temporary setback was followed by a streak of good fortune for the Earp party. Virgil Earp was appointed temporary town marshal, a position which became permanent when the incumbent, then on a short leave of absence from Tombstone, decided never to come back. The three stage robbers were killed in gun plays elsewhere. Doc Holliday, who had been jailed for attempted robbery and murder on the deposition of his much-abused (but usually loyal) mate, Kate Elder, was freed when Wyatt, insisting that Sheriff Behan had plied Kate with Demon Rum and made her sign a paper of whose contents she was ignorant, supplied Doc with an alibi. But Ike Clanton soon tore up the pea patch: under the impression that Wyatt hadn't kept his proposal concerning the three stage robbers a secret, he began to clamor that the Earps were telling lies about him, falsely claiming that the Clantons had agreed to sell out their friends for base coin. Wyatt, we may assume, began sweating: after this indiscretion, who could tell what else Ike might spill? In any case, for whatever reasons, it was high time that the partnership was dissolved.

To account for the trouble between the Earps and the Clantons and provide some sort of justification for what was to come, Wyatt began talking very loudly about law and order and Behan's rather cozy relationship with certain rustlers and other varmints; lending an air of legality to the upcoming showdown, Virgil Earp deputized Wyatt, Morgan, and Doc Holliday. Several attempts were then made to goad members of the Clanton faction into a fight.

On the afternoon of October 26 Sheriff Behan, having heard talk of an impending battle, walked up to the Earps where they were gathered in front of Hafford's saloon and told Virgil that he should attempt to disarm the Clantons, whereupon that officer, rather belligerently for a lawman, replied that he would instead give them a chance to fight it out. Behan then went down the street to see the Clantons and McLaurys in the alley behind the OK Corral, where they were apparently preparing to leave Tombstone. Behan asked them to disarm; Ike and Tom McLaury said they had no arms, while Billy Clanton and Frank McLaury declined to give theirs up.

Coming down the street, the Earps brushed Behan aside along with his protests when he came out and begged them to stop, then spread out to face their opponents in the most famous passage at arms in American history or legend. It lasted perhaps thirty seconds, at the end of which time Tom, Frank, and Billy were dead, Ike Clanton fled, and Virgil and Morgan Earp wounded. A strip of skin was torn from Doc Holliday's back by a bullet which had somehow contrived to glance off his gunbelt.

Wrote one eyewitness, who saw the fight from a window (and who refers to the McLaurys by the almost universal contemporary misspelling "McLowery"):

> I called my father's attention to what looked like a shooting to come off. Ike Clanton stood facing up the street, and as he saw the Earp crowd coming he ducked behind the gate and ran into the corral. The Earps levelled their guns and called out "hands-up!" The two McLowery boys and Billy Clanton put their hands above their heads and the Earp crowd fired into them. The McLowery boys fell at the first firing. Billy Clanton was shot through the right wrist; I saw his hand fall limp and backwards. The next fire he fell to the ground and as he did so he reached over with his left hand, got out his six-shooter and started to fire back at the Earps. . . .
>
> My father was wild over what he saw, and cried out, "That cold blooded murder!" He wanted to take my shotgun and go into the scrap. I said . . . "This is nothing but a bunch of stage-robbers splitting, and killing one another to keep any evidence from getting out."

Virgil was promptly fired as town marshal, and many of the town's law-abiding citizens seemed oddly ungrateful to the Earps for slaying the Clanton dragon. (Some went so far as to form a committee to inform them that if any more of this went on, the citizens themselves would act without regard to law.) A preliminary hearing took place and, despite a mass of damaging testimony—people swearing that two of the Clanton-McLaury men were unarmed, that the dead men had had their hands up, and so on—the Earps beat the rap, perhaps because the justice of the peace was a good friend who declined even to have them bound over for trial and declared them "fully justified in committing these homicides."

On December 28 Virgil Earp was crippled for life when he was shotgunned by persons unknown as he left the Oriental Saloon, and on March 18, 1882, Morgan Earp was killed by a bullet fired through a poolroom window as he chalked up. Packing the crippled Virgil and the rest of the Earp clan off to California, Wyatt proceeded in conjunction with some like-minded souls to murder several men he apparently considered responsible for his brothers' shootings, then rode off over the horizon to escape charges of murder and abandon his wife in California. Mattie Earp, whose husband had for reasons of his own kept their marriage a secret and would do so until his death, finally realized that Wyatt was not going to join her and returned to Arizona. There, destitute, she turned to prostitution in order to survive until she decided that surviving wasn't worth it and took a fatal dose of laudanum.

He left Cochise County, alas! untamed. (Tombstone itself, I should note, did not really come to be too violent a town until shortly after the Earps left. Only six men had been killed within the city limits in 1881, three of them by the Earps.) A few months later President Arthur threatened to proclaim martial law over the area if conditions didn't improve; this they did under the aegis of John Slaughter, a short, unimpressive-looking rancher who cleaned up the county very effectively but has thus far failed to become a national hero. While Sheriff Slaughter was doing this, Wyatt went on to pursue his Western career as gambler, saloon owner, and cheat; as late as 1911 (at age sixty-three) he was accused of complicity in a con game in Los Angeles, where he eventually died, leaving behind him an earthly life that makes Wild Bill Hickok look pretty good no matter what you think of him.

Not that it mattered much. Stuart Lake came along and begat *Frontier Marshal*, which in turn begat, in Frank Waters's words, "dozens of other books, pulp-paper yarns, movie thrillers galore, radio serials, a national TV series, Wyatt Earp hats, vests, toy pistols, tin badges—a fictitious legend of preposterous proportions. It is the cream of the jest that in Tombstone itself is now reenacted yearly the unjustified three-man murder outside the OK Corral on which the Earps' claim to fame largely rests today." The ritual reenactment of that historic slaughter had begun with the 1929 "Helldorado Week" celebration, named after a successful if not always accurate book by a former Tombstone deputy who, oddly enough, felt the Earps to be murderers. This tourist attraction left its satisfied customers with lightened wallets and somewhat warped notions of life in frontier Tombstone; what with blanks being fired off right and left and a fake Boot Hill extension being set up for disinterested mourners, it all seemed pretty queer to old-timer Billy Fourr, who couldn't recall his home town as having been quite so violent and so full of heavily bearded galoots waving six-guns. "Don't you remember," he asked, "that away back there in 1881, when you were mayor, the men seldom grew anything but a moustache, and there was a city ordinance forbidding anyone but a peace officer to carry firearms within the city limits?"

Former *Tombstone Epitaph* editor John P. Clum was, in the words of historian Odie B. Faulk, "speaking for all the men who had actually built Tombstone" when he replied. (The *Epitaph* had supported the Earps.)

"Well, Billy," said he scornfully, "you must remember that we were not giving a Helldorado show away back there in 1881."

This replay at the OK Corral was roughly similar to that played out at the fake "actual" corral for a 1970 Timex "Appointment with Destiny" television special. Narrated by Lorne Greene of "Bonanza" fame, it told of the Earp-Clanton feud in semidocumentary fashion, with "interviews" of participants and a slow-motion reconstruction of the corral fight "as though cameras had been on hand to record the event." Most of the film was even shot in black-and-white and given a sepia tint to suggest nineteenth-century photography (rather unnecessary since people back then could see in color just as well as they can now), and a commendable effort was made to tell the "real" story. But unfortunately the main sourcebook for the program appears to have been

Wyatt Earp, Frontier Marshal, an understandable error considering that its version of the conflict had already been echoed in several hundred other books and it was quite possible to overlook those anti-Earp books already published. The documentary's real value to the viewer lay in the way it revealed Hollywood's failure to remain faithful even to the Stuart Lake version of the Earp saga.

It was only natural that Lake's godlike *Saturday Evening Post* hero, who had never lost a fight and possessed no earthly vices to speak of, be transferred onto celluloid, and in due course he was. In fact one studio, Twentieth Century-Fox, transferred him three times in twelve years, although fictitious names were used for the 1934 *Frontier Marshal,* George O'Brien playing "Michael Wyatt." *Wyatt Earp* was also dropped from the title of the second version, a Randolph Scott vehicle shot by Alan *(Sands of Iwo Jima)* Dwan in 1939. But this time producer Darryl Zanuck revealed himself as a master of the Name prior to shooting. Was the film really based on the life of Wyatt Earp? asked Peter Bogdanovich of Dwan in an interview years later.

"No. Zanuck just decided to call him Wyatt Earp. . . . We never meant it to *be* Wyatt Earp. We were just making *Frontier Marshal* and that could be any frontier marshal." But the use of the Name brought a protest from Wyatt's widow, Josephine Sarah Marcus—that same "Sadie" for whose favors Earp and Sheriff Behan had earlier competed, and who was very sensitive about her late husband's image. (She didn't even like Stuart Lake's book, though it's hard to imagine what could have displeased her.) Fox finally had to make a settlement with Mrs. Earp since she had objected to Randolph Scott's love affair with Nancy Kelly, but since by 1939 the legend of the heroic frontier marshal—which, like most legends, possessed a certain monetary potential— had been firmly established, it may have been worth it to have Dwan's hero named Wyatt Earp. Save for a comparative handful of scholars, genuine Southwesterners, and miscellaneous folk who'd been exposed to anti-Earp material in books such as Lockwood's *Pioneer Days in Arizona,* just about everybody accepted Lake's vision of Earp as Western warrior-saint and town-tamer supreme.

In 1942 Earp's old hangout got a movie named after it: *Tombstone, the Town Too Tough to Die,* released by Paramount and based on *Tombstone: An Iliad of the Southwest,* a starry-eyed semifiction by Chicago newspaperman Walter Noble Burns, who liked to tell lies about the Old West (I doubt if he could really help himself) and who, like Lake, had actually talked with the heroic Wyatt before scribbling out his prose-poem ode to Earp. Although his book had actually appeared before Lake's, in 1927, it had not really made too much difference in establishing the legend, but of course by 1942 anything about Earp was potentially profitable. The final result, of course, bore little resemblance even to the Burns version of history. The OK Corral battle itself was surprisingly downplayed, with just a few seconds of the Earps and Doc blasting the Clantons (not the chief villains here), but as usual Wyatt (Richard

Dix) saves the day, fulfilling the expectations of the prologue. This was supposedly spoken by the state of Arizona itself ("I am the voice of the past . . . . for my existence, I am indebted to one man"); *Tombstone* was the only film ever to claim that Wyatt had saved an entire Western territory from destruction, though they never got around to explaining just how he'd managed it by killing a few badmen.

Wyatt's troublesome widow died in 1944, so there were no objections from that quarter when Earp (Henry Fonda) enjoyed a fictional romance with *My Darling Clementine* in 1946, the same year that Stuart Lake threatened to sic his lawyers on Frank Waters. *Clementine*, Fox's third version of the Earp saga, was also the most admired, and remains a classic of the Western film. It is rather sad that such a highly regarded work should be made in tribute to a nonhero like Earp, so we had best accept it on its own terms as one would *Macbeth*—as a work of art rather than just another Hollywood inaccuracy— and try not to see the real Wyatt peering out at us from behind the screen.

The funny thing is that *Clementine*'s director, John Ford, had talked extensively with its aging hero years before producing this ludicrously distorted film of Lake's ludicrously distorted "biography"—and seems to have believed that he was dramatizing at least the basic facts of the case.

> I knew Wyatt Earp. In the very early silent days, a couple of times a year, he would come up to visit pals, cowboys he knew in Tombstone; a lot of them were in my company. I think I was an assistant prop boy then and I used to give him a chair and a cup of coffee. . . . Wyatt was a friend of mine. In fact, I still have his rifle in the corner of my bedroom.

Some way to treat a friend! Not only did Ford kill off *two* of Wyatt's brothers prior to the OK Corral fight (the only one who did die at Tombstone, Morgan, is allowed to ride out of town at the end), but in the battle itself he liquidated Wyatt's loyal chum, Doc Holliday, who, as enigmatically played by Victor Mature, is an ex-surgeon rather than an ex-dentist and a power in Tombstone prior to Wyatt's arrival. (Ford later admitted that this death, at least, was unhistorical.) James Earp, a crippled Civil War veteran and the eldest brother, is portrayed by Don Garner as the youngest, born in 1864 (rather late to fight against the Confederacy) and killed at age eighteen while protecting the Earps' cattle from the Clantons, an unnatural clan of bestial ruffians presided over by the wicked Old Man Clanton (Walter Brennan).

Billy Clanton is metamorphosed from callow youth to ruthless killer John Ireland, who shoots Doc's fictitious half-breed girl friend, Chihauhau (Linda Darnell), before being killed himself by Virge. Finally Old Man Clanton invites Morg and Wyatt down to the OK Corral for the ultimate showdown: joined by Doc, galvanized into action by his girl's murder, and armed only with revolvers, the Earps employ a stagecoach driven by two sympathetic citizens as a decoy and manage to kill off the Clantons even though the latter all have rifles. Doc Holliday, the romantic tubercular, is slain when he coughs and leaves himself unable to shoot for a moment.

Said Ford: "[Wyatt] told me about the fight at the OK Corral. So in *My Darling Clementine*, we did it exactly the way it had been. They didn't just walk up the street and start banging away at each other; it was a clever military maneuver."

Especially getting your opponent to raise his hands before you shoot—damn smart. Makes you wonder just what Wyatt *did* tell Ford, and how much the director "remembered" by looking at the script, which even gives the year of the fight as 1882. Ford may have intended to re-create a historical event, but his screenwriters certainly hadn't.

A year after audiences all across American watched parfit gentil marshal and future savior Henry Fonda dance with Eastern nurse Cathy Downs on the foundations of a half-completed church symbolizing pioneer America—the other dancers clearing the floor for their revered prairie knight and his "lady fair"—Alvira Earp, the last of the original Earp party, died in Los Angeles, aged ninety-nine. It is to be hoped that she never saw Ford's movie, in which her beloved husband (Tim Holt) was shot by Walter Brennan.

By this time one might suppose that people would be getting sick of Wyatt Earp, but as the legend was retold differently each time, it retained its eternal appeal, and could even accommodate an occasional "off-beat" portrayal, such as Will Geer's in Anthony Mann's *Winchester '73* (1950). Here, as marshal of Dodge City, Wyatt is an aging, paunchy, child-loving father figure who appears briefly to preside over a Centennial Fourth of July celebration. Even though Greer's Wyatt seems about ready for retirement (and five years before the OK Corral fracas, too), there clings to him the aura of efficient marshal and all-around Good Joe—not surprisingly, since the film was based on a story by Stuart Lake himself.

In 1955 the release of *Wichita* was accompanied by the premiere of a TV series starring a previously unknown Hugh O'Brian and entitled "The Life and Legend of Wyatt Earp." Even as this highly successful show continued to take its weekly toll of prime-time badmen and reach into America's homes to perpetuate the legend in all its fraudulent glory, Paramount served up another large helping of Earp, offering what TV couldn't: not only glossy Technicolor but also awe-inspiring VistaVision and big-name stars. (Only the best for this American legend.) The winningly named *Gunfight at the OK Corral* (1957) was supposedly based on a mere magazine article, but in practice this meant that the article's title was appropriated for the film; grounded solidly in the Stuart Lake tradition, it starred Burt Lancaster as Earp and was scripted by famed novelist Leon Uris.

If Burt's Wyatt was in the familiar heroic mold, Kirk Douglas's Doc Holliday was in the familiar enigmatic mood. As in Ford's film, he's the most intriguing character on screen, a brooding, bad-tempered and dying gambler with a past who, through his friendship with Wyatt, ends up fighting on the

The Earps have a rendezvous with destiny and the Clantons in *Gunfight at the OK Corral*. (Museum of Modern Art/Filmn Stills Archive)

side of Good and only kills people who need it anyway. As an understanding bartender remarks to Wyatt (just after seeing Doc deftly toss a knife into the chest of a bothersome cowboy):* "I've never seen Doc pick a fight. Trouble just seems to find him."

Indeed.

While the projectionist struggles to repair a break in the film, we shall take a brief and belated look at the career of this persecuted, tragic hero, dogged as he is by an unrelenting fate.

John H. Holliday, a frail blond man coughing blood into his blue handkerchief—in one Bat Masterson's words, "a weakling who could not have whipped a healthy fifteen-year-old boy in a go-as-you-please fist fight"— seems hardly the man to be played by such robust silverscreen heroes as Kirk and Vic, especially as his chief role in life was that of a petty gambler with a nasty habit of killing people he didn't like. The first of those numerous unfortunates to feel the effects of the Holliday temper were allegedly several Negroes whom he found wading in his childhood swimming hole. Such a sight

---

*A neat trick, but scarcely an advisable tactic unless no other course is open: according to Harry K. McEvoy's *Knife Throwing: A Practical Guide*, the odds against making a knife hit point-first while throwing at an unknown distance are about eight to one. Even if a thrower should prove lucky, a man fatally hit in the chest might still have plenty of time to shoot his opponent due to the knife's lack of instant "stopping power."

proved too much for the sentimental Holliday, a mere lad at the time: he took up a gun and let fly. The score of killed and wounded in this incident is the subject of some minor controversy, and there may have been only one fatality—if, indeed, the shooting ever took place.

The Georgia-born Holliday was apparently told to seek healthier climes after he found his lungs giving out. Accordingly, he saddled up and rode out for the wide-open spaces, fatalistic courage supposedly strengthened by the knowledge that he was not long for this earth in any event. Having learned dentistry as an apprentice, he hung out his shingle in Dallas, but seems to have done more drilling with his six-gun than anything else, working on but a handful of mouths as he earned his bread at cards. Intent on mastering all the necessary arts of a professional gamesman, Holliday put himself through a rigorous schooling in the use of firearms, one of which he eventually used in an exchange of shots (ineffective) with a saloon owner. Leaving for Jacksboro, Doc allegedly shot several more men in disputes over the painted pasteboards and eventually fled to Denver, where he had an argument with one Bud Ryan over a card game and, instead of shooting him, slashed him across the face with a knife. In later years, we are told, Bud derived a good deal of satisfaction from pointing out the scar as the work of the infamous Doc Holliday.

No doubt sadly aware of the way trouble just seemed to find him, Doc nevertheless tried to outrun it. In Dodge City, he again set up practice—at least long enough to get up a gambling stake—and took out an ad in the *Dodge City Times* stating that "where satisfaction is not given money will be refunded." It is not known whether any ever was.

While at the "Queen of the Cowtowns" Doc became the loyal friend and fervent admirer of Wyatt Earp, who found him good company despite what Mr. Masterson described as Doc's "mean disposition and ungovernable temper"; their friendship remains perhaps the most intriguing part of the Earp saga. While in Las Vegas, New Mexico, Doc killed a man (who seems to have deserved it) and eventually joined Wyatt in Tombstone. There he helped preserve law and order as previously described, fleeing Arizona with Earp. In Leadville, Colorado, he tried to kill a man who had offended him, but failed. He died in a sanatorium at Glenwood Springs, Colorado, in 1887, the fatalistic dentist surprised and· perhaps somewhat annoyed that he didn't cash in with his boots on—and no doubt unrepentant concerning the trails of bodies he'd left behind him. When asked if his conscience troubled him, he reportedly replied, "No, I coughed that up with my lungs years ago."

But back to our story. After Burt Earp and Kirk Holliday start interfering with the Clantons' evil-doing, the latter force them as required into the climatic shoot-out, in this case at a very large corral identified by signs saying "OK" and nailed up on high posts. Since the battle itself figured so exclusively in the title, the fans obviously couldn't be disappointed by a mere thirty-second brawl, so, after that great image of the black-clad Earps tromping down the street to their blood-bespattered destiny, there ensues a long, complex battle in which wagons and other handy items are employed as cover, scores of shots are exchanged, and a defecting Clanton partisan is gunned down by his pals for an added thrill. After most resistance has been eliminated, Burt chases young-boy-gone-bad Billy Clanton (Dennis Hopper, John Ireland having graduated to playing the sinister Johnny Ringo in this film) into Fly's Photographic Gallery, where Ike Clanton had fled during the real "battle" to avoid Holliday's bullets; he is about to shoot the lad (reluctantly) when Doc does it for him, causing Billy to fall from a second-story railing and go crash.

After this, Frankie Laine, who'd been providing us with a running song-commentary throughout the film, sings all about the "three killers that died" in the "Gunfight at the OK Coraaaalllllll. . . ." Frankie was later chosen to sing the title song of Mel Brooks's 1974 farce *Blazing Saddles*, in which all comedy was intentional.

Gunfight was directed by John *(Bad Day at Black Rock)* Sturges, who in 1962 was inexplicably quoted as saying: "Western characters must not be glamorized. I'm a Westerner myself, and I can tell you I don't go for that Stuart Lake baloney."

Although professedly displeased with its creator, Sturges nevertheless returned to the Earp legend years after his first treatment, as did the old master John Ford. Jimmy Stewart played an aging Wyatt and Arthur Kennedy an unusually plump and healthy Doc Holliday in the Dodge City sequence of Ford's 1964 *Cheyenne Autumn*, intended by the director as a kind of intermission in an otherwise tragic story. Sans lawman's badge and dressed in an immaculate white suit, the middle-aged Earp is seen playing cards and puffing on a cigar in the saloon where he apparently makes his living, which is just about all of Dodge that we're allowed to see; when confronted by a belligerent cowboy, this revisionist Wyatt does not tell him to step outside so they can settle things, but instead shoots him through the foot with a concealed derringer, subsequently complaining about the bullet hole he's made in his own coat pocket. Then he goes reluctantly out to lead the apprehensive citizens in pursuit of Cheyenne warriors he knows to be nowhere around. "It actually happened that way," said Ford, although in fact it seems not to have happened that way.

The nature of this scene has led to some theorizing as to whether this changing interpretation of the Earp myth reflected Ford's own increasingly pessimistic view of the Old West; in *Visions of Yesterday* Jeffrey Richards even sees it as a sort of epilogue to *My Darling Clementine*, showing how "the formerly tragic and heroic figures of the winning of the West have become crafty, tired old men, content to rest on their laurels." There are problems with this interpretation. In the first place, the Dodge City sequence is set in 1878, three years before the Tombstone troubles—and yet Wyatt, instead of a young stalwart destined for future greatness, is already in his fifties (or at least

Stewart was during the filming). *Autumn* would also be in violation of *Clementine*'s narrative if this sequence were intended as a postscript, since Doc should already have been dead. The sequence would *seem* to indicate instead an awareness that the Earp myth was never all it had been cracked up to be; rather than a tired, corrupt ex-hero, Ford offers instead simply a more realistic picture of the Wyatt Earp of history, gambler and opportunist. (By 1964, after all, anti-Earp data had received fairly wide circulation in a number of popular sources, including certain nationally known magazines.)

The only trouble with this second theory is that the Bogdanovich interview in which Ford claimed to have recreated the OK Corral fight exactly as it had happened (and by implication at least the broad outline of Wyatt's Tombstone career, since the director never mentioned any change in his concept of Wyatt as Hero) took place in 1966, after he'd already shot *Autumn*'s Dodge City sequence—the effect of which Warner Brothers ruined in initial engagements by inserting an actual intermission in its center. In subsequent showings the second half, which had followed the studio's intermission, was deleted, leaving the actual burlesque "pursuit" of the Indians unshown and Stewart's cameo appearance unjustified. The broad comedy and seeming irrelevance of the sequence had disturbed or irritated many critics and viewers of the drama, and with the point of the sequence eliminated, what remained must have seened like an especially cheap and distasteful attempt to cash in on the Earp name in a film supposedly recounting a great American tragedy.

John Sturges's sort-of-sequel to *Gunfight at the OK Corral* was *Hour of the Gun* (1967). Scripted by Edward Anhalt, it opened with the following prologue:

This Picture is Based on Fact. This Is the Way It Happened.

Something of an exaggeration here. But one may say this of *Hour:* at the time it was the most faithful to the Lake scripture of all Earp films, and, as if to underscore its extravagant claim, was shot in a harsh, gritty, and naturalistic style far removed from the big-budget gloss of *Gunfight*. Sturges begins by serving up the OK Corral scrap again, but this time he gives the lie to his earlier work by making it a stand-up fight lasting only a few seconds. Most of the film's length is given over to the shootings of Morg and Virge (more or less as they happened) and Wyatt's hunting down of the ambushers (more or less as Lake made it up); the main fictional fictions added to Lake's fact-fictions are the continued presence of Doc Holliday—who tags along to save Earp's life once or twice, serve as a chorus on the action, and cough—the transformation of Ike Clanton (Robert Ryan) into a powerful criminal mastermind, and Wyatt's killing of same down in Old Mexico.

Since Wyatt (James Garner) is motivated primarily by a lust for vengeance rather than a love of law and order, he naturally seems less noble than in previous films—especially as he seems to enjoy giving each of his brothers' attackers some opening or chance to draw so that Wyatt can grimly shoot him down under the cover of his badge rather than take him, moving Doc (Jason Robards) to remark, "Those aren't arrest warrants, those are hunting licenses!" Jack Nachbar—who, perhaps basing his statement on the Stuart Lake version, called *Hour* "the most accurate filmed retelling" of the Earp story—contrasted Ford's idealist hero with Sturges's avenger hero and remarked that "obviously between 1946 and 1967 there were some important changes in the legend of Wyatt Earp." This depends on what one means by "legend." The Earp myth as established by Lake was a written rather than an oral one, with one writer unknowingly passing the lies onto another (or to the public) rather than some old cracker-barrel philosopher wheezing out tales of the Earp brothers through his beard to enraptured future storytellers: as such it had remained relatively constant since 1931, except for some debunkers who sometimes reached a respectable audience but whom Hollywood felt obliged to ignore, and only the approach to the same basic material had changed in keeping with the more "realistic" and less morally certain sixties. ("WYATT EARP," ran the ads. "HERO WITH A BADGE, OR COLD-BLOODED KILLER?") An audience in 1946 would have been far less likely to accept an unadulterated version of Lake's implacable, somewhat frightening lawman, even if his moral position went unquestioned by a cynical Doc Holliday; as Nachbar remarks, though the conventional formula of the "civilizer" pitting himself against the forces of chaos may still be evident, "heroes are no longer necessarily heroic, the civilized no longer necessarily civilized."

In 1970 Arthur Penn passed up the chance to satirize Earp along with Hickok in his *Little Big Man*, but then Earp's role in the original novel was of little importance: he merely asks the hero why he had called Earp's name, receives the truthful answer, "What I done was belch," and knocks the tactless Jack Crabb down with his fist, subsequently cold-cocking him with a pistol barrel. In 1971 came the first full-length anti-Earp film, *Doc*, written by journalist Pete Hamill and shot in Spain by Frank Perry, who claimed that his film pierced "the western myth's special heart of darkness." It didn't, but it did give us, along with enough inaccuracy to suit any Cecil B. De Mille fan, Harris Yulin as a short, unattractive Wyatt who makes hypocritical speeches about law and order, Stacy Keach as a brooding, tortured Doc, and Faye Dunaway as Kate Elder, a whore with both heart and tooth of gold. (She greets Doc with a salutation of "Hello, Bones," whereupon he replies, "Hello, bitch.") There were supposed to be overtones of homosexuality in this version of the famous friendship, but Yulin allegedly refused to speak the lines which would have positively established fact and act.

The critics were not particularly kind, some seeing in *Doc*—no doubt correctly—the influence of seventies disillusionment and the debunking tendency seen at work in movies such as *This Is the West That Was* rather than a desire to dramatize the truth. Jay Cocks, writing for *Time*, characterized it as "another Western for swingers" and "so redolent of a kind of New York café society chic that the Tombstone saloon might as well have been re-christened

Elaine's," while the "general air of charade" was underscored by brownish sets photographed with washes of white light so that the film resembled "an underdone French fry." As for minor New York City official John Scanlan and Dan Greenberg, author of *How to Be a Jewish Mother* (who played, respectively, a bartender and *Tombstone Epitaph* editor John P. Clum), Cocks sneered that they stood out "like two polo players at a rodeo."

The irony is that *Doc* is interesting mainly for the things it is trying to debunk. It is the stuff of legends—the challenges, the brawls, the gunfights—that sustains attention. Perry and Hamill are simply swallowed whole by the myth they hoped to destroy.

Some critics were apparently also swallowed up by the myth, such as Howard Thompson, who was not opposed to a debunking of Earp and Holliday, but found *Doc*'s efforts toward this end a bit too much to stomach and subsequently wrote in the *New York Times* that "the climax, when these two bland egotists serenely slaughter a clan of seven, who are apparently ready to 'talk,' is a pious, gory jolt that yanks the rug from under the whole picture. What realistic history book yielded this incident?"

What history book indeed? Did he bother to investigate? I doubt it. Of course, no "clan of seven" was ever slaughtered at the OK Corral (and the movie is so vague that we're not sure just *why* they were killed), but since most critics cannot afford the habit of dashing off to do research every time they must confront a so-called historical Western, I fear that Mr. Thompson had been influenced in his readiness to scoff by viewing previous Earp movies. Perhaps this particular myth has become just too big among those unacquainted with the written record for anyone to combat successfully; it's gone too far. Any future film account of the real Wyatt's activities, no matter how closely it adheres to the truth, may ironically seem merely a trendy product of our jaded, cynical modern era, a debunking age in which not even the flag, Mom, and apple pie are held sacred, let alone a great Westerner paid homage by such directors as John Ford. If a dozen anti-Earp films were to be made over a thirty- or forty-year period (a depressing business!), things might be different: it would cast a shadow of doubt, if nothing else.

One of Wyatt's friends in both real life and the movies was a man who, like the illustrious Hickok, became a legend in his own time, folks eagerly making up fantastic stories about him long before he was safely dead. Although he has, like Earp and Hickok, appeared in a number of films glorifying his peace-officer role, he is perhaps best "remembered" as portrayed by Gene Barry in the 1957 series that bore his name: "Bat Masterson." As the title song ran:

> Of all the legends of the West
> One name stands out above the rest. . . .

Bat Masterson . . . yeah, he was a cool one, all right. Cool, elegant, and highly cultured—downright foppish, in fact, laying down the law to the rough element in a flawless patrician drawl while fondling his silver-topped, gun-concealing cane, matched in tasteful nattiness by his white gloves, his fancy vest, and a bowler hat perched over clean-shaven, aristocratic features. Of necessity all his TV adventures were fictitious, since the real Masterson could scarcely have killed or roughed up enough badmen to satisfy the demands of a weekly show even if he'd set himself a quota; taken as a whole, these tales from the box inevitably surpassed in collective mayhem even those grisly legends and unlikely newspaper stories already clustering round the Masterson name during Bat's own Western career. Against one such newspaper article—picked up by a Missouri paper from the *New York Sun*, entitled "Bat's Bullets," and repeating the popular assertion that Masterson had already slain twenty-six men by the age of twenty-seven—the *Atchison* (Kansas) *Champion* editorialized, under the headline "TOO MUCH BLOOD":

> We do not stickle about a few tubs of gore, more or less, nor have we any disposition to haggle over a corpse or two, but when it comes to a miscount or overlap of [at least] a dozen, no conscientious journalist, who values truth as well as the honor of our State, should keep silent.

Keeping silent was one thing Bat didn't do. In the finest tradition of the Western tale-spinner, he managed to keep a straight face when confronted with his legend, while sometimes confirming even the wildest of body counts put to him by inquisitive reporters. But aside from any Indians he may or may not have killed, Bat's only victim appears to have been a Corporal Melvin King of the Fourth Cavalry. The story goes that, upon finding Bat in the company of saloon girl Molly Brennan—admired by both men—in a Sweetwater, Texas, dance hall, King pulled out his revolver and started blasting, killing the girl (who had supposedly thrown herself in front of Bat) and wounding Masterson, who, however, managed to draw his own weapon and shoot the soldier through the heart despite the bullet lodged in his pelvis. But one account claims that a number of other people were shooting at the same time, so there remains the slight possibility that Masterson never killed anybody.

If the real Bat failed to approach Gene Barry in kills scored, (which is not to disparage him, of course), he also came in second regarding polish, although he did dress well, carry a (nonexplosive) cane in addition to a silver-plated Colt, and possess a gentlemanly bearing. Though sometimes mistaken for an Eastern dude, he was no aristocrat, and for that matter neither were most of his screen doubles, the Barry character being an exception and very much a gimmick.

Born in Quebec Province in 1853 (his family trekking westward for ten years and reaching Kansas in 1871), William Barclay Masterson—original name Bartholemew Masterson, which accounts for the "Bat"—spent his early adult years as a railroad subcontractor, scout, and buffalo hunter, violating the Indian treaties of the moment in pursuit of the shaggy beasts so vital to the survival of the free Plains tribes. His first really newsworthy experience came in 1874 with the second battle of Adobe Walls, during which he was the youngest of a small band of hide-hunters who held that Texas trading post against hundreds of properly resentful red men. The Corporal King incident and Bat's wounding came in 1876.

In Dodge City, where the cattle trade was replacing the shipment of buffalo hides as the town's excuse for being (its original name was "Buffalo City"), Bat thrived as a gambler and part owner of a combination saloon-dancehall-whorehouse. In June of 1877 he was fined $15 and costs after being severely beaten about the head with a revolver and thrown into jail by city marshal Larry Deger, whom he had grabbed around the neck from behind in order to allow a drunken but otherwise harmless acquaintance to escape the lawman's clutches. In November Bat ran against Deger for Ford County sheriff and won by three votes. Headquartered at Dodge and getting off to a fine start with the capture of some train robbers (who were not actually within his jurisdiction when he captured them), he proved an efficient and popular officer.

Unfortunately young Bat had no bloody gunfights whatsoever during his term of office, though he occasionally used his walking stick or pistol barrel to pound sense into malefactors' heads and his brother Ed, the well-respected city marshal, was killed by a drunken cowboy whom he in turn slew along with one of his accomplices. Although it wasn't part of his job as county officer, Bat played his part in policing Dodge City itself. But despite the killings which occurred from time to time (seven during his own two years as sheriff), bawdy Dodge wasn't quite up to Hollywood standards when it came to wildness, and Bat, who also happened to be a deputy U.S. marshal, even had time to lead a group of hired volunteers to fight for the Atchison, Topeka, and Santa Fe railroad* in its violent dispute with the Denver and Rio Grande** over a strategic right of way. This particular group was bloodlessly arrested by local officials armed with a writ of injunction against the Santa Fe, and the Rio Grande got possession of the gorge in question. Bat also had some spare hours to spend dealing out the cards and maintaining close contacts with such fellow celebrities of the saloon and gambling element as Wyatt Earp, whose life he once saved during a scuffle with some irate Missourians. Their membership in the cowtown sporting crowd—which, of course, played a major if largely unheralded role in the winning of the West—caused such cowtown lawmen to be considered mere "fighting pimps" by disgruntled cowboys, who, not surprisingly, sometimes found themselves cheated in the prairie Sodoms where they came to drink, gamble, and whore. Fortunately, municipal opinion

*Immortalized by the song "The Atchison, Topeka and the Santa Fe" in the 1945 Judy Garland musical *The Harvey Girls*.

**Immortalized by the 1952 *Denver and Rio*, in which the title railway is good and the other the evil railway justly beaten in the war, though there really wasn't *that* much difference between the two other than the not unimportant fact that the Denver won.

and economics seldom required the suppression of such activities by members of the fraternity who happened to wear badges; the usual practice was to enrich the city coffers by levying taxes on gamblers and whores in the guise of fines.

After being defeated for reelection in 1880 by bartender George Hinkle (possibly a reaction to some of Masterson's less wholesome political cronies), Bat left for Colorado to deal cards and unsuccessfully look for gold. Then it was back to Dodge, where the 1880 census listed his occupation vaguely as "laborer" and his "concubine" of the moment as one nineteen-year-old Annie Ladue. Then to Tombstone, where he dealt faro at friend Wyatt's Oriental Saloon. Then back to Dodge to help his brother James, who had had a falling out with his partner in the saloon business and their bartender. Somebody got word to Bat, who, not knowing whether he would arrive to help Jim or simply avenge him, came a-gunning for both men and, upon leaping from the train bearing him to Dodge at about 11:50—almost high noon!—encountered the objects of his ire on the street. Firing somehow commenced, both sides took cover, and Bat, who by all accounts was an excellent shot, emptied his six-gun without noticeable effect. Some unknown marksman—an impressionable bystander, perhaps—put a bullet through the bartender's lung, after which everybody was arrested and Bat fined $8 for disturbing the peace. The *Dodge City Times*, formerly a pro-Masterson paper, professed to be very upset: "The firing on the street by Bat Masterson, and jeopardizing the lives of citizens, is severely condemned by our people, and the good opinion many citizens had of Bat has been changed to one of contempt." But although Bat left Dodge under a cloud, he would, on one of his later visits, be voted the most popular man in town.

Favoring other Western locales with his presence, Bat served briefly as marshal of Trinidad, Colorado, and centered his sporting and gambling activities at Denver, from which he was asked to depart in 1900 due to a binge of alcoholic rowdiness—apparently brought on by his depression over local woman suffrage. Visiting New York in 1902, he found himself under arrest and charged with cheating a rich Mormon elder out of $16,000 with marked cards—the first time Bat, renowned as an honest gambler (though he did have a lot of crooked friends), had ever been accused of such chicanery. He was freed for lack of evidence. Arrested again by city police for carrying a concealed pistol, he was rescued by an old acquaintance, ex-rancher and current president Teddy Roosevelt, a Wild West fan who appointed him a deputy U.S. marshal for New York's southern district after the aging Bat wisely declined a similar post in still-wild Arizona. Pursuing a colorful career as a respected sportswriter who numbered among his acquaintances such noted scribblers as Irwin S. Cobb, Damon Runyan, and Louella Parsons, Masterson died at his desk at the *New York Morning Telegraph* in 1921, legend-becrusted and ripe for the plucking by screenwriters of easy virtue.

The first plucking of consequence came in 1943 with *The Woman of the Town*. A sentimental tale, this film centers around a purely invented romance between sheriff Bat (Albert Dekker) and dance-hall singer Dora Hand (Claire Trevor, the whore with a heart of gold from Ford's *Stagecoach*). Miss Hand, alias Fannie Keenan, was a popular variety entertainer; in 1878, she was murdered in her sleep by one Jim Kenedy, who fired through the door of the house where she was staying under the mistaken impression that Dodge City mayor James "Dog" Kelley was sleeping there that night. Pursued by a Masterson-led posse (thus the link between murder victim and lawman), the assassin was cornered and brought down with a crippling shoulder wound, possibly inflicted by Masterson's .50 Sharps; when he learned of his mistake, Kenedy was rather crestfallen over killing an innocent woman and, perhaps, over the fact that he'd missed Kelley. Inevitably, Miss Trevor's Dora dies in a manner more reminiscent of the legendary Molly Brannan.

Going rapidly downhill, we encounter the 1954 *Masterson of Kansas*, directed by William *(House on Haunted Hill)* Castle for notorious low-budget producer Sam Katzman, who gave us all the usual bald-faced lies solemnly palmed off as documentary fact, complete with narration: "That's the way it was that bright July day when Bat Masterson went out to meet Doc Holliday." The meeting is, of course, a showdown, with the valiant sheriff of Dodge City (no such office) facing down James Griffith as the deadly D.D.S., who hates Bat (George Montgomery) for some unexplained reason. The two are stopped by Wyatt Earp (Bruce Cowling), who doesn't want to see his two best friends kill each other and, naturally, doesn't have to; after diving into a Wild West plot of impeccable cliché, we come up to find the three noble gunmen united in a just cause, striding down the main street of Hayes [*sic*] City and killing five badmen without breaking step. In between shootings Bat reminisces to heroine Nancy Gates about Molly's tragic death and how he got his nickname—by plugging lots of bats when he was a kid. At the end, having gotten the girl, wiped out the baddies, stopped a lynching, and nipped a full-scale Indian uprising in the bud, Bat rides off alone into the red, red sunset. "Out West they'll always remember him . . . as Masterson of Kansas."

Not that Hollywood could ever let them forget. In 1957, for instance, Bat appeared not only in his own show but also in *Gunfight at the OK Corral*, while veteran Joel McCrea did his Bat in the 1959 *The Gunfight at Dodge City*, which had absolutely nothing to do with Bat's inaccurate shooting on behalf of his brother Jim. The latest word on Masterson—and a very ungenerous word it is, too—comes in Don Siegel's *The Shootist* (1976), set in 1901. After hero-worshiping youth Ron Howard presciently quotes from Bat Masterson's observations on the qualities of courage, firearms proficiency, and delibera-tion required by the successful gunfighter (observations he wrote down in 1907 for articles in the magazine *Human Life*), aged man-killer J. B. Books (John Wayne in his last film) replies: "Well, Masterson always was full of . . . sheep-dip." Like several other things in this film adaptation, Wayne's language was somewhat watered down; the original noun Books used in the Glendon Swarthout novel was considerably stronger.

Once upon a time there lived a man named Bill Tilghman, who in his day was one of the Wild West's most widely admired peace officers. Serving as city marshal of Dodge (after quitting the saloon business, possibly because the town's increasingly "civilized" intolerance made law enforcement and the bar seem less compatible), and later as a federal and local lawman in Oklahoma, Tilghman earned the respect even of his enemies, one of whom, the notorious desperado Bill Doolin, declined to bushwhack him when given the opportunity, remarking simply that Tilghman was "too good a man to be shot in the back." After he was finally killed in the line of duty in 1924—aged seventy— his body lay in state for three days in the rotunda of the capitol building at Oklahoma City. He has been well "written up" in many general accounts of Western lawlessness and is the subject of several full-length biographies, including one by his wife, Zoe, and another by Floyd Miller which, in 1967, was condensed for publication in *Reader's Digest*.

Odds are you've never heard of him—perhaps because old Bill never got an "epic" Western or TV show made about him and thus has little claim to being a genuine "Western legend" as defined by the film industry. A similar fate befell lawmen such as Heck Thomas, Chris Madsen, and Harry Morse; for some reason or other those who could have made them stars chose to ignore them. Perhaps their names weren't considered sufficiently attractive or catchy (*Tilghman?* How do you pronounce it?), or perhaps they just lacked a superb publicist such as Stuart Lake. It couldn't have been because the right people were wholly unaware of them, for producers and screenwriters—whose invention sometimes flags when it comes to making up authentic-sounding "Western" names—have been known to do at least some historical reading in order to find vicious killers who can, with a wave of the corporate wand, be polished into shining symbols of the law's two-gun majesty. On occasion they have even used a legitimate figure such as Oklahoma lawyer and lawman Temple Houston (the inspiration for the character Yancy Cravat in Edna Ferber's novel *Cimarron*), who briefly appeared as hero of a 1964 TV series. But mostly the right people seemed to think that Bat, Wyatt, and Wild Bill were the only lawmen worthy of the name, and when lawmen were unavailable—back in that hectic Western-loving decade of TV beginning in the mid-fifties—it became necessary to invent them.

One such manufactured video hero was the noble "marshal" Clay Allison, who never held a peace officer's commission and was nothing better than a Tennessee-born thug who had been discharged from the Confederate Army for mental instability and whose exploits included riding down a cowtown street naked (save for gunbelt, boots, and the inevitable Stetson), killing several of what he considered to be belligerent Negroes, and shooting up, at irregular intervals, the town of Las Animas, Colorado. One writer, Dane Coolidge, finding that the so-called Wolf of the Washita had not a single redeeming trait, seized desperately on an alleged incident in which Clay gave some money to the widow of a man he had killed (for no particular reason) as proof that he wasn't all bad, and went on to regret, with a tiny nostalgic sigh, that the

Bill Tilghman, a peace officer for almost half a century at the time of his death. (Western History Collections, University of Oklahoma Library)

"need" for such men had passed. (Actually Clay seems to have killed no one in this affair, instead simply smashing up a printing press.) Eventually, as all men must, Allison died—in an unromantic wagon accident.

Why was Allison, whose name had been totally unknown to the public and whose talents for killing had generally been employed in the pursuit of something other than justice, picked out over better men? I don't know; his name wasn't particularly dramatic, and was certainly nothing to compare with that of Johnny Ringo, who also got his own show and deserved it, being a Tombstone alcoholic, gambler, rustler, and general no-good. A well-educated man of mystery, he has been an object of considerable fascination to Western writers, especially the bad ones; sometimes seen as a death-obsessed, brooding tragic hero, he ended with a bullet through his head, possibly a suicide, possibly done in by some unknown public benefactor. (Wyatt Earp, among others, has been suspected.) But his name had the clank-of-money sound that all producers love, and he was duly resurrected by Don Durant, in a form far different from that assumed by John Ireland in *Gunfight at the OK Corral*. Johnny's original and rather banal name had, apparently, been Ringgold, but he supposedly changed it so that his female relatives would not be heartbroken over his violent and debauched life, should they chance to hear of Johnny Ringo's misdeeds.

Among Roy Bean's roles as true man of the West were those of swindler, jail escapee, horseback duelist, and guest of honor at a lynching bee (he survived with a permanently stiff neck). But his early, and for that matter middle-aged, exploits need not concern us, since he only got started down the road to glory in the early 1880s, when he managed to get himself appointed justice of the peace and establish at the small West Texas tent city of Vinegaroon an extremely informal court which doubled as a saloon—becoming, as he liked to brag, "The Law West of the Pecos." Word of Bean's unorthodox rulings finally moved state authorities to dispatch Judge T. A. Falvey to the scene, where he witnessed Bean deliver a pistol-flaunting harangue to a hung jury on the order of the following: "It may be all right in some places for juries to get so high and mighty that they can't agree on anything. But that ain't the way it goes in this district. I know there's some argument about jurisdiction. But we ain't got time to fool with such nonsense out here because we're too far away from any other kind of jurisdiction. So I've got the right to chain the pack of you to the post out there until you can get together. And that's what I'm aimin' to do."

A verdict of guilty was soon brought in, Bean explaining to Falvey: "It's this way: If I can't finish off a case here in my court, then there's a lot of trouble. Some Ranger has to haul the prisoner to Fort Stockton and the last time that happened the Ranger had to travel 600 miles and he was out twelve days before he got back. . . . And as for this case we just got rid of, everybody knows that fella's guilty. He just had a couple of friends on the jury."

Faced with such logic, Falvey went back to report that all was well at Vinegaroon—which it was, sort of, since with the help of a few doughty Texas Rangers Bean had established a rough form of order in a tough town where none had existed previously. Not until the end of railway construction work resulted in Vinegaroon's folding itself up and stealing away did Bean move his court to the whistle-stop of Langtry and really begin confusing his own best interests with those of justice. (There was little legal precedent for fining a dead man for carrying a concealed weapon.) Bean christened his judicial beer joint "The Jersey Lilly," in misspelled honor of English actress Lillie Langtry, with whom Bean carried on a long-range, one-way love affair years before and years after he got to see her on stage at San Antonio in '88, giving a yellowed magazine picture of her an honored place behind the bar. He also claimed to

The Law West of the Pecos. (Western History Collections, University of Oklahoma Library)

have named the town after her, although the Southern Pacific Railway insisted that the hamlet bore the name of one of its own dignitaries.

Life at the bar of judgment produced an abundant supply of anecdotes. Once, having ridden out to preside over a coroner's jury examining ten men crushed by falling bridge timbers, His Honor declared that all ten had come by their deaths accidentally, whereupon one juror dared throw a monkey wrench into the wheels of justice by pointing out that one of the men was still breathing. "What are you talking about?" demanded Bean, in one of several quoted versions. "When I ride thirty miles on horseback to say somebody's officially dead, then he's officially dead. And I'm not going to be called back two-three hours from now and ride another thirty miles to make it more official." He was always the practical sort.

Bean expanded his reputation as a frontier eccentric by swindling tourists and droppers-in, fining men 90¢ for lacking change of a dollar, or hauling them up before the court for not liking the judge's beer. The judge tried to make sure that everyone voted the right way whenever he came up for reelection (sometimes stuffing the ballot box, just in case), and as he clung doggedly on, his fame spread across America; an especially bright moment of glory came when he arranged to host the eagerly watched and quite illegal Maher-Fitzsimmons prizefight in 1896, moving the contest across the border into Mexico. He had already been a truly legendary figure for perhaps a score of years when the Jersey Lily herself came to call on his judicial habitat— shortly after his death in 1903 at the age of somewhere around eighty. She accepted the gift of his revolver, remarked that "he must have been a remarkable man," and donated sixty dollars to "start a school library." Years before, after Bean had taken pen in hand to inform her of the naming of Langtry, she had written in reply offering to have a municipal drinking fountain erected there in his honor; she was dissuaded by his disclosure that nobody in the town ever drank water.

Being of a theatrical turn of mind himself, Roy Bean would probably have loved being the subject of extravagant fictions, and in any event his "true story," while an attractive source of inspiration, probably wouldn't make much of a narrative; so it seems rather inappropriate to criticize his screen portrayals too harshly, except perhaps for such as the early one featured in Sam Goldwyn's 1940 production of *The Westerner*, directed by William Wyler.

His Honor dispenses beer and justice while trying a horse thief at Langtry in 1900. (Western History Collections, University of Oklahoma Library)

While buckskinned Gary Cooper was the eponymous hero of the tale, Walter Brennan got to carry off another Oscar as Best Supporting Actor and play the only real character in the film (all others being, as a small-print disclaimer at the end of the opening credits duly noted, purely fictitious). Bean, who finally has to be shot down by his friend Cooper, is unjustly depicted as a tool of ruthless cattlemen, who burns out and kills small farmers and is much given to legal lynchings; he starts out in high style by hanging a sodbuster for shooting a steer, replying to his victim's plea of accidental bovicide that he should have taken better aim when firing at the cowboy he'd intended to hit. (The real Bean, of course, never hanged anybody.)* The studio reconstruction of Bean's saloon—actually the one he had built after somebody burned down the first in 1899—was fairly accurate, perhaps because the refurbished original was still being maintained as a tourist attraction.

In the fabulous fifties came the near-inevitable TV series "Judge Roy Bean" its benign hero (Edgar Buchanan) bearing only a slight resemblance to the rather sinister jurist Victor Jory portrayed in *A Time for Dying* (1969). Inspired by some apocryphal tales that had found their way into reputable history texts and in any case must have seemed too good to waste, writer-director Budd Boetticher made Bean into a blackly humorous semivillain who does both good deeds and bad and is quite capable of treating a condemned prisoner to a lyric description of the four seasons' diverse beauties before bellowing out: "But you won't be here to see none of 'em!" It was actually another Southwestern judge who employed a variant of this unnerving act, but as the personification and symbol of all such picturesque lawgivers (and there were many), Bean has naturally had such anecdotes credited to his account.

Still more of the black humor characteristic of Bean movies was found in John Huston's *The Life and Times of Judge Roy Bean* (1972), which had little to do with either, though it did feature a bear who credibly impersonated the judge's beer-guzzling bruin Bruno. Bean himself was played by a bearded, gruff-voiced Paul Newman. "Maybe this isn't the way it was," ran the prologue. "It's the way it should have been."[4] Maybe. As Huston described it:

> It's an extravagant concoction, not in money, but in *idea*. Bean was basically a con man. His fortune was made in his saloon short-changing the passengers of the Southern Pacific Railroad. We ignored the historical facts and made him into a hanging, shooting judge—lots of killing, but it's all on the romantic side.

One of the more romantic killings was that of Bad Bob, the albino gunfighter (Stacy Keach), who dresses in traditional gunman's black setting off his white skin and hair, has a human skull mounted on his saddle horn, pulls onions from the ground to devour them on the spot, drinks from a scalding coffeepot

---

*But this scene was still shown in 1975 when *The Westerner* received an award as a classic Western film from the National Cowboy Hall of Fame and Western Heritage Center in Oklahoma City, dedicated to preserving the memory of the pioneer days.

Judge Bean and Judge Colt. Paul Newman relaxes on the job in a publicity still for *The Life and Times of Judge Roy Bean*. (Museum of Modern Art/Film Stills Archive)

that he grips with his bare hands, and challenges the judge to a gunfight shortly before Bean, in a pleasing bit of special-effects work, shoots him in the back and blows into him a large hole through which the audience can see the street behind him. Milius's script has bandit Bean set up as judge-saloonkeeper on the almost empty desert, establish justice, and find growing up about him a thriving town; after Langtry has been taken over by shysters, Bean disappears into the desert, only to return in the 1920s as a white-bearded, mystical avenger to cleanse (destroy) the town and eliminate the corrupting influence of twentieth-century gangsters in an explosive, fiery climax. In between this municipal growth and death Bean lords it arbitrarily over the town, peddles booze, and deals out death with gun and noose, shooting a drunken cowboy for daring to put a bullet through a portrait of his darling Lillie (Ava Gardner). Although, being abnormally fussy ("pompous"?) about such things, I still have reservations about the use of real names in such films, criticizing *Bean* on historical grounds seems fruitless since it's a bit too far out for anyone to believe; indeed, it might almost leave the viewer thinking that Bean was a purely fictitious character, although his saloon was once again reconstructed with some care.

Anyway, I like the blunt honesty of that statement: "We ignored the historical facts." Would that all filmmakers were so honest!

NOTES

1. Cooper was a great admirer of Hickok, but admitted that his hero was inclined to be a bit overhasty on the trigger. Speaking of the Mike Williams affair, Coop cited it as just one more example of the shell-game axiom that the hand is quicker than the eye.

2. Paramount executives first asked De Mille not to kill Wild Bill and then, after he had perversely said that he could not remake history to that extent, requested that Bill at least be killed by Charles Bickford instead of the contemptible McCall. "But," wrote De Mille primly, "history was adhered to, and the audience did not object to the much more effective, as well as truer, tragedy of Hickok's being killed by a 'little rat' rather than by a more manly villain." Apparently the great crowd pleaser had badly misread public sentiment, for contemporary audiences, and some critics as well, *were* bothered by the unhappy ending. Frank Nugent confessed himself "vaguely puzzled" as to why this particular fact was retained, and added: "We hated to see Calamity Jane cheated that way."

3. In the valuable *Focus on the Western*, editor Jack Nachbar writes of his childhood Western fandom: "So predictably ritualistic were the gunplay, fistfights and riding on the screen and so religious was my attendance that once, when I had got to the theater a few minutes late and alone to see *Calamity Jane and Sam Bass*, I unthinkingly betrayed my Catholic school upbringing and genuflected by the side of my seat."

4. In a note to his published screenplay, writer John Milius was more belligerent about it: "To pompous historians—any similarity to historical characters, living or dead, is purely accidental. If this story is not the way it was—then it's the way it should have been and furthermore the author does not give a plug damn." But he felt that his script had been turned into a "Beverly Hills western" because certain scenes showing his hero's crueler side had been toned down. "Roy Bean is an obsessed man. . . . He sits out there in the desert and he's got this great vision of law and order and civilization and he kills people and does anything in the name of progress. I love those kinds of people. That's the American spirit!"

ADDENDUM

Reviewing my account of Wyatt Earp's career, I realize that I have presented too one-sided and speculative a picture to satisfy his partisans—who will doubtless scorn me as an irresponsible "debunker." My apologies: perhaps it was the detail about his wife that provoked a venom I normally reserve for pretentious directors. One alternate and eminently reasonable view of the Earp controversy, expressed by Glen G. Boyer in *The Suppressed Murder of Wyatt Earp* (the murder being that of the real man by the fictional alter ego), holds that, while no superhero, Wyatt had been unfairly treated by critics partly in reaction to the hyperbole of the Stuart Lake saga. Lake himself made Wyatt seem responsible for much of *Frontier Marshal* by fabricating numerous quotes from Earp, who was not interviewed by Lake to the extent his book would imply.

3
Lead Poisoning
or Don't Shoot with Your Eyes Closed

God created men; Colonel Colt made them equal.
—FRONTIER MAXIM

Fair play is a jewel, but I don't care for jewelry.
—JOHN KING FISHER

Before resuming our examination of individual Western heroes, we shall pause to consider a Type—the steely-eyed professional whose six-guns blaze out death with admirable efficiency and who personifies the anarchic violence of the untamed frontier. Although the current name for this type was employed as early as 1917 for the title of the William S. Hart film *The Gun Fighter*, it was not terribly popular during the actual heyday of the being, between 1860 and 1900. The earliest contemporary reference to a "gunfighter" unearthed by Joseph Rosa in his researches was printed in 1874; such references were few and far between, and although Bat Masterson wrote that the term was a common one, he preferred "man-killer," as did Teddy Roosevelt and other contemporary writers. Wrote Western novelist Eugene Manlove Rhodes in his introduction to Cunningham's *Triggernometry: A Gallery of Gunfighters:* "In the old days we said 'gunman'—a word exactly comparable with 'swordsman.' Because of the modern gangster, the word gunman now [1941] carries the implication of coward, of baby killer . . . the safe and the shameless!" Cunningham himself added that when the word "gunfighter" *was* used, it would have applied primarily to a peace officer or law-abiding killer rather than a low-life, criminal gunman. Other names for the man-killer, used with

74

comparative rarity, included "pistoleer" and "shootist," although this latter term was applied mostly to prominent target shots or exhibition marksmen.

No matter. *We,* loyal Western fans, know just what he is and does. We know that he excels in all forms of gunplay, but that he is at his best, his most dazzling, when he faces his mortal enemy of the moment in the walkdown, where firearmed combat is stripped to its bare essentials. In its classic and best-remembered form, two men face each other on an otherwise empty street and walk slowly toward one another, arms slightly bent, hands curled to grasp at revolver handles. The badman draws first, but with the speed of a snake's tongue the hero whips out his .45 and fires once from the hip. Shot through the body, the villain grimaces, sinks slowly into the dust and dies, the hero watching unmoved. Delivered from their oppressor, the townspeople drift slowly back into the street.

The origins of this "walkdown," the duel now thought of as characteristic of Western fiction, are uncertain; perhaps its development was inevitable, considering the opportunity it grants for a confrontation giving no undue advantage to either hero or villain. We can, however, be sure that it was largely the product of art rather than of life.

This is not to imply that there was no ceremony to Western gunfights. On the simplest level there were spontaneous gunplays resulting from a real or imagined offense committed on the spot, bad temper, drunkenness, or a meeting between two parties who had had it in for each other. If one of the parties proved to be weaponless, his opponent might thoughtfully wait until he had secured a pistol, as in Cheyenne's Levy-Harrison duel of 1877.

Sometimes, however, the duelist with such an advantage behaved with far less consideration. In 1840 a Texan named Jackson determined to kill another Texan named Goodbread with what was destined to be the first shot fired in the bloody Regulators-Moderators feud, but when cornered by his rifle-toting adversary Goodbread reportedly protested that there was really nothing to fight over. "Besides," he added, "I'm unarmed."

"So much the better!" exclaimed Jackson, shooting him.

Other fights had a bit more planning behind them. One type of prearranged gun battle—prearranged by one side, at least—was described in 1894 by playwright Bronson Howard, intent on refuting the quaint European notion that disputatious Yankees commonly drew lots for a pistol with which the winner shot himself in what, on the Continent, was termed "the American duel."

If there is any such thing as [a peculiarly] "American" duel, it is what is familiarly known as "shooting on sight." The challenger sends word to his enemy that he will shoot him the next time he sees him, and thereupon the latter arms himself, and takes his walks abroad with much caution, until the two meet, when both begin a brisk fusillade with their revolvers, and one of them is usually killed, together with from four to six of the bystanders. This sort of duel would never do for a sparsely-populated country like Italy; and as for the other and falsely called "American duel," it lacks everything that could recommend it to the lover of athletic sports.

There were even a few set-piece duels on the European plan, with six-gun or rifle usually replacing the traditional single-shot pistol, as well as such variations as the close-range "handkerchief duel," requiring that each participant grip with his hand or teeth a bandana stretched between them as they went at it with guns or knives. A tolerant frontier code, grounded to a degree in sheer necessity (but also in the more formal *code duello*, which did not become an anachronism in the United States until well into the nineteenth century), was recognized in many regions and permitted a man to kill in defense of his life, honor, or rights. Provided the fight was a reasonably fair one, the winner, if he were ever brought to trial in the first place, might very well get off as did Bill Hickok after shooting Dave Tutt. Bill may have erred by doing his shooting in town, but hadn't Tutt had an even break?[1]

It is the Hickok-Tutt duel that seems to have come closest to the fictional walkdown—at least according to Colonel Nichols's description of the incident, which he apparently got from a reliable witness before rewriting the man's words in a quaint "frontier" patois. Others claim that both combatants had guns in hand as they approached one another, but whether or not it happened as Nichols set it down—Tutt drawing first and the shots coming so close

Gary Cooper, in splendid but pathetic isolation, idiotically walks out to face the four killers in *High Noon*, revolver still in his holster. (Museum of Modern Art/Film Stills Archive)

together that one couldn't say which came first—his was the most widely known account, and its influence is hard to gauge. Here, for anyone who wanted to use them, were all the elements of the clichéd movie or TV showdown.

Bernard De Voto, on the other hand, claimed in a 1955 issue of *Harper's* that one should look to Owen Wister's *The Virginian* (1902), a tremendously popular success and the first "respectable" six-gun novel as opposed to the subliterary dime variety. (Of course, Wister may have been influenced by Nichols.) Like his friends Frederic Remington and Theodore Roosevelt, Wister was one of those upper-class Easterners who would play a key role in shaping the national vision of the Old West; his book not only popularized the phrase "When you call me that, *smile*" and set the pattern for much future fiction, but also shaped the way in which real Westerners viewed themselves and their own recent past. Wrote Wister's daughter Fanny Kemble Wister after visiting Wyoming in 1911: "Everybody in the West seemed to have read *The Virginian,* and as soon as they heard my father's name would speak to him about it. . . . It was written as fiction but has become history." After the novel was criticized for its Western characters' mode of speech, one bona fide cowboy confessed: "Well, maybe we didn't talk that way before Mr. Wister wrote his book, but we sure all talked that way after the book was published." Thus far the book has inspired four films—the third and most famous version, released in 1929 and starring Gary Cooper, was among the first talking Westerns—and a TV series unusual in its ninety-minute length.

De Voto did not criticize Wister too severely for originating the walkdown: "No doubt it is implicit in the myth of the Old West, and somebody else would have invented it if Owen Wister hadn't." But in fact Wister's climactic gunfight differed in several crucial aspects from the subsequent battles it is accused of inspiring. After the villain, Trampas, has impulsively given his enemy until sundown to leave town, the nameless hero is careful to have two buddies following him at a distance to prevent ambush. Trampas already has his gun drawn when the two men confront each other, and from the way Wister wrote this oddly dreamlike passage, it is impossible to say at precisely what moment the Virginian begins to shoot Trampas. Shortly before the actual showdown takes place Trampas, who has already shot one man in the back, reproaches himself for not keeping his mouth shut and waiting for a chance to dry-gulch the hero when nobody's looking. In many a movie duel the hero seems oddly smug about his safety from a shot in the back even though he has no "seconds" watching his rear—perhaps because the villain is inevitably forced by the screenwriter (by whatever contrivance or inconsistency) to play fair and square even though he may have played dirty on previous occasions; his gun, to his cost, remains holstered until the moment of truth.

The deciding factor in such walkdowns is speed in drawing, which, of course, *was* crucial in many gunfights, a fact widely recognized at the time. Wrote G. A. Custer of conditions on the post–Civil War Kansas frontier, "The quarrel is not from a word to a blow, but from a word to the revolver, and he who can draw and fire first is the best man." Most of the more experienced killers, if not exactly lightning-swift at clearing leather, at least took pains not to be particularly slow, and there were a number of methods—such as sawing off barrel sights lest they snag on shoulder scabbard or concealing frock coat—used to increase speed. Chief among these was simple practice, and many stories of extremely fast shooting (some of them true) are to be found in gunfight annals.

But speed was less important than the ability to do exactly the right thing under pressure; gunmen like Hickok might occasionally behave in an overly cautious manner and plug some innocent bystander, but they were able to take their time in a hurry when their own lives were at stake—unlike some men who, due to the natural anxiety that results from being shot at, might exchange several inaccurate pistol volleys when within a yard of each other. An extra moment taken to aim might prove decisive while the man who could draw and shoot in the blink of an eye blazed away without hitting anything; the important bullet was not the first fired, but the first to strike home, and for this reason hip-shooting, so common in films, was usually rejected in favor of firing from the shoulder level. (Stacey Keach goes so far as to teach this to a young would-be gunfighter—whom he later kills at the OK Corral—in *Doc*.)

Fiction has, of course, elevated the fast draw into what sometimes seems the be-all and end-all of the gunfight; rarely does anyone speak of accuracy, which is taken for granted. Hollywood's emphasis on leather-slapping gave employment to many a latter-day fast gun hired to teach the art to stars such as Audie Murphy—who, incidentally, was soon outdrawing his tutor and was alleged to be the fastest Hollywood gun of the 1950s with either blank or live ammo.[2] Besides being rigorously drilled, an actor might profit from shrewd editing, a skilled stand-in, or, like Charles Bronson in *Showdown at Boot Hill* (1958), fast-motion photography.

The movie gunfighter, given his working conditions, can be forgiven his preoccupation with speed. Things might be different if he were allowed the option of hauling his gun out first in a walkdown or similar confrontation, but often this is a privilege reserved for villains. The Western hero is an expert in violence, but the last-draw rule symbolizes the restraint with which he administers it. We are aware that the just man has been forced to use his gun by the misdeeds of his opponent; nevertheless, the final shoot-out is often initiated only by the villain's immediate, physical provocation in drawing first. As Robert Warshow wrote in his classic 1954 essay on the movie Westerner: "The Westerner could not fulfill himself if the moment did not finally come when he can shoot his enemy down. But because that moment is so thoroughly the expression of his being, it must be kept pure."

A real gunman, concerned less with purity than with simple survival, would usually have his gun already out if he expected trouble, although there were cases when it might be considered improper to draw first. If, for instance, one wished to provoke a fight by accusing someone of being a liar, it was usually up to him to make the first move toward a gun; then after you shot him you could claim self-defense. One might, of course, ignore such niceties if nobody was looking, but it is usually a point of honor for a movie hero to give the other fellow a "chance," a point often carried to the seemingly dangerous extremes of Robert Aldrich's *Vera Cruz*. At the denouement Gary Cooper, with Winchester, has the drop on Burt Lancaster, a former ally who has betrayed Cooper (as well as both sides in the Mexican struggle against Maximilian) and just murdered an unarmed man in cold blood—and who now asks for an even break before Cooper executes him. Hesitating briefly, Cooper obligingly lays his rifle down and both men square off. After a last, sneering reference to Coop's "old soft spot," Burt draws first and, as luck would have it, dies. It would have been quite embarrassing to both Cooper and the cause of justice had Lancaster won out, but since we know that isn't about to happen Cooper's gesture seems less an act of rash chivalry than a cost-free formality, a sacrificial rite legitimizing Burt's execution. Clearly, Lancaster must die, yet Cooper cannot simply shoot him down like the dog he is. He has to have that break—an *even* break.

Of course, one might say, *that* was in 1954. For the first four or five decades of Western film production many heroes tended to be, in John Wayne's words, "too goddamn sweet and pure to be dirty fighters," whether the fight was a hand-to-hand brawl in which only the villain could kick and throw chairs or a gunfight with the badman firing first: such were the commonly accepted standards of "heroic" conduct, especially when the kids were watching, which was nearly always. Then, too, censors usually took a dim view of any killings by good guys which were not "self-defense" in the strictest sense of the term, even if they were necessary to impose justice on an essentially lawless environment.

Yet there are many ways in which such killings can be done *after* both men have their guns out, and far more screen heavies have perished sans benefit of a contrived draw-and-shot contest; the walkdown is a less common movie situation than one would imagine. The draw-last custom often persisted even after writers no longer worried about preserving heroic illusions or satisfying censors and could have villains killed off ruthlessly. (In Penn's *The Misssouri Breaks* Marlon Brando, as a hammy hired gun who loves his work, whittles down a band of rustlers by such foul means as firing his rifle through the back wall of an outhouse and into its occupant; the long-awaited showdown consists of amiable horse thief and avenger Jack Nicholson, the closest thing to a good guy the film has, cutting the throat of the "regulator" while he sleeps.) Letting the other man have first crack may owe its continued practice to an intrinsic appeal rather than to any surviving notions about the inevitability of fair play; the hero with a sense of honor retains his attractiveness, but the walkdown may prove a protagonist simply the best gunman, rather than the best man.

Even the more unscrupulous heroes of the sixties and seventies, usually at their seamiest in Italian-made Westerns, often find themselves behaving in accordance with the Hollywood code. At the climax of *The Good, the Bad and the Ugly*, "good" Clint Eastwood doesn't just suddenly shoot down his two rivals in lust for a buried cache of gold, but instead arranges with "Bad" Lee Van Cleef and "Ugly" Eli Wallach a memorable three-cornered duel in a desolate graveyard.[3] After roughly two and a half minutes of nervous eyes shifting and hands edging slowly up toward gun butts, Van Cleef draws first and falls into a handy grave after being shot by Eastwood, who can afford to spare Wallach for some sadistic pyschological torture since "the Good" had previously removed the shells from his erstwhile pal's revolver. Even a true hero might hesitate over giving Van Cleef such a chance; unlike the noble swordsman who let a disarmed foe retrieve his rapier, the pistoleer who allowed his enemy first reach was giving him not an "even break," but a breathtaking advantage, since, as gunfight buff E. B. Mann writes, "it takes even a man with quick reactions 20 to 25 hundredths of a second to respond to any 'signal.'" Therefore, in a duel "between men of anything like equal skill, the man who *started* to draw first would always win."

The only way to have a completely "fair" quick-draw contest would be to have both men begin on a signal, European-style, a technique used most strikingly in Lamont Johnson's *A Gunfight* (1971). Two gunmen (Johnny Cash and Kirk Douglas) stage a lethal fast-draw exhibition in a Mexican bullring, the survivor to receive a cut of the box-office take; their duel, if somewhat bizarre, is completely reasonable from a sportsman's point of view since both draw on a signal from a nearby church bell.

When the Hollywood pistoleer is required to fire two or more shots in rapid succession, he usually resorts to fanning, pressing back the trigger of his revolver while slapping back the hammer repeatedly with his free hand. "I suspect," *Guns and Ammo* editor Howard French wrote to me, "that you will find that the film industry is responsible for the image of fanning." And so it would seem, despite occasional celebration of the trick in hayburner literature. Perhaps the fastest way to empty a six-gun, it looks quite impressive, but it was usually impossible to hit anything this way since the slamming of the hammer and the powerful recoil of a live .45 round were highly detrimental to accuracy. In consequence, fanning was practically unknown in the West, except perhaps for purposes of sport. Plainsman George "Cimarron" Bolds testified to having seen but one demonstration during his eventful life in the Wild West, the marksman being a character in Dodge "we called the 'Jersey Kid' simply because he came from New Jersey," who attempted to look the gunman with a moustache, black hat, and fancy vest. He had, according to Bolds, come west after reading a lot of dime novels.

> He was on the brag about how good he was with a gun, but no one paid any attention to him. One day in the Long Branch[4] he started to pick on a young Texan who was drifting through—just a saddle tramp. The Texan didn't answer the Kid and moved away. Finally the Kid said something you don't say unless you want to back it up with your hardware. They stepped out into the street and the Kid started fanning. The bullets flew everywhere. The Texan drew also but just calmly aimed and fired.

Someone sent the Kid's folks a telegram and the local undertaker arranged for the body to be shipped back East. That was the only fanning I ever saw in my life.

Fanning was also a bit hard on the single-action's mechanism, very distressing if you still worried about such things after you were dead. At best, it might be useful to a man outnumbered at close quarters; the spray of bullets could, if nothing else, have a considerable demoralizing effect on one's intended victims. For the Western actor, fanning is an entirely different type of lifesaver, serving to conceal his usual inability to thumb-cock his six-gun fast enough for several rapid shots. Lack of experience plays a part in this disability, as does the use of a blank-loaded gun, which doesn't handle like a .45 firing live ammo. Our actor can usually cock his gun quickly only while drawing, and some give the impression that even this is beyond them by palming back the hammer for a single shot "from the leather." Amateurish behavior of this sort need not show up on screen if creative editing is employed, and if all else fails one can give the actor a double-action revolver, although these were never very popular with gunfighters.

Better yet might be to give the man a rifle or shotgun when he goes in for serious killing, as opposed to a minor brawl or assassination. But the gun in "gunfighter" means revolver, and it is on this relatively inefficient weapon that the hero too often relies, especially in Westerns made when only bad guys were supposed to take "unfair" advantage. In *The Plainsman* Gary Cooper might take up a Winchester to kill an Indian or two, but he was equally if not more comfortable picking off the redskins with his pistols from a hundred yards away. Shotguns were nasty and required no skill. Though the rifle had been the glory of the sharp-eyed backwoods hero whose exploits unfolded in the prerevolver era (such as Davy Crockett with his Betsy, or James Fenimore Cooper's Leatherstocking with his "Killdeer") and remained the chief weapon of some postrevolver heroes such as Jimmy Stewart in *Winchester '73*, it is the pistol which has held most of the romance in the classic West of fiction—a romance receiving due recognition even in some films which acknowledge the rifle's superiority. In Leon's *A Fistful of Dollars* (1964), an uncredited remake of Akira Kurosawa's cynical samurai adventure *Yojimbo*,[5] the chief Mexican villain quotes an alleged proverb to the effect that when a man with a rifle meets a man with a pistol, the man with the pistol is a dead man. Clint Eastwood, as "The Man with No Name," thinks otherwise and kills the rifle-armed epigrammist in a showdown, but as he is a superman the maxim may still have some application to lesser beings.

Despite some lapses, John Ford usually kept his Western heroes behaving sensibly, disdaining pistol gymnastics ("none of this so-called quick-draw stuff") and often making use of the rifle, perhaps because the voice of experience had been heard during his silent-movie days: "If we had a gunfight, we'd talk it over with someone who'd been an old lawman—like Pardner Jones—and he'd tell us how it would have happened."[6] In his TV series "The Rifleman" Chuck Connors was to flaunt convention by neglecting

John Wayne has Ricky Nelson and other friends to help him, but still relies on his Winchester as Sheriff John T. Chance in *Rio Bravo*. (Museum of Modern Art/Film Stills Archive)

even to *wear* a handgun and lugging around a Winchester instead, but in this he merely followed the lead of John Wayne in Ford's *Stagecoach*. The Winchester has in fact been that actor's favored weapon; in 1969 Andrew Sarris, doing a little *Village Voice* retrospective on Wayne's career after he'd won an Oscar for *True Grit*, and comparing him with other actors who made a habit of "flaunting virility and swaggering about with six shooters at the ready," noted approvingly that he was "more likely to outlast his opponents than to outdraw them, and ever since *Stagecoach* he has never hesitated to use the rifle, an instrument more efficient, if less phallic, than the six shooter."

Such down-to-earth behavior by an actor who has come to symbolize the Western hero merely reassures us that our beloved, mythic man-killer need not rely on phony theatrics or misplaced chivalry to retain the essential aura of romance—although he may indulge in the occasional quixotic gesture, like the one-eyed Rooster Cogburn's glorious *True Grit* charge against four bandits, Wayne clutching the reins in his teeth as he fires pistol and rifle. The Duke's brand of common sense appears even more admirable when compared with the idiocy of Marshal Will Kane (Gary Cooper) in Fred Zinnemann's 1952 "classic" *High Noon*, a totally phony, embarrassingly overpraised "anti-Western" drama allegorically warning, it seemed, against the collective cowardice of the McCarthy witch-hunt era in a heavy-handed style typical of producer Stanley Kramer. (Robert Warshow coined the term "anti-Western" in writing of films which used the Western form to criticize the ills of modern society.) After almost ninety minutes of "running around like a wet chicken trying to get people to help him" (Howard Hawks's phrase), and running up against his fellow citizens' unconvincingly presented moral cowardice, Cooper finally has to face single-handed the four killers due to come into town at high noon. His natural reaction is to meet them out in the open, armed with two measly six-guns, behavior which might be believable in a cool expert confident of his ability to handle all comers—such as Cooper's own Bill Hickok some fifteen years before—but which isn't in a frightened, supposedly more "realistic" hero quite reluctant to meet the danger his imagined duty calls on him to face. After making a complete mess of the situation, Coop can lay claim to killing only three of the varmints; his Quaker wife (Grace Kelly) abandons her pacifist principles just in time to account for another member of the foursome. In an essay on Howard Hawks in which he compared *High Noon* to *Rio Bravo*, Andrew Sarris complained:

> Zinnemann tries to have it both ways. He spends most of the film on the pathos of Cooper's helplessness, and then denies Cooper any sensible defense. . . . If Zinnemann had wanted to sustain his realistic approach, he could have had Cooper mow his assailants down with a shotgun. Instead *High Noon*, like most anti-Westerns, degenerates into a wasteful choreography of violent arabesques. Cooper warns his would-be murderers that he is behind them, ducks behind buildings, runs into a hayloft which is promptly 'set afire, darts behind horses, wagons, and fences, and limits himself to the range of his six-shooter.[7]

Sarris's mention of a shotgun brings to mind the conduct of a real-life lawman who, though faced with only one badman come to test his mettle, procured such a weapon and, as his would-be assassin rode down the street, jumped out from behind a rain barrel and leveled his scattergun at the desperado—who unbuckled his guns and rode quietly out of town. But it is not necessary that one have any extensive knowledge of the "real West" to recognize the imbecility of *High Noon*'s final gunfight, which seems to me rather obvious, though only a few critics seem to have noticed it and many students of the cinema continue to view Coop's behavior as perfectly correct even if they don't particularly like the rest of the movie. In his 1974 *Violence in the Arts*, for instance, John Fraser makes this evaluation: "Much of Zinnemann's *High Noon* . . . may have been *Kitsch*, but the final showdown wasn't." Howard Hawks, on the other hand, was so disgusted by the film that, as he often liked to tell, he made *Rio Bravo* partly as an antidote, with John Wayne's Sheriff Chance, the compleat Hawksian professional, bringing about the downfall of a superior force of gunmen with a little help from his friends and the judicious use of assorted firearms and dynamite—plus, of course, the sort of luck reserved almost exclusively for heroes.

When the Ringo Kid stalks down a twilit Lordsburg street in search of the three Plummer boys with only three bullets left in his Winchester, we can rest assured that he'll be able to kill one man with each of them. Whatever his flaws, the gunfighter remains a man apart and generally favored by the gods. At his most conservative he will contain an element of wish fulfillment, especially as the majority of Westerns, despite any "realist" trappings, have always been primarily escapist in intent. Sometimes he seems a Christ figure, like the ethereal Alan Ladd in George Stevens's celebrated *Shane* (1953), or an indeterminate sort of supernatural avenger, like the invincible Stranger played by Clint Eastwood in his own 1973 *High Plains Drifter* (which many took to be a ghost story but which, Eastwood later said, wasn't specifically intended as such). At one point in South American director Alejandro Jodorowsky's gory, surrealist fantasy *El Topo* (1971), the seemingly invulnerable hero even declares himself to be God.

But in most cases this hero *is* seen operating in a believable world where whatever "fantasy" exists is couched in strictly realistic and credible terms; often the most "mythic" of gunfighter heroes, such as Shane, perform no feats not within the capabilities of a real gunman. It seems just a bit much for such a hero to dash about shooting guns out of people's hands or shooting to wound.

Such kindly acts are not confined to kiddie shows such as the old "Lone Ranger" series, the do-gooding hero of which followed his radio predecessor in using his silver bullets only to smash guns or nick shoulders; they are also seen in more serious adventures such as Sturges's *The Magnificent Seven*, in which Yul Brynner warms up for more serious battles ahead by winging two rowdies in the arm as they draw—fanning, yet. Even dastardly villains sometimes indulge: in Robert Benton's completely cynical *Bad Company* (1972), a fat highwayman casually shoots the gun from a boy's hand, later going on to reminisce about the notorious Curly Bill Brocious and his famous gun spin.[8]

In films where the shootist is allowed free rein in killing people, trick shooting leads to some inconsistencies: why are some villains merely rendered harmless while others die, even when they present the same kind of threat? Terribly unfair—and even if it doesn't resemble life, a story should have some internal harmony and obey its own conventions. We find the same inconsistency in certain written accounts; Stuart Lake's Wyatt Earp was represented as disarming foemen with a literal shot in the arm, but he certainly didn't try to wing anybody at the OK Corral, where at point-blank range the Earps failed to kill three men without incurring three wounds themselves. Such acts were prudent for a gunman only when the other fellow's gun was pointed somewhere else: according to Jim Herron's eyewitness account in *Fifty Years on the Owlhoot Trail*, Texas badman (and sometime marshal of Austin) Ben Thompson once saw a man in a saloon twirling a six-gun and rashly pointing it at some of the men along the bar, and reacted accordingly.

> I suddenly heard a shot, and this gun-flashing fellow let out a squeal like a javelina. His gun flew out of his hand and went clattering across the board floor, and as he grasped his hand in pain I could see he was minus a perfectly good finger. . . . A small fellow walked over from a card table, blew smoke away from his own revolver, and spoke sharply to the injured man. . . . Thompson said later he had no intention of killing him. But he was suspicious that the fellow might turn the gun on him just to make himself a record.

Herron's anecdote is perhaps less illustrative of Thompson's good aim than of his *idée fixe:* avoiding violent death. It was one he shared with many other man-killers, such as Wild Bill, described by one cowtown eyewitness as simply "Cat-eyed! He *slid* into a room, watching the whole crowd like a hawk. He looked like a man who lived in expectation of getting killed." It was claimed that one could count the number of experienced gunmen in a room just by counting those men sitting with their backs to the wall—an exaggeration, but one grounded in a sensible precaution. Hickok himself was killed shortly after some friends had teased him into, for once, sitting with his back to a door—a fact which, when called to mind later, must have caused these companions great pain.

Despite his watchfulness on the above-mentioned occasion, Thompson, who often went looking for trouble and had careless drinking habits (he was finally killed during an ambush inside an Austin theater, along with his gunman friend "King" Fisher), was less cautious than most pistoleers. Unlike the Hollywood gunman, the typical expert man-killer had no use for a confrontation with one of his own kind; with a true professional's respect for another professional's ability, he usually kept his distance. A few stories to the contrary might be cited, but as a rule confrontations between true experts were limited to crabwise sidling and long-distance growling. There was little desire to hunt up other gunfighters and test one's speed against theirs—a good thing, too, since it wouldn't have proved anything. (The man who draws first, remember.)

Ambitious movie shootists, having never heard of such things as "reaction time," continue to seek out the fellow professional, perhaps a weary gunman hero who, having hoped to "hang up his guns" for good, must buckle them on once more and sally forth to confront one or more lightning-fast challengers. Occasionally the hero is hounded because of a reputation he doesn't even *deserve*, like peace-loving if neurotic storekeeper Glenn Ford in the ludicrously exaggerated "Freudian" Western *The Fastest Gun Alive* (1956). Ford, whose gun bears some notches denoting men killed by its previous owner,[9] finally escapes his rep by way of the old false-burial routine, erecting a tombstone with his own name on it.

Occasionally two duelists will be so intent on the "sporting" aspects of gunplay that they neglect completely the important business of killing each other. In the made-for-TV *The Gun and the Pulpit* (1974), a gunfighter turned phony preacher (a cunningly cast Marjoe Gortner) faces another sure-shot in front of a number of witnesses; the men draw and fire, their two shots resounding as one—and both missing. This is in itself novel, but even more curious is their behavior afterwards. Rather than fire again, both lower their weapons and stand blinking at each other until Marjoe asks quietly, "You want to try again?" The other doesn't and rides off.

Gregory Peck as the tragic—yet romantic—Jimmy Ringo in *The Gunfighter*. The suffering of the gunman is, in the words of Frank Waters, "what makes him our favorite hero." (Museum of Modern Art/Film Stills Archive)

This premise of one champion seeking trials at arms with others was probably just as inevitable as the walkdown, the gunfighter being, in another of his several roles, the New World's substitute for those doughty knights who, when not rescuing fair maidens, zealously hacked each other up to no good purpose. But the premise was given an immeasurable boost by Henry King's 1950 *The Gunfighter*. (Part of the film's influence may have been due to a belief that King's movie was not only "realistic" but also based on the life of an actual gunman, since the prologue implied as much.) The drama starred Gregory Peck, moustache sorrowfully drooped, as tired badman Jimmy—*not* Johnny—Ringo, trying to reform and plagued by some old enemies as well as by several young punks out to make a name for themselves; one of the latter finally kills him in an unfair fight. As he lies dying, the tragic hero tells the punk that, rather than have him arrested, he will let him go free, doomed to inherit the mantle of Ringo's rep and live in cat-eyed fear until some other glory hunter kills him in much the same way.

Except perhaps for the overly message-laden ending (far better to try and get the kid hanged, lest he go free to change his name and ride off leaving his reputation behind, after having been warned by his considerate victim of what lies ahead), this original premise was somewhat reasonable. It was the petty gunman or town bully, the green young 'un, and the dude showoff who actually seemed most inclined to seek out men of reputation (though even such seekers as these were comparatively rare), and it was the relative unknown who sought to make a "name" for himself through violence.

Sometimes this took the form of shooting the first person he found convenient, simply to enable him to say that he had "killed his man." Wrote Mark Twain of mining camps in 1860s Nevada: "That was the very expression used. . . . I knew two youths who tried to 'kill their men' for no other reason— and got killed themselves for their pains." One's rewards were naturally greater upon killing someone of importance, but although a reputation *might*, conceivably, attract trouble, it would at the same time tend to keep away all but the most foolhardy amateurs, who usually ended in much the same condition as the Jersey Kid. The big-name gunmen themselves had *not* deliberately set out to "become" gunfighters, even though some of them were naturally inclined toward violence.

The thematic cliché of a gunfighter's reputation leading to an endless number of self-defense killings (and/or the death of the hero) served Hollywood as a handy brush with which to whitewash several bad citizens into misunderstood victims of circumstance, as in 1953's *Jack Slade*, directed by and starring Mark Stevens. A written prologue to this one quotes, out of context, from Twain's *Roughing it* to prove that Slade was really a civilizing influence on the frontier; indeed, so beneficial and widely appreciated was his influence that he was hanged by Montana vigilantes in 1864.[10]

A similar cleansing miracle was performed in Raoul Walsh's *The Lawless Breed* (1952), ostensibly based on the posthumous memoirs of John Wesley Hardin[11] and starring Rock Hudson as an oh-so-remorseful sort who really hates being forced to kill all those people in self-defense. The real Hardin, short on remorse and long on self-righteousness, was in the process of growing up fast in 1868 Texas when he precociously killed his first man at age fifteen; he was popularly believed to have killed forty men—"not countin' Mexicans and Injuns," as the saying went—and became a child's bogeyman: "Wes Hardin'll git-chi if ya don't watch out!" Wes expecially liked killing Negroes. Arrested in 1877 and jailed for seventeen years, he studied law in prison, but reverted to his old bullying habits soon after his pardon[12] and was finally shot in the back of the head as he shot dice in an El Paso saloon; the assassin was a constable whose life Hardin had previously threatened. El Paso being El Paso and Hardin being Hardin, John Selman was acquitted after claiming self-defense.

Hardin's end probably surprised no one. Although the unwritten frontier code held it improper—at least most of the time—to shoot a man in the back, while he was unarmed, or from ambush, when a widely respected gunman was killed it was usually through violation of one or more of the rules. In each case the killer expressed with deeds the hard-boiled philosophy articulated by the legendary Jack McCall and, for that matter, John Wayne in *El Dorado*. "You never even gave me a chance," mutters head opposition gunman Christopher George, who had earlier prevented his men from back-shooting Wayne in the hope of an even showdown, only to find himself blasted by a rifle at close range. Bringing a last ironic smile to his opponent's lips with the compliment, the ever-practical Duke replies, "You're too good to give a chance to."

Having adequately covered the art of shooting people, it only remains to explore what does and doesn't happen when the bullets strike home. No matter how generously administered, movie violence often seems much tamer in its effects than the equivalent action in the real world, whether the action is an immense Western saloon brawl in which heavy chairs break harmlessly over human heads (instead of simply breaking the heads, as God intended) or gunfights in which the losers, hit by .45 slugs, wince and double up before crumpling slowly to the ground. Sometimes they fail even to crumple immediately, as in the aftermath of that Cooper-Lancaster shoot-out in *Vera Cruz*. As the smoke clears, we see both men still standing; Burt smiles and twirls his gun into his holster. But we know that Coop hasn't missed: after several seconds of fake suspense, Burt sinks to the ground.

Considerably less grace was exhibited by real frontier victims, but not because of any defective aesthetic sense. The revolver was preferred by gunmen and others in .44 and .45 (also the most common calibers for Winchester rifles) precisely because one could almost always knock a man down with one shot by using such large bullets, taking him out of the fight temporarily even if he wasn't seriously hurt. At the very least such a bullet would probably send a man staggering back a few yards, while even a spent bullet or ricochet could have tremendous impact. (In order to test the Peacemaker's capabilities the U.S. Army once sent marksmen to shoot at cows in the Chicago stockyards and found that the .45 could easily bowl over a half-ton steer, even if no vital spot were hit.) The user of smaller-caliber guns, such as Hickok with his 1851 Colt Navy .36s, enjoyed weaker recoil but also took the chance that his enemy, even if fatally hit, might well remain standing and able to shoot back.

A trend toward increasing realism in the area of bullet impact began, slowly, in the post–World War II years. The death of innocent farmer Elisha Cook, Jr., goaded into a gunfight by devilish hired killer Jack Palance in *Shane*—a scene which still retains considerable force—was the first Western shooting to use wires pulling a man through the air as though blasted back. But others were slow to follow suit until the increasingly "realistic" sixties and seventies, when, although proper dying was still often neglected, the use of wires was sometimes coupled with dedicated actors simply doing their best to fall back realistically. (Men shot while on rooftops or cliffs, however, must of necessity pitch *forward* most of the time so that they can fall horrifyingly through the air to the ground.)

Filmic deaths of the late sixties and seventies also inclined toward greater gore than the bloodless clutchings-at-the-chest of earlier days. Tiny explosive charges planted under clothing or artificial skin provided impressive effects as they burst open packets of ersatz blood, and with the breakdown of censorship and whatever inhibitions had previously existed, a Sam Peckinpah, who came to scorn the mayhem in all those old-fashioned horse operas ("You always expected them to get up again") could leap exultantly into the slaughter pen for his own 1969 *The Wild Bunch*, most of its countless killings shot in an affectionate slow motion, the purpose of which (unless it was simply to aestheticize violence) was difficult to fathom.[13] In such cases things may get so obsessively bloody, with an insistence on lingering over the nastier portions, that what we see might legitimately be termed gratuitous realism. Moviemakers, or their flacks, occasionally claim that they want to show everything in awful detail so we'll realize how terrible violence is and so on, but since nearly all Westerns are ultimately proviolence and prokilling (provided that the right people are the victims), such emphasis on the purely physical aspects of murdering and maiming, more likely to excite disgust than pity, would seem to serve some other purpose. Like traditional epics, the Western can easily accommodate both the graphic depiction of violence and the romance of the man who employs it correctly.

The realistic, full-color bloodletting of the Peckinpah era has been accompanied by modification of the victim's traditionally cavalier attitude toward "minor wounds," which becomes particularly hard to take when he gets hit smack-dab in the middle of his shoulder and all well-wishers are assured that it's nothing serious and that he'll be up and around in no time—whereas Civil War medical records tell us that about one-third of all those shot in the shoulder joint during that conflict died. The heavy, slow-moving lead slugs of the classic gunfight era usually made a mess of the muscle, tendons, and blood vessels of a meaty area like the shoulder, commonly mushrooming on

Warren Oates and Ben Johnson, hit rather badly by Mexican slugs in *The Wild Bunch*, react accordingly. (Museum of Modern Art/Film Stills Archive)

contact with any bone. When part of a limb was thus shattered, amputation, often resulting in death, was the usual procedure. Frontier medical care was seldom of the best (perhaps one-fourth of Western practitioners were actually certified doctors at a time when it was not too difficult to become one), and even the best the times could offer might not be good enough. Back at the turn of the century Raoul Walsh, himself a cowboy and no stranger to such atmospheric events as shootings and hangings, served as assistant to a French-born Montana doctor and thus had a chance to observe first-hand the picturesque, devil-may-care attitude toward sanitation he shared with many another frontier sawbones.

One day he was operating on a man who had been shot in the stomach. When the doctor told me to hold the small gut out of his way, it was slippery. Echinelle then hung a couple of loops of intestine over a nearby hatrack. Soon he was probing unconcernedly for the bullet, with ashes dropping into the wound from his eternal cigar. He found the bullet and dropped it onto the floor. Then he unhooked the loops from the hatrack, sluiced them with saline solution, and closed the patient up. I helped with the stitching. The man lived. I played poker with him more than once before I left Montana. But I never told him about the loops.

Seeing this, of course, never disillusioned Walsh into making sordid or depressing oaters when he himself rode further west into Hollywood. The Western adventure can survive anything, whether gallons of blood, unchivalrous good guys, or (though they haven't shown up yet) intestines on the hatrack and cigar ashes in the wounds. It may even thrive on them. And aren't you glad?

NOTES

1. A less admirable reason behind public tolerance of such private brawls was, of course, the notion that most of those killed really weren't worth crying over. "Generally," wrote Teddy Roosevelt, "everyone is heartily glad to hear of the death of either of the contestants, and the only regret is that the other survives."

2. Unlike Murphy, some actors who were just blurs of motion using blanks never had the pleasure of trying their speed with real bullets, and some learned their art from equally inexperienced instructors such as David Sharpe, who in 1941 coached Jack Beutel in handling the sixes for *The Outlaw*. Sharpe was fast, of course, but even if he had used live rounds, he could never have hit anything; photographs taken for *Life* revealed that he involuntarily closed his eyes when pulling the trigger. Viewing a still of Sharpe in action, one irate reader wrote in to point out that he couldn't even *carry* his guns properly, for the "line of fire of the revolver as held by Mr. Sharpe would hit an opponent below the knees at ten feet and miss him totally at fifteen feet." Many modern fast-draw enthusiasts, largely influenced by gunfighter films, continue to use blanks or wax bullets and so earn the scorn of certain "legitimate" shooters; other, more daring souls use real slugs and occasionally blow painful .45 holes in themselves by ineptly practicing what they fondly believe to have been the Western gunman's specialty.

3. Each of the three was identified with his adjective by written captions at the beginning and end of the film, just in case we couldn't guess who was who. But it is actually quite easy to figure out who is supposed to be the hero in most of these spaghetti oaters; despite his customary lack of scruples and noble "cause," he is usually provided with some moral edge, no matter how slight, over his enemies—as well as with final victory over them.

4. This Dodge City saloon was named after Long Branch, New Jersey, and was never owned and operated by Miss Kitty (Amanda Blake) of the TV series "Gunsmoke," which starred James Arness as Marshal Dillon from 1955 to 1975. In the index of Miller and Snell's *Great Gunfighers of the Kansas Cowtowns* can be found this entry under D: "Dillon, Matt: no police officer by this name ever served in early Dodge City. Sorry." Just so we get *that* cleared up; but tourist-hungry Dodge erected a statue of him anyway. Our frontier heritage . . .

5. Similarly, the American-made films *The Magnificent Seven* (1960) and *The Outrage* (1964) were Western remakes of Kurosawa's *Seven Samurai* and *Rashomon*; Kurosawa himself had been greatly influenced by Hollywood Westerns.

6. Such a conversation could be quite unsettling. Top Western screenwriter Borden Chase recalled in a 1971 *Film Comment* interview that after writing a number of screenplays he was privileged to converse with some aged Westerners: "When I got done talking with the old timers, I didn't think I could ever write another Western." One day in a bar Chase was present when a friend asked a grizzled ex-lawman if he had ever told anyone to go for his gun: "And he says, 'What the hell, do you think I want to get myself killed?' . . . He told me stories in that bar that just destroyed my idea of what the West had been."

7. In Robert Altman's *McCabe and Mrs. Miller* (1971) the hero, a smalltime pimp and entrepreneur (Warren Beatty), finds himself in a *High Noon*-ish situation when he elects to face three gunmen hired by a powerful mining company to kill him. He too is limited to the range of his six-gun, but not through choice, since Altman cleverly separates him from his shotgun: back-shooting and employing trickery, McCabe manages to kill all three gunmen, but unfortunately incurs a mortal wound in the process, and his heroism in standing up for the "small businessman" is ironically viewed as a futile gesture which goes not only unappreciated, but also unnoticed by the townspeople.

8. The "Curly Bill" or "road agent's" spin was the method by which badman Brocious killed Fred White, first marshal of Tombstone, presenting his Colt to White butt forward and with his finger inside the trigger guard, then twirling it into a firing position and cocking it before—said Bill—it went off accidentally. Nice to mention this showy if not terribly practical trick, but Bill wasn't associated with it until after 1880, almost

twenty years too late for Benton's Civil War toughs. Curly Bill was later inflated by certain writers into a supervillain whom Wyatt Earp claimed to have killed during a large-scale gunfight; played by Edgar Buchanan, he was chief menace in *Tombstone*. More recently, Clint Eastwood can be seen trying out the spin on two unsuspecting hooligans in his *The Outlaw Josey Wales* (1976), the hero of which was described in the ads, with a minimum of hyperbole, as "an army of one."

9. Reputable gunmen did not mutilate their weapons in this manner, although such notches were sometimes used in figures of speech. As Jim Herron said of the gunmen he knew, rather than really mark their guns, they "just talked about it."

10. In *Roughing It* Twain, who had once met Slade and found him "so friendly and so gentle-spoken that I warmed to him in spite of his awful history," recounts a number of grisly anecdotes concerning the hero, though most are of dubious authenticity. My favorite is a fast-draw story with a difference: "One day on the plains he had an angry dispute with one of his wagon-drivers, and both drew their revolvers. But the driver was the quicker artist, and had his weapon cocked first. So Slade said it was a pity to waste life on so small a matter, and proposed that the pistols be thrown on the ground and the quarrel settled by a fistfight. The unsuspecting driver agreed, and threw down his pistol—whereupon Slade laughed at his simplicity, and shot him dead!"

11. Not to be confused with the John Wesley Hard*ing* of the Bob Dylan song and record album, who never shot an honest man and was a friend to the poor besides; Dylan simply liked the name and added a "g" presumably to remove it from any relationship with the original owner. Hardin seems to have had only two other screen appearances to date, one of them a burlesque by Jack Elam in the lousy Frank Sinatra vehicle *Dirty Dingus Magee* (1970). Perhaps his quasi-religious name, derived from that of Methodism's founder, prevented him from romping through further filmed adventures.

12. Although the specific charge had been second-degree murder, Hardin's previous record made the sentence seem like rank injustice to killer Bill Longley, then awaiting execution after a roughly similar career. "Don't you think it is rather hard," wrote Bill to the governor, "to kill me for my sins and give Wes Hardin only twenty-five years for the crimes he has committed?" The governor made no reply and Longley swung off as scheduled, later being compensated in the 1950s with a TV show generically named "The Texan."

13. In addition to neutralizing the impact of the terrifying speed at which most violence takes place, slow motion sometimes distances the viewer by making him all too conscious that it's just a movie, while the fancy special-effects gimmicks used to simulate wounds and dismemberment may occasionally start him wondering just *how* that character got his limb blown away instead of submitting to the illusion. Very often that which is unseen, or merely implied, is most effective. Much of the Old West's authentic gore must have been obscured at the moment of violence anyway by the black-powder cartridges, which produced a large cloud of white smoke (hardly an aid to accuracy) between shooter and target at each shot. So-called "smokeless powder" cartridges first became widely available in the mid-1890s.

4
The Robin Hood Factory
or Can't Keep a Bad Man Down

Simply, America was the land where people still believed in
heroes: George Washington; Billy the Kid; Lincoln,
Jefferson . . .
—NORMAN MAILER

Funny how things get twisted, ain't it?
—BRODERICK CRAWFORD
in *When the Daltons Rode*

Some years back a delver into the occult (whose name I no longer remember)
decided to have a chat with the shade of Robin Hood, that noble outlaw of
medieval England. After emerging from the séance, the psychic scientist
reported that this hero had revealed himself as a bloodthirsty bandit who
"gloated over his evil deeds." Even worse, the fair Maid Marian was exposed
as a slatternly nympho.

This is not, of course, the Merrie Robyn of whom the poets sing—that
Anglo-Saxon outlaw-hero who robs from the rich, gives to the poor, and battles
against tyranny. But the confession, or whatever it was, somehow seems to
present a more believable version. If a Robin Hood ever existed—and that
séance seems about as good a piece of evidence as any—the odds are against
his having been a dashing Errol Flynn or Douglas Fairbanks; thieves rarely
are, despite the fact that people in every age have glamorized them.[1] It is a
loathsome villain indeed who can find no admirers.

America seems to be among the most popular havens of the mythic outlaw-hero, something reformed Western badman Emmett Dalton couldn't help noticing.

> One thing puzzled me profoundly for a long time when I began taking thought in prison: The curiously inconsistent attitude of the American public toward its malefactors. . . .
>
> Why has the free-running reprobate always been so extolled? Is it because he symbolizes the undying anarchy in the heart of almost every man? Because he has the rude courage of his desires? Represent the rogue as a man fighting against odds—even against the police—and we tacitly encourage him. Give him the slightest pretext of a "cause," and we follow in his train—in spirit, at least. He becomes our fighting vicar against aristocracy, against power, against the law, against the upstart, the pretender, the smugly virtuous and the pompously successful person or corporation whom we envy. He becomes a very hero of democracy.
>
> . . . With scarce secret complaisance we thrill at his maraudings—until he sticks a gun under our own nose. Then he becomes a dastardly villain.

The most compelling of all reasons for identifying with the criminal is, perhaps, a secret desire to be Bad—to unleash the monsters of the id and go killing, raping, robbing, or what have you. To defuse the nastier implications of outlaw worship, those who actually do such things must become heroes, or at least victims, rather than mere lawbreakers driven by greed or dark compulsion. Lawlessness must become a self-sacrificing struggle against wrong, armed robbery a rudimentary Share the Wealth plan, and murder— well, they all deserved it anyway. Once embarked upon his illicit career, the outlaw typically comports himself with honor, behaving kindly toward women, children, and animals, though not always in that order. Jack Schaefer, author of *Shane*, has referred to the Western version of this frequently unconscious process as "gilding the stinkweed."

The weeds have, as a rule, been kept well watered by Hollywood, which, ever keen to the bloodlust and baser sentiments of the masses, has responded almost since its founding with scores of nauseating film "biographies" depicting good badmen robbing, killing, and—especially after enforcement of the film industry's Production Code in 1934—usually dying. This code, instituted in 1930 by the Motion Picture Producers and Distributors of America and administered by its president, Will Hays, dictated that "the sympathy of the audience shall never be thrown to the side of crime, wrongdoing, evil or sin. . . . [Crimes] shall never be presented in such a way as to throw sympathy with the criminal as against the law and justice or to inspire others with a desire for imitation." Such an absurd regulation was, of course, unenforceable; in practice it was normally translated to mean that the criminal could be as admirable and as justified in his misdeeds as the writer could make him, and that the audience could root for him all the way— provided he were adequately punished at the end. Thus did Hollywood uphold the nation's moral standards while setting up homicidal icons for the youth of

America to worship and, incidentally, profiting greatly thereby.

Perhaps it is this consuming lust for gold which, held in common, forges a bond of sympathy between the film producer and an equally ambitious capitalist such as Jesse James.

During the 1850s, abolitionist groups encouraged the migration of like-minded settlers into Kansas for the purpose of voting to exclude slavery, while proslavery Missourians sent bands of murderous "border ruffians" across the border to cast their ballots for human bondage and terrorize the Kansans; these, in turn, organized to defend themselves and often do a little terrorizing of their own. Conditions did not improve with the coming of the Civil War, which gave free rein to the extremists and cutthroats on both sides.

Alexander Franklin James, born in 1843, was introduced to the pleasures of fratricidal violence early in the war when he joined former horse thief William Quantrill and his band of raiders, a command made up in large part of brigands whose allegiance to the Confederacy proved a wonderful excuse for whatever deviltry they chose to commit. Together with such future business partners as Cole Younger, Frank participated in the 1863 raid on Lawrence, Kansas, during which Quantrill's men killed roughly 150 men and boys and burned most of the town to the ground. At the time of this exploit Frank's brother Jesse, a thin youth whose blue eyes blinked constantly (he had granulated eyelids) was considered too young for such things, but he more than made up for it later; as a seventeen-year-old guerrilla, he was present at the 1864 Centralia massacre led by Quantrill lieutenant William "Bloody Bill" Anderson, whose nickname requires no explanation.

After the war many of Quantrill's men continued in their old, comfortable groove of looting and shooting, while many others settled down to a peaceable life, as did the James boys—temporarily. But pushing a plough can get to be a frightful bore, so in 1866 the brothers and some of their friends (starting with the new crime of armed bank robbery pioneered by one Edward Green in 1863) launched a criminal career characterized by moderate success and unnecessary brutality: the bandits are generally "credited" not only with robbing some twelve banks, seven trains, two stagecoaches, and one state fair over a fifteen-year period for an estimated take of $250,000, but also with murdering some sixteen people along the way. The more refined sort of bank or train robber, such as Bill Doolin, usually abstained from killing unless he "had" to, and Doolin himself once expelled from his gang a member who had needlessly slain an old parson with the words: "You're too damn low to associate with a high-class gang of train robbers!" Jesse's crew proved themselves a lower breed of owlhoot.

After some six years of simple bank robbery and murder, Jesse and his gang held up the Kansas City Fair in spectacular fashion, a small girl being shot in the leg by a horseman aiming at the ticket seller. The take was small ($978), but there was an important fringe benefit, for Major John N. Edwards, editor of

Jesse and Frank James as young men. (Minnesota Historical Society)

the *Kansas City Times,* was inspired by the event to write a singular paean to "The Chivalry of Crime":

> The nineteenth century with its Sybaritic civilization is not the social soil for men who might have sat with *Arthur* at the Round Table, ridden at tourney with Sir Lancelot or won the colors of *Guinevere;* men who might have shattered the casque of *Brian de Bois Guilbert,* shivered a lance with *Ivanhoe* or won the smile of the Hebrew maiden; and men who could have met *Turpin* and *Duval* and robbed them of their illgotten booty on Hounslow Heath.
>
> Such as these are they who awed the multitude on Thursday. . . . What they did we condemn. but the way they did it we cannot help admiring. . . . It was as though three bandits had come to us from the storied Odenwald, with the halo of medieval chivalry upon their garments and shown us how the things were done that poets sing of. No where else in the United States or in the civilized world, probably, could this thing have been done.

Shortly after the appearance of this editorial Edwards's paper received a letter supposedly sent by the bandits, claiming that "we rob the rich and give to the poor" and signed with the names of three famous English highwaymen of the eighteenth century: Jack Shephard, Dick Turpin, and Claude Duval. No letter was sent to the rival *Daily Journal of Commerce*, which had seemingly imagined the proper "social soil" for the bandits to be several feet below ground: "More audacious villains than the perpetrators of this robbery, or those more deserving of hanging to a limb do not exist at this moment."

Major Edwards, himself an alcoholic Confederate veteran, would soon drop all that "what they did we condemn" nonsense and become the loudest, most influential, and most obnoxious of the James boys' defenders, who argued in somewhat contradictory fashion that (a) the brothers had in fact committed no crimes and were merely being hounded by Damnyankee oppressors, (b) they'd only committed *some* of the crimes being laid at their door, and anyway (c) they'd been driven to it by the aforesaid Damnyankees and were only taking revenge on their persecutors for unspecified offenses. Since a bandit-hero who commits no crimes is of little interest to anyone, only the revenge and driven-to-it excuses are of any importance to the enduring legend, and neither held water. Most of the banks robbed by the outlaws were in the South, and most of the men they murdered, Southerners. (After one Missouri holdup, a local newspaper concluded that the robbers were doubtless ex-Union irregulars from Kansas.) Unlike some former guerrillas, Jesse and Frank were never persecuted by Missouri Unionists and lived peacefully at their mother's home until evidence of their crimes caught up with them in 1869 and forced them to flee; during this period Jesse joined the local Baptist church and was baptized, thus conforming to the Ambrose Bierce definition of a Christian as "one who follows the teachings of Christ in so far as they are not inconsistent with a life of sin."

Even after their initial flight the brothers rarely fit the popular conception of hounded fugitives, sometimes being shielded by sympathetic (or intimidated) Missourians, sometimes merely concealing their identities, a relatively simple process in those days. They did reveal their identities to a lucky few; Mark Twain writes that Jesse introduced himself to the writer one day in a small Missouri town, after recognizing him and remarking, "Guess you and I are 'bout the greatest in our line."

Some time after their visit to the fair, the boys decided to branch out into a new form of mayhem recently introduced to America by Indiana's Reno brothers: train robbery. This they achieved by loosening a rail over which an Iowa passenger train was to travel, in the hope of wrecking it. Fortunately only the engine toppled over; the engineer was killed and the merry band of pranksters, fast on their way to becoming national heroes, robbed all the passengers. By this time the Pinkerton Detective Agency had been retained by some of their victims to destroy the gang, but in January of 1875, on what became known as the Night of Blood, its operatives inadvertently increased public sympathy for the Jameses and added fuel to the persecution myth. Surrounding the house of Jesse's mother, Mrs. Zerelda Samuel, they tossed a large flare through the window to illuminate those within. Jesse's stepfather apparently shoved it into the fireplace and it exploded, killing a nine-year-old boy and tearing off Mrs. Samuel's right arm. Jesse and Frank were not at home.

Later that year somebody thought up a resolution praising the Jameses and Youngers as "brave," "gallant," and "honorable," granting amnesty for whatever they had done during the war (an unnecessary yet significant gesture), and offering fair trials where postwar crimes were concerned; lacking the eulogistic flourishes, a revised resolution was introduced into the Missouri legislature but failed to pass. In the meantime its intended beneficiaries continued business as usual, interrupted only by the adverse denouement of the 1876 Northfield raid. Here the citizens, never having seen *High Noon*, and unaware that they were entertaining America's Robin Hoods, secured guns (along with rocks for throwing) and shot the gang up, killing two lesser bandits. Another was killed and Jim, Cole, and Bob Younger captured by Minnesota possemen two weeks later. Jesse and Frank escaped.

Somewhat daunted, the brothers settled down to a three-year stay in Nashville under assumed names; Jesse's was "J. B. Howard." In 1879 they stitched together a new gang out of rather shoddy material and made the past live again until Bob Ford, a recently recruited member, shot Jesse in the back of the head as he stood on a chair to straighten a picture in his home at Saint Joseph, Missouri. A reward of $10,000 per James had been posted by the governor.

This cold-blooded slaying, well merited though it was, upset even some of the anti-James Missourians, especially after Governor Crittenden pardoned Bob Ford and his brother Charlie upon their conviction for Jesse's murder. Major Edwards' reaction was predictably overwrought:

> Tear the two bears from the flag of Missouri! Put thereon in place of them as more appropriate, a thief blowing out the brains of an unarmed victim, and a brazen harlot, naked to the waist and splashed to the brows in blood!

A more rational newsman urged: "Let the senseless gush stop, and let his deeds and memory be forgotten." But Jesse's death had already assured him a place in the Wild West gallery of heroes, for the "betrayal" theme has been essential to the growth of almost every good-badman myth since Robin Hood and Turpin. One cannot be defeated in fair fight with the forces of law, for that would imply the fallibility of the hero and possibly the justice of his fate; betrayal makes the Western blackguard into a frontier Christ done in by a lesser Judas, whose sins pale beside that of the traitor. Sam Bass, an especially interesting example of the phenomenon, was an amiable if inept train robber (one writer went so far as to call him a "stupid oaf") who may or may not have killed one man and who was shot to death by Texas Rangers after being betrayed by associate Jim Murphy. In no time at all someone had made up an extremely popular song which praised Sam's predictable personal qualities ("A kinder-hearted fellow you'd never hope to see") while singling out Murphy for special obloquy.[2]

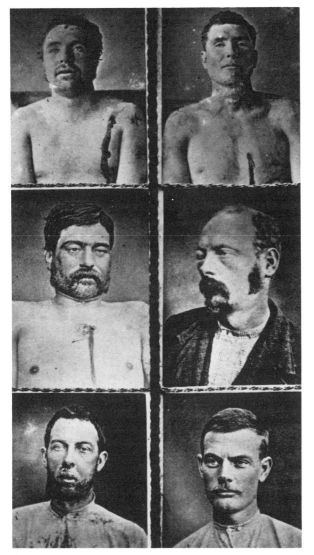

Pictures of these outlaws killed or captured at Northfield were widely distributed in the form of souvenir cards commemorating the famous raid. *Top row:* Clell Miller and Bill Chadwell, both killed. *Middle row:* Charlie Pitts (killed), and Cole Younger. *Bottom row:* Jim and Bob Younger. (Minnesota Historical Society)

And so it was with Jesse. Many of the supposedly skeptical denizens of the Show Me State (and others) proved disgustingly gullible when it came to swallowing the lies told about his nobility and generosity, such as the key fable in which Jesse gives a poor widow lady, about to be foreclosed on, enough money to pay off a rascally banker, the legendary knight of the road later waylaying the capitalist and retrieving all the loot. Since movies had yet to be invented, the home folks contented themselves with telling stories about Jesse, reading trashy biographies and dime novels about him, and singing the anonymous ballad, the chorus of which ran mournfully:

> Jesse had a wife to mourn for his life
> Three children, they were brave.
> But that dirty little coward that shot Mr. Howard
> Has laid Jesse James in his grave.

The "dirty little coward" himself went on stage to reenact his treachery for the public, while Mrs. Samuel, not to be outdone by any base assassin, showed tourists around Jesse's old farm, sold them pebbles from his grave (regularly replenished from a nearby creek) at two bits a shot, and unloaded enough horseshoes from the brothers' trusty steeds to "fill a wagonbed." On Jesse's tombstone, resting over a $500 coffin (one wag suggested that the bandit would be taken for a banker by the folks on the other side), she caused this epitaph to be inscribed:

In Loving Remembrance of My Beloved Son

JESSE JAMES

Died April 3, 1882
Aged 34 Years, 6 Months, 28 Days
Murdered by a Traitor and a Coward
Whose Name Is Not Worthy to Appear Here

But there was some doubt in the public mind concerning the body in that expensive coffin. "The people held their breath when they heard of Jesse's death," ran the song, "and wondered how he ever came to die." How *could* this god have perished, even by treachery? Surely he still lived—and all the proof to the contrary made not a bit of difference. Such was the need for a killer-hero to worship, a need apparently existing to this day, when Missouri communities hold celebrations to commemorate their Jesse's bestial crimes and youngsters proudly flaunt their Jesse James T shirts. The crop of idols harvested from our Old West is indeed an odd one; as C. L. Sonnichsen once wrote, "It looks as if the American people have gone shopping for heroes and come back with whatever they could find."

Although most of the cheap paperback "dime novels" dealing with the James Boys during the nineteenth century wrote them up as bold Robin Hoods, others cast them as sadistic butchers, and several publishing firms, such as the famed house of Beadle and Adams, discontinued or simply refrained from publishing novels about the brothers as they tended to glamorize outlawry and were therefore, or so the theory went, bad for business. (Many people were convinced that dime novels had a horrific effect on children in any case, much as moral crusaders in the 1950s were to view dime comic books as guidebooks for the road to hell.) The American film industry followed a different course by getting all the mileage it could out of the James myth and, doubtless in the belief that righteous crime had a better chance of paying, depicted Jesse and his pards with comparatively few exceptions as put-upon heroes; the financial results are too varied for any definitive judgment on the soundness of this approach. The granddaddy of all such films was Essanay's *The James Boys in Missouri*, released in 1908 when the business was in its infancy and Frank James still living.

The first full-length feature inspired by the James story was produced by a company formed specifically for that purpose, members of the James family owning stock. Entitled *Under the Black Flag*—signifying no quarter asked or given, the usual conditions under which border-war partisans operated—and released in 1921, it starred Jesse's son Jesse Edward, usually billed as Jesse James, Jr. A young Eastern dude is represented as falling for old Jesse's granddaughter and wondering whether her family background is acceptable. She has him read a biography of Frank and Jesse and the flashbacks begin, showing the innocent brothers driven to lives as fugitives due to their wartime backgrounds. His decision is as expected.

Black Flag was a flop, but this in itself did not prove that crime couldn't pay, nor did it prevent Paramount from coming up with its own large-scale *Jesse James* in 1927. This time Jesse James, Jr., was on hand only as a "technical advisor"—perhaps just to insure that nothing detrimental to the memory of Saint Jesse was permitted on screen—and ordained Presbyterian minister Fred Thomson co-starred with his trick horse Silver King. Even the evil Quantrill was glamorized, and in interviews Thomson, who had chosen the story treatment himself and claimed to have been flooded with fan mail from Jessephiles after its production was announced, stated publicly that the luckless lads had been driven to it. "It was always the bullion hoarded by some carpet-bagger that he and his boys were after," said Fred. "Never did they rob the poor and needy." Since Thomson was not terribly bright, it probably never occurred to him that the reason Jesse generally neglected to rob the "poor and needy" was that they had little worth stealing.

Despite all the fan mail, Thomson's movie also proved a box-office disappointment. Partly at fault were the high prices charged exhibitors for the "epic" and one of those periodic slumps in the popularity of Westerns, but there was also a surprising amount of loud moral condemnation, as well as censorship trouble in Missouri and several other states. (The film did spark a movement to erect a monument to Jesse, but this effort mercifully failed.)

Leaping ahead to 1938, we find Henry King convincing Darryl F. Zanuck at Twentieth Century-Fox to let him direct an epic treatment of the James story. Perhaps he felt that the time was right for such a film because the Great Depression had cost banks and other businesses whatever prestige they had enjoyed during the smugly prosperous twenties, reinforcing their traditional role as targets for popular resentment. No expense would be spared.

As if to distract from the less than inspiring motives behind the making of the picture, director King evidently felt obliged to spout some hypocritical and sanctimonious claptrap about morality. Of *course* they'd known more about Jesse than they'd put in the picture: the research department, he said, had been digging up facts a year before production began, and they also had access to Pinkerton's newspaper files on Jesse.

> But what we were trying to do was create a Jesse James who would be worthy of the legend, for we knew that no matter what we or any other creators of fiction did now, the legend would persist. Our effort was to make the legend a better one, morally as well as dramatically. If we succeeded it was well worth the effort, which involved a long location trip to the Jesse James country, the use of Technicolor and the great expense of the production.

Filmmakers are devoted to legend—one might say slavishly so. Whenever a director is caught ravishing truth and elevating some Western ruffian into a god, he almost invariably falls back on the excuse that he was actually dramatizing (or, more impressively, "interpreting") a legend or myth—which in the Wild West context, however, usually means dramatizing or interpreting some other clown's delusion or misconception, sustained more by ignorance or muddled thinking than by the qualities of the tale. It would be refreshing if we could find a director as dedicated to basic historical fact as the mass of them seem to be to "legends" conceived by drunken lunatics and perpetuated by the mass media.

When you get right down to it, there is no real Jesse James legend anyway—or, more precisely, there is only the standardized outline of the classic outlaw-hero story with Jesse's name hung on it, and had King's real purpose been to concoct a simple Western morality play, he could have changed all the names and come up with the same, rather pedestrian story. But the Name was too important to discard, especially when so much money was involved.

Let us imagine topflight screenwriter Nunnally Johnson looking over all that meticulously gathered research material, discarding as irrelevant the accounts of gratuitous cruelty, searching desperately for some bit of persecution that will justify the boys' extended crime spree, and, since the popular myth proves groundless, finding none. But wait! The Night of Blood! Of course . . . all we have to do is move it *ahead* of the crimes and make a few other simple changes.

So it is that Jesse (Tyrone Power) finds himself victimized by the villainous St. Louis–Midland railroad, though its sole offense against the real Jesse was offering a reward for his capture after being robbed by him. Personified by that favorite thirties heavy, Brian Donlevy, the St. Louis–Midland blows up Jesse's ma (Jane Darwell) when she declines to sell the family land for a right of way at a measly price, thereby forcing Jesse and his folksy, tobacco-chewing

Henry Fonda and Tyrone Power at bay in Henry King's *Jesse James*. For Jesse's granddaughter Jo Frances, all resemblance between the film and history could be summed up by saying that "once there was a man named James and he rode a horse." (Museum of Modern Art/Film Stills Archive)

brother (Henry Fonda) onto the owlhoot trail. From then on, in Technicolored glory, the two siblings and their chosen cohorts loot the St. Louis–Midland, rob equally greedy banks, and shoot such deserving individuals as goon Donlevy, who draws first. They are publicly defended by a friendly newspaper editor (Henry Hull), who, with respect to the brothers' foes and various others, keeps yelling, "Shoot 'em down like dogs!"

Finally trying to settle down to some cozy domesticity, Jesse falls victim to Bobby Ford, who aims his gun at the innocent outlaw's enticing back as he straightens the (sob) "God Bless Our Home" motto on the wall. (Ford himself, a mild-looking man of twenty-one at the time, was played to the scurvy hilt by John Carradine.) Poor Jesse is laid in his grave under a tombstone with the proper inscription (minus a fond mother's dedication, of course) and Henry Hull intones the eulogy, saying that, although he was a thief and killer, he was really a product of the times and not at all a bad sort of fella.

Persuading millions of viewers, both in America and overseas, with its romantic yet (relatively) believable drama, *Jesse James* left many of those not already misinformed with the impression that its hero, the train wrecker and murderer, was indeed the Robin Hood of the legend—a shameful lie motivated only by money and an act of gross irresponsibility, especially as the falsehoods of the picture were sure to reach many more people than the truth of the printed record (that which survived the attentions of pro-James biographers) ever could. There is not really an excess of morality in perpetuating a "legend" such as this, although helping to destroy it might be praiseworthy. Of course, one need not do either: if you can't say anything good about the man, just say nothing at all.

It might be of service to the paying public if a filmmaker who, like King, insisted on making a "historical" outlaw film merely placed at the beginning of the movie a disclaimer, clearly identifying what follows as a deliberate falsification of the known facts and giving some pertinent data on its supposed subject. This procedure would cramp the artist's style no more than any other form of truth in packaging; Jesse and his comrades are little more than commercial products to be sold for cash just like any other—and why should they be sold under false labels? By this method we rational people could have the truth and the filmmakers would still be free to play around with their absurd "legends." I think it an admirable solution; however, since the profits derived from such films might conceivably be reduced if their makers confessed too openly their style of "legend-making," viewer ignorance must be maintained if not actually encouraged.

King's ersatz folktale premiered in January of 1939 on a Friday the thirteenth, but it did great business anyway and was Fox's biggest hit of the year despite a minor scandal concerning a spectacular scene in which the brothers, attempting to elude a posse, leap their steeds from a high cliff into the water below; the horses in question, after being blindfolded, had been thrown approximately seventy feet into a lake by means of a greased slide, with fatal results for at least one.

Fox's glossy immorality play was so successful that there just had to be a sequel for 1940. True, Jesse was no more, but Frank was still around, and hadn't Henry Fonda's performance overshadowed Power's anyway? To satisfy fans of the earlier film, the sequel would receive the same Technicolor and first-rate production values, plus the services of a renowned foreign director responsible for such films as *M*, *Metropolis*, and *Doktor Mabuse der Spieler*.

In 1933, Fritz Lang had endured a meeting with German propaganda chieftain Joseph Goebbels, who told him that Der Fuehrer, having seen his pictures, had concluded that this was the man to make the big Nazi epics. The Austrian-born Lang balked at the prospect of glorifying Nazi thugs on film and fled to breathe the free, invigorating air of America—where, after making several noteworthy films, he would be assigned to direct *The Return of Frank James*, glorifying a wholesome American thug. Shortly after Lang had received his final naturalization papers, the *New York Times* ran the headline:

FOOTNOTE ON A PATRIOTIC OCCASION

Fritz Lang, U.S. Citizen,
Celebrates by Making
A Horse Opera

"My contribution extended to the script, although in a minor capacity," said Lang later, adding, "I greatly enjoyed doing it." (He would have enjoyed it even more had he been allowed to do it as an accurate and realistic study of Frank James. But his employers at Fox could never have allowed *that*.)[3] *The Return* cast Frank as an avenger who goes after the Ford boys following their pardon. But since the Hays Office, though technically banning only the endorsement of revenge in "modern" times, might not have allowed him his happy ending if he'd killed them himself, the Ford brothers are disposed of most conveniently: one falls off a cliff and the other is shot by one of Frank's pals, the hero thereby keeping his hands clean.

Fonda's role as avenger was one which many Missourians expected the real Frank, a balding, sanctimonious weasel, to assume after Jesse's murder. This he did not do; instead he continued in hiding, finally surrendering to Governor Crittenden because he was tired of running and leaving Charlie and Bob Ford to, respectively, commit suicide and get blown away with a shotgun by a man who thought it a good idea. For various reasons, chiefly sob-sistering, they were never able to convict him of anything and he died free in 1915 after occupying a number of jobs, including those of doorman, shoe salesman, and bit player in two theatrical productions. (He did not play himself.)

In 1902 Frank sought a court order to prevent the stage melodrama *The James Boys in Missouri* from playing in Kansas City as part of an attempt to live down his envied past. "The dad-binged play glorifies these outlaws and makes heroes of them," he complained, perhaps a tad unconvincingly. "That's the main thing I object to. It's injurious to the youth of the country. It's positively harmful. I am told that the Gilliss Theater was packed to the doors last night, and that most of those there were men and boys. What will be the effect upon these men to see the acts of a train robber and outlaw glorified?"

But few if any in Hollywood knew or cared what Frank James had thought, and such sociological questions as he saw fit to raise mattered little compared with the positive effect said glorification had on the box office. As was the case with Fred Thomson, even the most pious could indulge with a clear conscience: soon after Zanuck released his *Jesse James*, the low-budget Republic studio produced *Days of Jesse James*, starring singing cowboy Roy Rogers as a friend of the good badman. Roy, the meetings of whose fan clubs always began with prayer, followed this with *Jesse James at Bay* (1941), in which he played both Jesse and an evil lookalike who endangers the Robin Hood legend through his cruel depredations.

In 1946 RKO Radio, in *Frankenstein Meets the Wolf Man* fashion, had Jesse teamed up with a host of other "real" badmen to confront Randolph Scott in

Badman's Territory, although it turns out the James boys *really* weren't such bad guys after all. When applied to horror films, such a technique usually foreshadowed at least a temporary end to a character's vitality and his degeneration into burlesque *(Abbott and Costello Meet Frankenstein)*, but Jesse still had a lot of life left in him, as shown by such items as Republic's 1949 *Jesse James Jr.* (which did not star Jesse James Jr.), Columbia's *Jesse James vs. the Daltons* (1953), and United Artists' tawdry *Jesse James' Women*. In 1949 Samuel Fuller *(Shock Corridor, The Big Red One)* made his directorial debut with a film actually featuring Bob Ford as protagonist, the inexpensive *I Shot Jesse James*. Here John Ireland's treachery seems even blacker than the real Ford's, since by rewriting history Fuller elevated him from mere hanger-on to Jesse's best friend, owing his life to "Mr. Howard"; but Ford gradually becomes a more sympathetic character as he faces the consequences of his act and finally rushes to an almost suicidal death. Perhaps part of this sympathetic treatment was tied in with Fuller's own feelings toward the American Robin Hood.

> I'll make it very brief about Mr. Robert Ford. I happen to like Robert Ford, because he did something which should have been done quite a bit earlier in the life of Jesse Woodson James. . . .
> Since I despise Mr. James (and would give my right eyeball to make the true story of Jesse James) I've always had sympathy for Robert Ford. One day, the real story of Jesse James will be made. It will shock people. Rough! Vicious! . . .
> I love the West. I read a lot about the West, and I'm shocked, I'm ashamed that in pictures they have not made the true story of the winning of the West . . . nothing to do with guns. Streets, roads, bridges, streams, forests—that's the winning of the West to me. Hard! Tremendous, tremendous fight. But we have, as you know, Cowboys and Indians and all that.

To give Hollywood its due, one might point out that the public could not endure too many Westerns dealing with hard work, though a few can be tolerated—and there are some who would argue that these should not really be called "Westerns" at all, despite their settings. (To Philip French, a nonviolent Western is as unthinkable as "a vegetarian steakhouse.") Fuller himself, a specialist in low-budget action flick, never made such a film; perhaps he himself was not terribly interested in nonviolent Westerns, or else, as with many of his projects, he was unable to find sufficient backing. One reason behind the glamorization of the Western badman is his unquestioned ability to liven things up; as Ramon F. Adams writes, "Without him, the more or less orderly process of settlement would have been as dull as neighborhood gossip in a country store."

In tune with current problems and the national *Angst*, Hollywood sold us juvenile delinquency films disguised as Westerns. Universal's *Kansas Raiders* (1950) starred Audie Murphy as Jesse and pointed out that Quantrill (Brian

Donlevy) had been a bad influence on the lad, who like his young comrades, would become an Old West delinquent after the end of the movie.

For 1957 Fox remade Jesse's saga and showed the world it couldn't even lie *consistently*. Director Nicholas Ray had originally desired to make the film a sort of stagebound, surrealistic examination of the legend in which the characters mused aloud on their mythic immortality, but this artsy-craftsy notion was soon quashed: Ray's *The True Story of Jesse James* emerged excelling in truth even the anonymous sex tales ("Raped on My Mother's Grave," etc.) in *True Story* magazine. Nunnally Johnson again contributed the screenplay, this time from a story by Walter Newman so that Jesse (Robert Wagner) becomes the victim not of capitalist greed but of Damnyankee tyranny, a theme even more appealing to some Southerners in the year of Little Rock. Fittingly, *The True Story* was adapted into a Dell Movie Classics comic book so as to brainwash all the little tots who hadn't seen the movie itself.

The sixties showed no improvement in the portrayal of Mr. James. *Young Jesse James* (1960) firmly established that Jesse had gone bad to avenge his dad's murder by Yankees; this of course never happened, but as his mother had already been sacrificed, it may have seemed wise to maintain a parental balance. In 1965 ABC spread its legs and offered to the discriminating viewer a TV series, "The Legend of Jesse James"; nobody was buying and the show was soon canceled. To round out the decade, Audie Murphy made a guest appearance as a rather benign Jesse down Texas way in *A Time for Dying*, which—oops, almost forgot to mention William Beaudine's Embassy Pictures classic of 1966, *Jesse James Meets Frankenstein's Daughter*.

For 1972 we got *The Great Northfield Minnesota Raid*, written and directed by Phil Kaufman with considerable black humor and, incidentally, the third Jesse film to include the words "great" and "raid," having been preceded in the 1950s by *The Great Missouri Raid* and *The Great Jesse James Raid*. Kaufman's neglected work was undoubtedly the best on the James theme, although one distortion of fact which struck me as particularly objectionable was the depiction of the Northfieldians as a pack of trigger-happy fools who go about lynching innocent people in the aftermath of the robbery attempt (the choir of Saint Olaf's College at Northfield generously contributed a hymn to the film). Seemingly out of place was an introductory montage with a crackerbarrel narrator telling how the James-Youngers rose up to save downtrodden Missouri and tar and feather the carpetbaggers. This was presumably intended to be ironic, since—despite the portrayal of the Pinkertons as meanies who bribe legislators so that they won't give the outlaws amnesty for their crimes—it has little connection with the way Kaufman handles his bandits: they are not the Robin Hoods we might have expected, but a mangy bunch of mostly dimwitted hardcases whose refrain of "we only rob the robbers" strikes one as exceedingly empty. Robert Duvall's crazed, callous Jesse, still obsessed with the border wars and making the Northfield robbery a "guerrilla raid," stands out as the least palatable of the gang, and the widow's-mortgage story is darkly satirized: Jesse waylays that banker all

Jesse the Baptist's got that old time religion . . .

. . . and the outlaw Cole Younger becomes an object of fascination for the crowd in *The Great Northfield Minnesota Raid.* (Both: Museum of Modern Art/Film Stills Archive)

right, but instead of just robbing him he shoots him (as in the legend's gorier, less popular version) and then plants evidence framing the widow for the crime, she being "just a Yankee." After the raid, which involves a tribute to the bad-banker cliché since it is revealed that the Northfield bank president is conning his patrons, Jesse murders the widow to prevent her revealing the gang's whereabouts and escapes with Frank in a stolen wagon, disguised in the widow's dress and wondering aloud whether Bob Ford would make a good member for the brothers' next gang.* We end on that real-life bit of showmanship during which Cole Younger, punctured by eleven slugs, stood up in the cart taking him to jail for the benefit of the assembled spectators; Cliff Robertson's good-humored Cole emerged as a somewhat likable rogue, if only by comparison with the evil Jesse.

After his little *beau geste*, Cole (as the film's narration told) served twenty-five years in prison, being paroled along with brother Jim in 1901; Bob had died of tuberculosis in 1889 and Jim committed suicide the year after his release. Soon after being freed Cole formed with Frank James the nostalgically named James-Younger Wild West show, although Cole just sat in the reserved-seat section to be stared at since his parole forbade him to exhibit himself and Frank merely enacted the role of passenger in a stagecoach robbery. Cole later went on the lecture circuit to insist that crime did not pay, but he still claimed that he had committed no crimes until Northfield, and then only out of ill-defined desperation. He died in 1916.

The Younger Brothers, a "true life" three-reel silent adventure, had premiered in 1915, but the siblings' first major film was Warners' 1941 *Badmen of Missouri*, part of a whitewashed badman cycle touched off by the immense success of *Jesse James*. In the midst of a montage sequence of Blue and Gray battling it out, the war's end, mortgage foreclosures, and repulsive Damnyankees in huge close-up telling honest farmers to get off their land, we are shown this preface:

DISHONEST MEN EXPLOITING THE MISFORTUNE OF THE SOUTH WERE DRIVING THE FARMERS FROM THE LAND. A FEW MEN REBELLED. AMONG THEM WERE THE THREE YOUNGER BROTHERS. BY THEIR ENEMIES THEY WERE CALLED BADMEN. MISSOURI CALLED THEM HEROES. THIS IS THEIR STORY.

Now that's what I call a fast-moving historical Western: all those lies told us even before the movie's fairly begun. Not only does the prologue claim that the Youngers were rebelling against land-grabbers and that the entire population of Missouri regarded them as heroes—it most certainly did not—but it even whittles down the number of brothers, eliminating the murderous John (killed

---

*Quite unromantic; but a distressed Universal executive apparently thought an earlier, fact-based scene showing Jesse so disguised while a Civil War guerrilla (hence Sam Fuller's description of the outlaw as "a half-assed homo") too much, and snipped it.

in an 1874 shoot-out with Pinkertons). What follows is even better, with old Mr. Younger slain, his land stolen, and his sons Cole, Bob, and Jim (Dennis Morgan, Wayne Morris, and Arthur Kennedy) framed for murder. In modern-day crime films those falsely accused usually try to clear themselves or just keep running, but in Westerns like this they always felt obliged to rob somebody, so the Youngers hold up a stagecoach, a seemingly irrelevant crime turned into an unalloyed act of virtue by placing on board the villain's comic-relief flunky, with a large sum of money wrung by the heavies from the downtrodden. This the Youngers redistribute so that a small army of sodbusters can pay off their mortgages in a king-sized version of the widow's-farm story. As Jim's girl friend, Jane Wyman tells the boys that murder and robbery aren't "the right way," in a pitiful attempt at fooling the Hays Office into thinking that we're not supposed to applaud the three robbers.

Next, the boys hold up a train, robbing the passengers—who all deserve it, I guess, except for an old friend whom the trio spares—and providentially capturing another fat wad from the land-grabber's flunky. As it happens, Jesse James (a depraved-looking Alan Baxter) is also on board and decides to link his destiny with the Youngers'; but, shocking though it may have been to those who'd seen Tyrone Power's portrayal two years before, he is revealed as a mere opportunist and not at all an idealistic killer like our heroes. "It's money we're all after, ain't it?" asks Jesse.

After James leaves the gang, the three brothers, unsullied by his mercenary presence, continue doing good, although they do have to shoot down a few citizens who try to stop them. Finally they purge the land of evil by killing the land-grabbers and, with Missouri apparently cleaned out of either villains or banks, go on to depredate all across the West until wounded and captured in Minnesota, where there were presumably few honest Southerners being shafted by carpetbaggers. The censors are satisfied by their incarceration, but the studio tries to turn even this into a happy ending by having plucky Jane assure Jim before the final clinch that there's talk of a pardon since, although the boys had done some bad things, "you did a lot of good things too." Despite her warning that "it may take a long time," we're led to believe that they'll be out in two shakes—certainly not that they'll have to wait a quarter century, with one brother already dead when the parole comes and a second still unable to take solid food because much of his jaw had been shot away at Northfield.

"Here is a picture the small-fry will like," suggested "T.S." in the *New York Times*.

After their release from prison the brothers got a Technicolor sequel, *The Younger Brothers* (1949), forcing them into crime again. But they never got as much exposure as they might have, since they'd been overshadowed by the more familiar James boys and were sometimes forced to play second fiddle to them as in *The True Story of Jesse James*. The year following Ray's biography, Cole popped up in his own star vehicle, but in a slightly different guise; plain old good badmen weren't quite as popular then as grim-eyed *pistoleros* and he became *Cole Younger, Gunfighter* (Frank Lovejoy).

Shining as a gilded buffalo chip, the James-Younger legend warmed the heart of many another stouthearted lad whose destiny led him to pick up the gun, live out a short and bloody life on the outlaw trail, finally get his guts blown out, and, if he were lucky, get a movie made about him. The most famous of these were the Dalton brothers, Grat, Bob, and Emmett, who, after turning in their U.S. marshals' badges (their brother Frank had been wearing one when he was killed in the line of duty), threw in with Bill Doolin and some other Oklahombres and were doing OK robbing banks and trains just like everybody else until Bob, leader of the gang, got delusions of grandeur. Hoping to "beat Jesse James," he planned the simultaneous robbery of two banks in the same town. On October 5, 1892, the three brothers and two accomplices rode into Coffeyville, Kansas, for a raid which did indeed "beat Jesse" in at least one respect: it was an even bigger fiasco than the Northfield raid, and although the Daltons succeeded in killing a shoemaker, a clerk, a merchant, and the local marshal, every bandit perished at the hands of armed citizens save Emmett, who was shot twenty-four times and therefore considered unfit to lynch.[4]

Emmett got life imprisonment for the shooting of two citizens, even though he modestly gave the credit to his dead brother Bob; he was pardoned in 1907 and thereafter walked the straight and narrow. (In the meantime still another Dalton brother, Bill, had gone bad and been killed by police.) In 1931 Emmett published *When the Daltons Rode*, written with Jack Jungmeyer, and in recounting the gang's crimes offered this explanation of their earliest jobs: the brothers had been falsely accused of complicity in a robbery and, once on the dodge, had felt a strong urge to do that of which they'd been accused. However, Emmet did concede that their later holdups had been completely voluntary, and despite its romanticism and factual shortcomings, his book did make *some* attempt to deglamorize the badman; in 1912 and 1918 he acted in films shot at Coffeyville and dramatizing his own version of the Dalton story, apparently with the same end in mind.

Although this last of the renegade Daltons was particularly insistent about setting the brothers up as horrible examples, he was ultimately thwarted by those who preferred them as social workers with guns, undeterred by the fact that at least one of the bandits in question hadn't wanted to be a hero and had professed himself ashamed of his own misdeeds. In 1937 Emmett Dalton died, leaving the folks at Universal, led by screenwriter Harold Shumate, to dance gleefully on his grave and pervert his book from a condemnation of the Dalton's outlawry into a mealymouthed celebration of the same in 1940; the studio was sufficiently crass to have Emmett's widow pose on the set for publicity stills with some of the stars who would help distort her husband's life. The chief players were Brian Donlevy (for once playing an honest badman instead of a shyster villain) as Grat, Broderick Crawford as a gangster-voiced Bob, Frank Albertson as Emmett, and Stuart Ervin as "Ben" Dalton added to make an even four. Andy Devine, playing the fictitious "Ozark," was tossed in for what passed as comic relief.

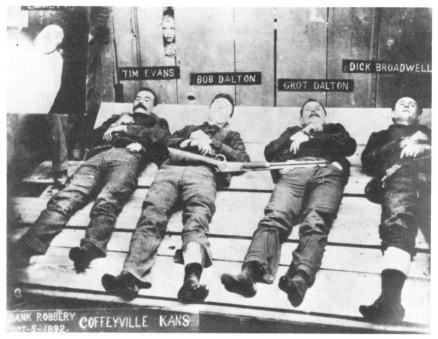

A young boy expresses interest in the outcome of the Coffeyville raid. Grat Dalton's name is here misspelled "Grot." (Kansas State Historical Society)

When the Daltons Rode was preceded by another of those bizarre studio prologues, this one claiming that what followed was "the story of the Dalton gang," and based mainly on "stories told round old campfires," which I suppose would have been some sort of cinematic first had these alleged campfire stories not existed solely in the mind of Mr. Shumate. The prologue did admit that there were "a few strands of fiction" woven in to improve the narrative, although it didn't say that had these strands been unwoven what remained would have been exceedingly threadbare.

The bad guys are again land-grabbers who seek the heroes' land for a railroad right of way and thereby force the brothers into thievery. Since he has an extra Dalton to fool around with, Shumate kills Ben off early, and despite ample justification for their crimes, the remaining Daltons are all soundly punished at Coffeyville—rather too soundly, since even Emmett, credited source for the screenplay, is killed. (Maybe it was thought that nobody'd notice.) But lest this defeat be misconstrued, it is arranged for all three to be shot down from a window by the evil banker responsible for the whole mess. This shyster then tries to pick off Randolph Scott, playing an invented lawyer who's been investigating his activities and just happens to be walking the streets at the time; but the dying Bob blasts the banker first. This leaves Scott free to marry Bob's girl—after a decent interval of mourning, it is to be hoped—and to provide the required happy ending.

Emmett Dalton, solid citizen. (Kansas State Historical Society)

Bosley Crowther wrote for the *New York Times:* "We wouldn't like to suggest that this is the true saga of the famous Dalton gang. But we will say that Brian Donlevy, Broderick Crawford, Andy Devine and others of the gang make some fine desperadoes; the picture itself is straight, fast action fare, and for folks who like plenty of shootin,' here is your gunpowder." This was typical of Crowther's condescending attitude toward the Western, an attitude widely held ever since it had been perceived as a distinct genre and which, in view of such films as *When the Daltons Rode*, was certainly not without cause. The "serious" Western, or at least the Western with pretentions to maturity, did not really come of age until after World War II, and some critics actually expressed hostility toward the notion of a more sophisticated approach.

The Daltons next turned up in *Badmen of Missouri*, with the Youngers encountering a wagon train of settlers driven off their land by the carpetbaggers. Among them are Ma Dalton and her young 'uns; upon hearing of the James gang's activities little Emmett pipes up with: "I'm gonna rob banks too when I grow up!" Ma doesn't like it, but we are comfortable in the knowledge that the child will grow up to carry on in the sacred tradition that is also his legacy.

The boys meet their Waterloo in *When the Daltons Rode* and prove once again that crime does not pay—at least not as long as the censors have anything to say about it. (Museum of Modern Art/Film Stills Archive)

Where the historical Daltons really went wrong was in not dying correctly: no treason was involved and they perished by virtue of their own stupidity at the hands of simple citizens. Emmett didn't get killed at all, and as he himself recognized, this was a serious drawback as far as becoming a hero went, since jail took much of the glamor away. Unlike their cousins the Youngers, the Daltons didn't even have an association with Jesse or the Confederacy's lost cause to help them; they never became folk heroes and there was no "legend." So as often as not they played the movie villain, as in RKO's *The Return of the Badmen*, a 1948 sequel to their previous renegade reunion promising "TEN TIMES THE THRILLS OF 'BADMAN'S TERRITORY'" with an outlaw lineup including the Youngers, Wild [*sic*] Bill Doolin, and a lad named William Bonney. Randolph Scott, formerly pro-Dalton, was the hero who set out to handle "THE TEN WORST KILLERS OF THE UNTAMED WEST . . . and the Lady they called 'Cheyenne.'" Recently they've shown up in TV productions, such as ABC's 1975 *The Last Day*, which narrator Harry Morgan said was "based on historical fact." Dealing only with the Coffeyville raid (which took perhaps twelve minutes), it had to be padded out to the necessary two-hours-including-commercials with a fictitious cliché subplot about a retired gunfighter (Richard Widmark) and the Dalton hirelings sent into

Coffeyville to eliminate this potential danger prior to the actual robbery. The Daltons, led by a cold-eyed Robert Conrad as Bob, were with the exception of Emmett unsentimentalized, and the story quite dull. NBC's three-hour *The Last Ride of the Dalton Gang* (1979) was somewhat more accurate and avoided the meat-extender approach by dealing with the gang's whole career; it even had a prologue and an epilogue showing the aged Emmett in Hollywood. Yet it persisted in having the bandits all gunned down at Coffeyville by a shyster conspiracy.

Back in those thrilling days of yesteryear, full-fledged female outlaws were extremely rare—that is, they *must* have been, considering the specimen whom the legend-makers chose to enshrine as "The Bandit Queen" and "The Female Jesse James." Born Myra Belle Shirley in 1848, she supposedly acted as a youthful spy for Quantrill's tarnished cavaliers before fleeing perilous Missouri for Texas with her family in 1864. In postwar Dallas Myra Belle had contact with a number of unrepentant ex-guerrillas; one of them was Cole Younger, alleged to have fathered her daughter Rosa Lee, later known as Pearl Younger. Others credit this conception to Jim Reed, her first husband (common-law, at any rate) and another of those conservative Quantrill vets who insisted on carrying on in the same old larcenous way after Apppomattox. Reed was shot to death in 1873, but Myra Belle was quick to recover from the tragedy and soon opened a Dallas livery stable offering the best in stolen horseflesh. The James-Younger bunch dropped by for an occasional visit.

Depositing her daughter and son Ed with relatives, Myra Belle took off for the Indian Territory to consort with some of Reed's old outlaw buddies. She came to dominate the gang, but never took a very active part in the actual horse thieving, whisky running, and cattle rustling; she could better serve the cause by handling their legal affairs, planning robberies, and fencing hot goods. What spare time she had was partly filled by persuading an impressive string of disreputable characters (nearly all of whom managed to get themselves killed off sooner or later) to share her bed.

Only in part did our heroine conform to the stereotyped image of the frontier hellcat. True, she did go about fully armed, and did refer to her two shiny six-shooters as her "babies." But she continued to wear dresses and refused to mount her horse astride, instead using a sidesaddle as was expected of a proper Victorian lady and graduate of the Carthage Female Academy. If she ever shot anybody, word of the event has not come down to us.

In 1880 Myra Belle made it into the big time of frontier legendry: she married a thoroughly bad Cherokee named Sam Starr (the happy couple moved into a cabin on the Canadian River which she nostalgically named Younger's Bend) and adopted the name Belle Starr, her sure ticket to immortality. When in 1883 Belle became the first woman ever tried for horse theft in Judge Isaac Parker's federal court,[5] she became the darling of Eastern newspaper reporters who would have yawned at a Myra Belle. Since the age of

The Bandit Queen and one of her many paramours, the Indian Blue Duck.
(Oklahoma State Historical Society and Hale Photo Supply)

photograhic news illustration had yet to arrive, no harsh visual reality was
required to intrude upon the reader's fantasies.

Among the most fervent pushers of the Starr mystique was *The National
Police Gazette*, which featured lurid pink pages and equally lurid stories
concerning lascivious clergymen, lynchings, heathen Chinee, and women who
wore bloomers to church. It was owned by one Richard Kyle Fox, of whom
Gene Smith has recently written, in his *The Police Gazette:* "The words 'good
taste' can be applied to him with as much reason as 'nice fellow' to Genghis
Khan. Vulgarity was his middle name." What better man for the job?

After Belle was gone, "the Pinky" said:

Of all women of the Cleopatra type, since the days of the Egyptian queen herself, the universe has produced none more remarkable than Belle Starr, the Bandit Queen. . . . She was more amorous than Antony's mistress, more relentless than Pharoah's daughter, and braver than Joan of Arc. Of her it may well be said that Mother Nature was indulging in one of her rarest freaks, when she produced such a novel specimen of womankind.

One might be tempted to laugh off such "journalistic" excesses, but their effect on the legend should not be underestimated. The wild tales originating with the *Police Gazette* and similar printed sources sank deep into the minds of Western as well as Eastern readers, to resurface later as authentic, first-hand recollections for the benefit of other writers pressing garrulous old-timers for facts concerning the Bandit Queen and other outlaw personalities.

After nine months in prison, Belle and Sam were back at Younger's Bend and in business. In 1886 Sam, wanted for robbing a post office, was killed under uninteresting circumstances, so Belle found solace in the arms of others; her last paramour appears to have been an Indian named Jim July. On February 2, 1889, while riding along a country road, Belle was murdered by someone who apparently knocked her off her horse with a load of buckshot in the back and then gave her a barrelful of turkey shot for good measure. This assassin was never found, but likely suspects included Jim July (who had allegedly offered one Milo Hoyt a whole $200 to kill "the old hag") and Belle's son Ed—with whom, it was whispered, Belle had had incestuous relations, but who hated her for her cruel treatment of him. Both men were later killed in gunfights, so it didn't matter.

On her tombstone, paid for by daughter Pearl with money earned at Fort Smith's Pea Green Bawdy House, was carved this tender sentiment, along with a picture of her horse Venus:

> Shed not for her the bitter tear,
> Nor give the heart to vain regret
> 'Tis but the casket that lies here,
> The gem that filled it sparkles yet.

Belle was buried with a pistol in her hand, but this was subsequently dug up and stolen by someone apparently immune to tender sentiments. A heroic bronze statue of her was later erected at Ponca City, Oklahoma, but God alone knows why.

In 1941 literary critic Burton Rascoe published his *Belle Starr: "The Bandit Queen,"* a biography that laid waste the myth of the glamorous Belle and, using to good effect a complete file of *Police Gazette* back issues, uncovered the embarrassing truth concerning the "recollections" of Mrs. Starr made by helpful informants. Mr. Rascoe tended to take a rather dim view of earlier Western chroniclers, although his own work contained a number of quite incomprehensible boners (he stated, for example, that Frank James had

A gripping scene from *Belle Starr*. (Museum of Modern Art/Film Stills Archive)

served twenty-one years in prison sorting gunny sacks, and took William McLeod Raines to task for truthfully writing in his *Famous Sheriffs and Western Outlaws* that Frank Dalton had been killed while a U.S. deputy marshal); despite such inaccuracies, Rascoe's work held the basic stuff of truth, which was very easily swamped by Twentieth Century-Fox since for every person who chanced to read Rascoe's biography there were several thousand who paid to see the 1941 *Belle Starr*, *"The Bandit Queen."* A wisp of Technicolor fluff coincidentally bearing the same name as Rascoe's work, it starred Gene Tierney as the glamorous frontier Amazon and ersatz Scarlett O'Hara, riding and shooting and having all sorts of simply *thrilling* adventures. The story never left Missouri (treated here as the stereotype of a

Deep South state, although it was split by "Northern" and "Southern" factions and never actually seceded), the catalysts for banditry were the familiar Yankee carpetbaggers, and the whitewashing extended even to race: Sam Starr became a lily-white guerrilla chieftain (Randolph Scott) who carries on after the surrender and is led astray by bad guys in the movement.[6] Equally original was the 1952 *Montana Belle* (why Montana?), starring Jane Russell and paying just as little attention to whatever facts the screenwriter happened to be aware of. Scenes requiring Russell to don masculine disguise presumed not only on the audience's intelligence (standard practice anyway) but also on its anatomical knowledge. Finally we had an Elizabeth Montgomery TV soap-opera version of *Belle Starr* (1980), which presented her as a sort of bored housewife who disrupts her family life by running around with outlaws.

On a lesser level—if we may speak here of a lesser level—we have Allied Artists' 1953 *Son of Belle Starr*, which was not about a suspected bastard and matricide getting himself killed while trying to throw two saloonkeepers out of their own saloon, and Fox's 1948 *Belle Starr's Daughter*, which was not about Pearl Younger's adventures as a Pea Green inmate and later the proud owner and operator of her very own brothel.

But enough of the sordid, small-time Belle Starr and her brood. Let us now contemplate reverently the hero who slouches even above Frank and Jesse; the hero who has been honored in scores of films, an Aaron Copland–scored ballet, a Billy Joel pop tune, hundreds of plays, dime novels, and shoddily written histories steeped in inky gore; the hero who can unite left- and right-winger in his universal legendry and, even in this cynical era, make strong men weep at the tragedy of his youthful demise.

Controversy has long raged over the real name and early life of this paragon, but it now seems reasonably certain that the innocent stripling destined to become Billy the Kid started out as William Bonney, then became Henry McCarty after his widowed mother resumed her maiden name, then became Henry Antrim after she remarried in 1873 only to die a little more than a year later. He was Henry McCarty again when nabbed for stealing clothes from a Chinese laundry at Silver City, New Mexico, in 1875. It was an unpromising beginning, but two years later the boy shot a blacksmith at Fort Grant, Arizona, who had first bullied him and then wrestled him to the ground; the victim may simply have got what he deserved, but a coroner's jury decided that "Henry Antrim" was unjustified in killing him.

The Kid, as he was nicknamed, fled into New Mexico and did a little cattle rustling; riding into Lincoln County, he was eventually hired as a cowboy by English-born rancher John Tunstall. Tunstall and lawyer Alexander McSween, financially supported by powerful rancher John Chisum, were then engaged in competition with Colonel J. S. Murphy and James Dolan, who had the backing of powerful business interests and territorial officials in their attempt to monopolize the county's trading activity. In opposing this rapacious foe Tunstall and McSween claimed to be waging a kind of idealistic crusade on

The boy all the fuss was about. Billy himself was allegedly displeased with this photograph, which has been reversed in printing so that the Kid's holster appears on his left hip. (*The Cattleman* magazine)

behalf of the Little People, but Tunstall, at least, seems to have thought the idea was to set up their own monopoly. "*Everything* in New Mexico that pays at *all*," he wrote home, "is worked by a 'ring.' . . . I am at work at present making such a ring & have succeeded admirably so far. . . . I propose to handle it in such a way as to get half of every dollar that is made in the county by any one." It was later the claim of several Lincoln County residents that Billy the Kid had been a member of the Murphy-Dolan faction before joining McSween.

On February 18, 1878, the legal maneuvering of the two parties escalated into violence: Tunstall was murdered by a Murphy-Dolan posse. The Kid was supposedly driven to a seething lust for vengeance by this slaying, but it is also possible that he was motivated by money paid him by the McSween faction. Either way, he was party to the murders of several Murphy-Dolan men. On April 1 county sheriff William Brady, a Dolan partisan, and several friends were walking down the town of Lincoln's main (and only) street when Billy and a quintet of other brave souls bushwhacked them from behind a fence gate; both Brady and deputy George Hind were killed by a volley of rifle fire in the back. A few indecisive skirmishes followed, and on July 15 McSween and his followers rode into Lincoln and attempted to seize the town. Failing, they retreated to the McSween house, where they were soon besieged. After several days of gunfire the Murphy-Dolan men managed to set the house on fire; McSween came out, allegedly with Bible in hand, and was of course riddled with bullets, as were three other men trying to flee the burning ruins. Billy and five others escaped.

With the Murphy-Dolan combine triumphant, these McSween warriors found themselves lacking an employer; along with Billy, who by now had reverted to using his old name of Bonney, they kept body and soul together by rustling stock, special attention being directed to the cattle of John Chisum on the theory that he owed them for services rendered in the Lincoln County War. That September Lew Wallace was appointed governor and offered a general amnesty for those involved in the war; the drawback was that it didn't apply to those under indictment for murder, but after Billy witnessed the shooting of a lawyer named Huston Chapman, he wrote to Wallace offering to tell what he knew in exchange for immunity. At a dramatic meeting with the Kid, Wallace agreed on condition that Billy surrender to stand trial for the murder of Sheriff Brady, as he could not be pardoned until he had been tried. The Kid responded by squealing like the proverbial stuck pig before a grand jury.

The boy wonder was then lodged in jail, but he apparently feared that the governor wouldn't keep up his end of the bargain and escaped before he could be tried. On January 10 he killed a Texan named Joe Grant (cause obscure) and bragged about it, the Las Vegas, New Mexico, *Gazette* reporting that the "daring young rascal seemed to enjoy the telling as well as the killing." Billy made a nuisance of himself by leading a gang of stock thieves, claiming all the while that he was being victimized by false impressions of his acts "put out by Chisum and his tools."

Meanwhile Billy's former friend Pat Garrett had been elected sheriff of Lincoln County to put an end to all this foolishness, and on December 18 he laid an ambush for the Kid's gang at Old Fort Sumner, their favorite hangout. One outlaw was killed, but the others escaped. Garrett's posse then trailed them to romantic Stinking Springs and managed to surround them. There was much shooting and one of Billy's close friends, Charlie Bowdre, was hit several times.

Billy shouted to Garrett that Bowdre wanted to come out, and Garrett agreed. The Kid then grabbed the fallen man and propped him up in front of the door; revealing himself to be an expert judge of bullet wounds, he informed Bowdre that he was dying, advised him to get revenge by shooting a few of Garrett's men before he died, and pushed him out the door. Bowdre staggered a few steps toward Garrett before falling and leaving both sides free to resume the lead-swapping. The Kid and his remaining friends finally surrendered and Billy was taken to the jail at Las Vegas, where a reporter interviewed him and pronounced him "in all, quite a handsome looking fellow, the only imperfections being two prominent front teeth slightly protruding like squirrel's teeth, and he has agreeable and winning ways."

The Kid was tried and sentenced to die for Brady's murder, and his letter of complaint to Governor Wallace did no good at all; as the Kid had already violated his end of the bargain by escaping, Wallace ignored him and concentrated on writing *Ben-Hur*. Transferred to the Lincoln courthouse-jail and left to contemplate his future as a bit of rope meat, Billy escaped after killing his two guards and Garrett began a new manhunt, which ended at old Fort Sumner on the night of June 14, 1881, with a shot in the dark in one Pete Maxwell's bedroom.

The *Silver City New Southwest and Grant City Herald* expressed the general press reaction in rejoicing that "the vulgar murderer and desperado known as 'Billy the Kid' has met his just deserts at last. . . . Despite the glamor of romance thrown about his dare-devil life by sensation writers, the fact is he was a low down vulgar cut-throat, with probably not one redeeming quality." No doubt the reporter imagined that such glamor would not long endure, much like the man at the *Kansas City Journal* who wrote that Billy had perished "like the commonest cur that ever fell before a bullet of the muncipal dog killer" and predicted that he who went and did likewise to the James boys would earn the lasting gratitude of the American public.

The death of New Mexico's most famous outlaw was national news, and the public's desire for further information was inevitably answered by those least qualified to do so; contemporary newspaper accounts of the Kid's doings were often garbled to an appalling degree, and at least one piece of garbling became an enduring part of the legend. A Santa Fe paper stated that Billy had boasted of killing twenty-one men, one for each year of his life; this boast, which he allegedly made on a number of occasions, was subsequently transformed into fact by other newspapers and perpetuated by countless writers. The dime novelists had a field day, but failed to give Billy the Robin Hood treatment one might expect. Instead—perhaps the better to ladle on the gore—they cast him as a sadistic archfiend dressed in outrageous costumes and equipped with a heart "only for anatomical purposes." The contrast between this interpretation and the later Robin Hood image would seem to indicate that the Kid's catchy nickname was the chief factor in the survival of his legend.

The first big step toward glorifying the Kid in print was taken by the least

Patrick F. Garrett. (Denver Public Library, Western History Department)

likely of all suspects—Pat Garrett, who in 1882 signed his name to an *Authentic Life of Billy the Kid* actually written by the eccentric journalist Ash Upson, who (he said) wished to "correct the thousand false impressions which have appeared in the public newspapers and in yellow-covered novels." Never one to let a dearth of available fact stand in his way, Upson reconstructed the Kid's life with the aid of his imagination and had him driven to crime when, at age twelve, he stabbed to death an anonymous loafer who had insulted his mother, a most praiseworthy crime in that Victorian era of filial piety. But although it became a source for later writers, the book was not a success, and its charitable interpretation was swamped by the antiheroic view.

The real turning point may have been the play *Billy the Kid*, first shown in 1906, in which the hero was driven to crime by an evil father who gets himself killed while wearing Billy's clothes so that pursuing lawmen assume it's the Kid ("To the law I am dead. Today my life begins anew. Come Nellie, we'll wander down life's pathways together, where the sun shines always". . .). By 1918 the play had been seen by millions and had helped establish a more positive image in the mind of the Eastern public, but Billy's written legend (if not orally transmitted Southwestern folktales, which were of secondary importance) appeared to be in a state of comparative stagnation, apparently for lack of those soft-headed scribes so willing to polish up the halos of other badmen. In 1925 one writer, who himself made a feeble effort at recreating the Kid as an idealist, was even asking rhetorically, "Who remembers Billy the Kid?"

But help, alas, was on the way. In 1926 Walter Noble Burns rode to the rescue with his *Saga of Billy the Kid*, its hopelessly romantic author visualizing the Kid as a ruthless murderer but also as a good-hearted angel of vengeance, who defied a corrupt law in the name of the righteous McSween-Tunstall cause. The book was heavily, not to say deliriously, fictionalized and incorporated into its flowery narrative tall tales from earlier and equally unreliable sources. But since the popularity of such "popular" Wild West histories has traditionally been in inverse proportion to their historical accuracy (Dee Brown provides one fairly recent example), it sold very well.

In one respect Burns parted company with many of the Kid's other fans by being (comparatively) kind to Pat Garrett, though he did hint that Garrett had done something unethical in tracking down his friend. The customary vilification of the "betrayer" had begun with a gaggle of outlaw buffs almost before Billy's grave had been filled in, one San Francisco paper going so far as to demand Garrett's trial for the Kid's "murder." The year following publication of Burns's "saga," Eugene Manlove Rhodes, a friend of the sheriff, was irked into writing for *Sunset Magazine* an article in which he commented: "Shameful, the way Garrett has been treated." None of this mattered, of course, to all those who insisted that Billy was still alive, somewhere . . . too clever even to die through treachery.

To be truly established as an authentic (that is, commercially manufactured) Western folk hero, the self-made badman simply *must* have a film made about him. This was done for New Mexico's Robin Hood in 1930, when King Vidor directed the first version of *Billy the Kid* for Metro-Goldwyn-Mayer. Burns's *Saga* was credited as the film's inspiration, but since a faithful adaptation of even his account, with fancy prose removed, would have left the Kid a shockingly murderous lad (as well as an anti-Semite who dismisses one victim with the words "He was only a Jew anyway"), inspiration was all it was. Vidor began outlining Billy's short life to producer Irving Thalberg as their limo sped toward the funeral of starlet Mabel Normand, opening up with Billy's first murder in defense of his mother's honor. "This bit of historical half-truth," Vidor later explained, "was emphasized in the hope of convincing Thalberg that all of the Kid's murders were understandable, if not entirely excusable. Then I took Billy through scenes of murder in self-defense, and murders on the side of justice if not the side of law." During the funeral Thalberg leaned over and whispered to Vidor, "Too many murders," momentarily confusing him. "The public won't accept it," the producer added, and Vidor realized that he was talking about Billy. On the way back to Culver City the story conference continued, Thalberg asking such vital questions as "Was Sheriff Pat Garrett his friend during the last five murders?"

On seeing what Vidor had wrought, Thalberg's fears concerning public acceptance were confirmed, and he immediately ordered the first reel reshot so as to provide more sympathetic motivation. "But he can't do that!" cried a university professor of dramatics, who just happened to be in the screening room and was happily ignorant of the world's ways.

Billy the Kid was shot simultaneously in standard 35mm and a new 70mm process, but the wide-screen version was shown in very few theaters. William S. Hart, whose own specialty had always been tales of "good badman,"[7] lent his name to the project and gave former football hero Johnny Mack Brown a six-gun which was supposed to have belonged to the Kid. Johnny Mack's Billy was only looking for justice, but his murders, well motivated though they were, seemed a tad ruthless as well as illegal, and this made the tacked-on happy ending all the more difficult to accept: soft-hearted deputy and villain's henchman Pat Garrett (Wallace Beery), rather than shooting the Kid, allows Billy and his gal to ride off into Old Mexico and safety. Fortunately for MGM, the 1930 Production Code would not be rigorously enforced for another four years.

Following the success of Republic's 1938 *Billy the Kid Returns*, starring Roy Rogers, that studio commenced a series of "B" pictures starring Bob Steele as Billy until he was transferred to the slightly classier "Three Mesquiteers" series. Following this, Producers Releasing Corporation, a poverty-row outfit of the lowest sort, caught the falling flag with their own seemingly endless stream of $12,000 cheapies starring Buster *(Flash Gordon)* Crabbe. From 1940 to 1942 Sam Newfield directed ten of them with such titles as *Billy the Kid's Fighting Pals*, *Billy the Kid in Texas*, and *Billy the Kid's Smoking Guns*. It was simply good business to let a big-name outlaw add distinction to what were essentially "Z"-grade oaters designed for people who would pay to sit through any Western no matter what its quality.

Even as Newfield spat up Billy after Billy, MGM was planning to grab more discriminating viewers with a remake of the Bonney story for 1941, this time in expensive Technicolor as befit Billy's epic stature and the then-current fashion for inaccurate badman sagas and big-budget Westerns. David Miller directed.

Met.
Fulton St.
Brooklyn   ROBERT TAYLOR
                   in M-G-M's TECHNICOLOR HIT!
                          'BILLY THE KID'
                   plus 'HELLO SUCKER'—Hugh
                                            Herbert

As in the 1930 version, Billy (again coached by William S. Hart) is driven by a need for vengeance and makes America a better place to live in through his ventilation of the villains, although Miller's version was prettier and more sentimental in keeping with the notions of MGM chief Louis B. Mayer, a lover of middle-class banality and the happy ending. But there was no happy ending for Billy this time—not with the draconic Production Code in full force. Aware that he must die for his (or society's?) sins, the left-handed Billy commits suicide by shifting his holster to the right hip so that he can't win the final gunfight with boyhood chum Brian Donlevy. Screenwriter Gene Fowler somehow managed to avoid having Taylor climb up onto a cross and call for hammer and nails.

Bosley Crowther knew it was all bosh, but liked it anyway, and his *New York Times* review was headed:

THE LEGENDARY WEST

Perhaps It Was All a Myth, but
It Is Still Good for Fast Moving
Pictures

Crowther began his defense of such films with a look at Rascoe's *Belle Starr*, its thesis that Fox's *Police Gazette* had had a great deal to do with the enduring fame of certain disreputable people, and Rascoe's belief that the Fox publishing empire had finally declined partly because of a change in the public taste regarding the treatment of outlaw themes. Crowther declined to accept this last and cited *Billy the Kid* as proof that the "old *Police Gazette* formula" was still a winner. But for Crowther this did not necessarily mean that public taste was especially low, since, he explained, a Western, "by common understanding," was "a purely fictitious type of film, accepted by adults who watch them as fantastic and implausible—but fun."

Robert Taylor uses his Peacemaker in the 1941 interpretation of *Billy the Kid.* **(Cinemabilia)**

Crowther mentioned the fact that "we" had recently been told by Fritz Lang that he would have preferred to make *The Return of Frank James* and *Western Union* as "realistic stories of the characters and accomplishments for which they were named." The reviewer called this aspiration commendable and thought it beyond question that such a film might be "a sensational thing"; there was "plenty of room for such a film, and we'd like to see Mr. Lang make one."

But there was also "plenty of room for good old-fashioned Westerns. . . . Granted this sort of thing is as phony as a miniature storm—granted the Daltons and the Youngers and Billy the Kid were all a pack of mangy highway robbers with no more honor and courage than wolves. We can still get lots of kick out of watching their fictional counterparts perform—assuming always, of course, that the performance itself is slick." Westerns were "pure escape pictures" and the formula would probably never change. Crowther suspected that Rascow was due for a shock when he saw the forthcoming screen version of his own *Belle Starr.*

Crowther's attitude toward Western history was most accommodating: it was perfectly all right for a film to claim historical accuracy while telling countless whoppers and lionizing back-shooters—just so long as the actors wore cowboy hats and rode horses. The Western did not count as a period film, biography, or anything else connected with reality; it was simply a *Western,* which everyone knew to be a fraud even as it claimed to be factual. (One wonders, then, why such claims were made in the first place. *Somebody* must have been fooled.)[8] A film telling the truth might be acceptable as a novelty, but one needn't deprive the Yahoos of their bang-bang. Such a view not only shortchanged history, but also the possibilities for the Western's artistic growth.

Mr. Rascoe (whose book had not in fact been used as the source for Fox's movie) was quick to reply to the *Times*, and in doing so supplied the other half of a rare public clash of pens between a defender of Western dementia and a partisan of truth. He had indeed seen *Billy the Kid*. Rascoe added that the scene at the theater when *he* went looked "like an unpopular wake" and went on to bemoan the fate of Lang and to attack *Billy the Kid*, the film industry, and Crowther in some detail. How unfortunate, he wrote, that all that effort should be "thrown away on a formula story, which is essentially shoddy and morally reprehensible," especially since a magnificent story could have been made simply by adhering to the facts—which, he felt, would have been such a welcome change that it "would have set the critics demanding Oscars for everybody concerned and drawn the fed-up moviegoers back into the moviehouses."* Believing that the *Police Gazette* had eventually declined not on moral grounds but because it had failed to change its outworn approach, Rascoe argued that Fox had possessed a far better moral sense than his 1941 counterparts and brains enough to see that some moral sense has traditionally been demanded by the paying public. He concluded:

> I am for the good American way of staying away from such socially dangerous and revolting exhibitions of an utter lack of a true moral sense. And I don't mean "morals" in the exclusively sexual sense, which seems to be about the only sense in which Hollywood understands the word. I mean a perception of the difference between good and evil—such a sense, for instance, that makes any decent-minded man, woman or child fail to see anything funny or right in the constant movie implication that it is contemptible to be an officer of the law, and courageous, brainy and resourceful to be a cold-blooded murderer, who always croaks so nobly in the end.

Rascoe's protest, needless to say, shook no moguls from their glorious complacency.

MGM's decision to remake Billy was at least partly inspired by a hatred of the superrich Howard Hughes and a determination to cut the ground out from under his production of *The Outlaw*, which Hughes had intended to call *Billy the Kid* until MGM beat him to the draw. Having already produced the

---

*Lang himself, who had thought to make a movie for 1942 showing the kid as a "moron" (which, in all justice, he wasn't, even though he does resemble one in a well-known photograph), later offered a different view: "But motion pictures have spread the legend, and because an audience is educated, they know from the films that Billy the Kid was a handsome, dashing outlaw, and if somebody would make him today as he really was, it would probably be so much against the grain of an audience that it couldn't be a success."

ultimate gangster film (Hawk's *Scarface*) and himself directed the ultimate badly written aviation war film *(Hell's Angels)*, the tycoon could think of nothing better than making the ultimate Western. And what better subject for the film than that ultimate western hero, Billy the Kid? Hughes's epic was not, however, to be the kind of dull and familiar tripe so roundly condemned by Burton Rascoe. It was instead to be a new and excitingly different kind of tripe.

The Outlaw would, above everything else, be the movie to bring S-E-X to the Western, and Hughes made sure to inform press agent Russell Birdwell, best known for the ballyhoo connected with *Gone with the Wind*, so that he could begin his promotional campaign before shooting began. The nature of this advance publicity led Joseph Breen, then head of the Hays Office (or Breen Office, as some now called it) to write to Hughes for a copy of Jules Furthman's script. Finding it unacceptable by 1940 standards, Breen suggested a number of changes, all of which Hughes neglected to make.

Howard Hawks was hired to direct the film, which would star amateur Jane Russell, Hughes's latest "discovery," as the fictitious Rio, a half-breed Maid Marian to neophyte Jack Beutel's Billy and Walter Huston's Doc Holliday. Hawks set to work, but then got a better offer from Warners and went off to make *Sergeant York* (1941) after telling Hughes he was unhappy with *The Outlaw*.[9] The furious millionaire promptly took over the direction himself, making rather a botch of it and losing the story of Billy the Kid somewhere in Miss Russell's cleavage, which Hughes took great pains to reveal by way of low-cut blouses. Hollywood legend even has the ingenious Hughes complaining, "We're not getting enough production out of Jane's breasts," and personally designing a special "heaving" brassiere based "on a very simple engineering principle."

In 1941, with *The Outlaw* still in the works, *Life* played a dirty trick on both MGM and Hughes with an illustrated article ("Billy the Kid: In Two Films about Him Hollywood Fakes History"), reproducing photographs of still-living eyewitnesses to both Billy's sneaky ambush of Sheriff Brady and his subsequent murderous jailbreak, as well as a rather poignant shot of the aged Don Roberto Brady seated beneath a portrait of his murdered father. Although *Life's* piece may have dissuaded some readers from going to see MGM's film (or encouraged them to see it, for all I know), it was perhaps, too early for *The Outlaw*, which due to the trials of filming and arguing with the Hays Office wasn't ready for release until 1943. Hughes's promotional antics included an attempt to get the film banned in San Francisco which culminated in the theater manager's arrest (quite good for business); the ads grew worse until even Darryl Zanuck, who thought little of glorifying murderers but drew the line at being vulgar (what was that Mr. Rascoe had said about Hollywood's moral understanding?), wrote to Joe Breen: "The whole advertising campaign on this picture is a disgrace to the Industry." Making use of God's own billboard, Hughes hired a skywriter to fly above Pasadena, trace "The Outlaw" in virginal white smoke, and then paint this cryptic symbol in the heavens:

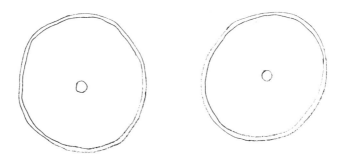

After thus whetting the public appetite, Hughes inexplicably withdrew *The Outlaw* from circulation and had the original negative squirreled away in a special lead-lined room. The film was rereleased in 1947 after another ad campaign which Hughes evidently intended as the ultimate in bad taste ("How Would You Like to Tussle with Russell?"). When the Advertising Code Authority complained, Hughes stopped submitting his ads for inspection and thereby violated the code of conduct set down by the Hays Office, which withdrew the seal of approval previously granted. Hughes brought suit against the MPPA (and lost) while simultaneously distributing prints to those exhibitors willing to take *The Outlaw* without benefit of seal and risk being picketed by certain selective guardians of the nation's moral fiber. Hughes had further troubles with various local censors, but apparently enough of what was intended as erotic remained to satisfy most customers of that era.

For there was more here than Russell's aerodynamically designed super-structure. Not only was the halfbreed Rio the mistress of Beutel's refreshingly unheroic Billy (who apparently rapes her in a conveniently darkened barn and behaves otherwise unchivalrously), but she was also that of his friend and enemy Holliday, who got there first. Although Hughes toned down some of the more lurid aspects of the Rio-Billy relationship, he failed to modify the callous, contemptuous attitude toward women pervading the film. The French critic André Bazin even theorized that the real uproar stemmed not from the breast acreage shown, but from violation of this unwritten rule: "It is forbidden to despise women."

"They're all alike," says Doc to Billy. "There isn't anything they wouldn't do for ya . . . or to ya." Billy himself says, "I don't trust 'em," having been embittered by a procession of females who've done him wrong. The true love, as opposed to lust, affair is between Doc and his strawberry roan; "I dote on him like rock candy," he says winningly. Doc loses the noble animal to a thief, Billy buys it (he says) from the thief, and after their first meeting the two badmen spend most of their time fighting over who really owns the horse, each trying to steal it away from the other. When Doc gets mad at Billy because the latter has been serviced by Rio, the Kid tries to pacify him by allowing him first pick: Doc can either keep Rio and let Billy ride off on the roan or take the horse himself. Doc chooses the horse and Billy is greatly disturbed by the decision, as is Rio.

Male love also enters the picture, with Sheriff Pat Garrett (Thomas Mitchell) jealous because his old friend Doc is befriending Billy and, worse, helping him to escape Garrett's clutches. If Doc's cooing over his strawberry roan seemed like a parody of the stereotyped movie cowboy's love for his horse, the entire film resembled nothing so much as a takeoff on those strong-male-friendship films which were a specialty of Howard Hawks and which Jules Furthman sometimes helped write for him.

Compromise though he might on matters sexual, Hughes defied the MPPA and its Production Code with his Vidor-like ending: after killing his friend Holliday, a depressed Garrett allows desperado Billy and trollop Rio to ride off toward the horizon. A written epilogue tells us that "some say" Billy the Kid was later shot by lawmen, others that he lived on—but with a guilty conscience. This merely implied moral retribution annoyed not only the Hays Office but also Garrett's children, who sued because Hughes had "cruelly and unjustifiably besmirched" Sheriff Pat, in direct violation of a contract with his descendants intended to guarantee that no aspersions would be cast "upon his character as a man or frontier peace officer." The trouble is that after a public figure's dead and buried you can make his fictional alter ego jump through whatever hoops you like.

Shifting allegiances prove troublesome in Howard Hughes's _The Outlaw_, a male love story with Jane Russell thrown in for good measure. The others are Thomas Mitchell, Walter Huston, and Jack Beutel. (Museum of Modern Art/Film Stills Archive)

The public lapped it up. Comparing the reaction of one British audience with that of an American crowd, Geoffrey Wagner, who went to see the film twice—presumably to gauge such reactions—wrote in his *Parade of Pleasure:*

I saw *The Outlaw,* for instance, in London, where it was treated as a hilarious farce by the audience; not so in Detroit, where the audience watched it to my surprise in stolid solemnity, broken by an occasional wolf-whistle at the great divide.

And Bosley Crowther said our folks didn't take Westerns seriously!

Billy had clearly come a long way since 1881. But there was more to come. Having already acted in several minor films, Texas-born Audie Murphy, most decorated soldier in American history, got his lengthy Western career off to a wretched start with Universal's *The Kid from Texas* (1949). Prior to shooting, Hollywood gossip columnist Hedda Hopper reported that it would be "a documentary type film and will tell of juvenile delinquency of 70 years ago and how 'The Kid' was a result of that youth problem." Seems everybody had juvenile delinquency on the brain back then, including J. Edgar Hoover, who, said Hedda, had offered to narrate the film. He didn't, and its "documentary" nature was likewise a promise unfulfilled.

THE TRUE, SAVAGE STORY
OF *BILLY THE KID.* . . .

21 men knew his fury . . .
only one woman knew his love!

Just another good, mixed-up kid caught up in a mess not of his own making. In 1950 one "Brushy Bill" Roberts confessed that he was Billy the Kid and unsuccessfully sought pardon from the governor of New Mexico for all crimes committed under that name. His story, told in Sonnichsen and Morrison's *Alias Billy the Kid,* even had a few points in its favor, but failed to convince the late Maurice Garland Fulton, leading authority on the Lincoln County War. Such Billy releases of this decade as *The Law vs. Billy the Kid* (1954) and *The Parson and the Outlaw* (1957) were fairly bland horse operas, but as so-called psychological Westerns were rather the rage during the 1950s (some films so described merely more complex in their approach to character, others pretentiously pseudo-Freudian), it was absolutely necessary that one be made to "explain" Billy's actions. Besides being the supreme outlaw hero, he is also an all-purpose one—"less interesting as a human being," to quote Peter Lyon, "than as a sort of glorified Rorschach ink blot by which one may elicit fantasies and so judge their inventors. . . . The face is blank, but it comes complete with a handy Do-It-Yourself Kit so that the features may be easily filled in."

Warners' 1958 *The Left-Handed Gun* was no cheap commercial whitewashing, no siree. Director Arthur Penn's lofty intention in making his first film was, in his own words, "to find, through the Billy the Kid myth, which is very alive in the United States, the deep myths of Greek tragedy. *The Left-Handed Gun* is Oedipus in the West." This seems doubtful. However, Penn also said on another occasion that "I didn't understand it when I was making it." The script, by Penn and Leslie Stevens, was reworked from a TV play by Gore Vidal, who disliked the result.

After a maudlin ballad about a "poor boy who never meant wrong" sung over the credits, Billy (Paul Newman) goes to work for the paternalistic Mr. Tunstall, who wants to make something of the penniless, illiterate lad (not actually illiterate, I should point out) but is murdered before he can get around to it. Newman then becomes antisocial, running around with those famous blue eyes, seen here in black-and-white, bulging out of his head and staring glassily. Although most of the supporting players also seem to be mentally ill and thus have an excuse to indulge in hysterical overacting, the star's version of James Dean on the Frontier topped them all. "Poor Mr. Newman," wrote Howard Thompson, "seems to be auditioning alternately for the Moscow Art Players and the Grand Ole Opry as he ambles about, brooding, grinning, or mumbling endlessly."

To avenge his father figure, Billy rides into Lincoln to have it out with Sheriff Brady, here made responsible for Tunstall's murder. It might have been quite disturbing even in a psychological Western to have the hero back-shoot members of the opposition with the help of several friends, so Penn, who has an abiding love for violent criminals but is insufficiently reckless to show them as they are,[10] has him step out alone and allow Brady and a henchman to draw first before fanning them both into eternity. Some time later we find Billy remarking to another intended victim, as he hands him a gunbelt and revolver, that he'd never kill a man "without a fair fight." The real Billy generally took care to do just that very thing; bushwhacking was ever so much safer.

Billy is finally betrayed by a traveling salesman disillusioned because the somewhat uncouth Kid doesn't come up to his idea of a hero. (Penn may have pretended that he was cutting down the legend, but in truth his Billy, aside from a few psychological quirks, is a far more heroic figure than the real Kid, or Burns's, ever was.) Realizing at last that for some reason he's "all dead inside" and mere physical existence is no longer worthwhile, Billy walks out to where his only slightly neurotic friend Pat Garrett waits and lets his hand speed toward an empty holster so he can play at being Christ again.

The holster was on his left hip; he *was* the Left-Handed Gun, wasn't he? Or was he? Even Penn wasn't really sure. "There's one famous photograph of Billy the Kid that shows him left-handed. There are those historians who claim that it's printed backwards. . . . That starts you wondering immediately about the truth, versus appearance. Was he left-handed, or has the passage of time reversed reality?" A great and deep question, but one which proves pointless when you take a close look and see that this picture, if printed so that the holster is on the left hip, clearly shows Billy's vest buttons to be on the left side (wrong) and his Winchester's loading gate on the rifle's left-hand breechplate (also wrong). But then, Penn rarely looked too closely at anything, perhaps out of fear that he might spy something unpleasant. What he does see he does his best to disguise; the real mystery here is why someone making a film so stuffed full of deliberate falsehoods should bother pondering things such as "myth" and "reality."

The film fared badly with domestic critics. Said Penn: "I only really regained confidence in myself when I read the critical reviews in the French press. They had seen it and understood it. It was a miracle." (You can't tell *what* those French will do.) Since then, the film has achieved something of a reputation here at home—not bad considering that the director hadn't understood what he was making. But at the time the die-hard American fan, if dissuaded from seeing *The Left-Handed Gun* by the generally bad reviews, really had nothing to worry about; he wouldn't have long to wait for the next bucket of slop praising the Kid's name. In 1961 the indestructible youth even took time off from his hectic movie career to co-star with his friend and destroyer Pat Garrett in a TV series called "The Tall Man." You could see *that* for nothing—and it was still too much.

That year also saw parts of the Kid turn up in Marlon Brando's long and expensive *One-Eyed Jacks*, based on Charles Neider's novel *The Authentic Death of Hendry Jones*, which was inspired in turn by the Burns version of the Kid's life; Brando's protagonist is in fact nicknamed "the Kid," although he's named Rio, like Jane Russell in *The Outlaw*. Since it is a Billy the Kid film only remotely and makes no claim to being even semifactual, it is relevant here largely because it used a theme rarely discernible in the Name films: Rio, apparently possessed of few real virtues, becomes the film's "hero" only through betrayal by bandit sidekick Dad Longworth (Karl Malden), who rides away with the loot from the gang's last robbery, leaving Rio for capture by the Mexican Rurales. Longworth later establishes himself as a sheriff in California (though the tolerant townspeople are aware of his bandit past) and becomes something of a Pat Garrett figure; escaping jail, Rio seeks out Longworth to wreak vengeance after an extended cat-and-mouse game. "You're a one-eyed jack in this town," he tells the sheriff at one point, "but I see the other side of your face." Finally shooting Longworth, Rio rides off with his enemy's disaffected Mexican stepdaughter. Earlier films had largely ignored the betrayal aspect of the Kid legend and concentrated on making Billy a good guy; in the more realistic *Jacks* only Rio's relative lack of hypocrisy makes him superior to Longworth.

In 1966 Billy took a fling at the horror movie with William Beaudine's *Billy the Kid vs. Dracula*—obviously a great film since it embraces not one but two of our culture's greatest legends—but soon came back home for Andrew V. McLaglen's *Chisum*, which, though made in 1970, looked at least ten years older. But this time he didn't get to be the star: Geoffrey Deuel's Kid was naturally overshadowed by John Wayne's portrayal of famed cattleman John Simpson Chisum, a person of honestly debatable merit who, though retaining professional gunmen on his payroll, disdained to wear a gun himself and had a plain-looking niece named Sallie who was rather stuck on Billy the Kid.

As played by the Duke (whose production company was, regrettably, responsible for this mess), Chisum becomes a brave, wise, generous, paternalistic soul who befriends the oppressed Indian and Mexican, wears a six-gun like your normal Western hero, and has a beautiful niece who's rather stuck on Billy the Kid, despite her fearfully muttering to Uncle John, "They say he killed his first man when he was twelve." Movie folk seem to make a point of consulting only outdated, romanticized history books outmoded decades ago, possibly because they best suit the film industry's peculiar needs. Long before *Chisum* was filmed, nearly all contemporary writers on the Kid were regarding him with disfavor, and Hollywood seemed almost the last place of media refuge for the heroic image.

Billy himself is looked upon as unduly wild and reckless, and his murders, though committed in a good cause, are strongly no-no'd by such friends as Chisum, who wants to work within the law as long as possible. As if to establish Billy's fundamental decency beyond question, it is pointed out to Chisum that the wayward boy is just like *he* was at that age. With Big John on their side, the McSweenites are of necessity pure good and the Murphy men pure evil: the real Chisum was careful to keep out of the Lincoln troubles except for bankrolling the opponents of Murphy-Dolan, but that would be too unheroic, so when McSween is murdered after an epic siege Chisum comes to the rescue like some Duke ex machina, stampeding a herd of cattle down the street and putting the baddies to rout. No unhappy endings here: Chisum engages Colonel Murphy (Forrest Tucker, who, as head villain, made an odd choice for narrator of the film's rotten title song) in a fistfight that ends when Murphy is impaled on a set of ornamental steerhorns. Benevolent capitalism has triumphed over selfish and greedy capitalism, and things settle down with an almost palpable air of middle-aged booj-wah complacency that is supposed to be a good thing, even if it doesn't leave much of the mythic West left; a youthful, anarchic irrelevance, Billy rides off to one day perish at Pat Garrett's hands and, though the film doesn't mention it, rustle Chisum's cattle. His bitter lament after landing in the jug at Lincoln ("Chisum got me into all this trouble") is likewise unforeshadowed.

A major, which is to say costly, motion picture in its own right, *Chisum* went on to play a small but acutely embarrassing part in our nation's political and legal history with a few choice remarks delivered by President Nixon to a gathering of law-enforcement officials. He had, it seems, seen the movie over the previous weekend: "In the end, as this movie particularly pointed out, even in the Old West, there was a time when there was no law. But the law eventually came, and the law was important from the standpoint of not only prosecuting the guilty, but also seeing that those who were guilty had a proper trial." After commenting on the unhappy tendency of extensive media coverage to glamorize those engaged in criminal activities, Mr. Nixon mentioned a recent case much in the headlines: "I noted, for example, the coverage of the Charles Manson case when I was in Los Angeles, front page every day in the papers. . . . Here is a man who was guilty, directly or indirectly, of eight murders without reason. Here is a man, yet who as far as the coverage was concerned, appeared to be rather a glamorous figure."

"MANSON GUILTY, NIXON DECLARES," ran the *Los Angeles Times* headline—front page, sure enough—which Manson himself frantically flashed at his jury in an attempt to create grounds for a mistrial. He failed, but *Chisum*'s political career was not yet over. It was shown as a reward to some young campaign workers by (appropriately enough, in view of the Duke's politics) conservative New York senatorial candidate James Buckley. Having little else to do, a *Times* reporter sought out some young Buckleyites' reactions.

Michael Edison said, "The similarity between that and anything real is hazy."

Leslie Pickens discerned a Vietnam War allegory: "Both sides were wrong and John Wayne came in as the third force."

"Far-fetched," replied Edison.

"Oh," said Daniel Drake, in recalling the Manson affair, "the President just likes John Wayne movies."

In 1973 Mr. Nixon could, had he so desired, have viewed in his private screening room two Billy the Kid films—which, through their mutual contradiction, would have quickly convinced him of the folly inherent in relying on movies for historical information. But by then he probably had too many other things on his mind.

"BILLY THE KID WAS A PUNK," ran the huge newspaper ads heralding the arrival of *Dirty Little Billy*, Columbia's nontribute to the youthful outlaw. But the film itself made no real attempt to depict his alleged rise to punkdom. Co-written by Charles Moss and director Stan Dragoti, it succeeded in presenting a negative image of the Kid, but, as it contained about as much fact as *The Outlaw*, seemed either just another stab at cashing in on the public's mood—though the perception of the mood had changed and the public was now supposed to want deglamorization and cynicism—or a reflection of its makers' purposeless iconoclasm. Like certain historical writers, such filmmakers seem quite prepared to forego accuracy so long as they can carry out their purely negative objective of myth-busting. Billy, whose contemporaries described him as both reasonably good-looking and possessed of a "charming" personality, was reduced to a nose-picking Michael J. Pollard, who spends most of his time behaving repulsively against a backdrop of wretched buildings and uninviting landscapes as far away from the "Golden West" as could be found: he finally shuffles off into the sunset, bound for further unwholesome adventures. Said the *Times:* " 'Dirty Little Billy' projects an unvarnished picture of the Old West. . . . Credit the team headed by Stan Dragoti, the television commercial director, who is making his movie bow with 'Dirty Little Billy,' "with giving us a realistically raw view of the beginnings of the Billy the Kid legend." Raw, certainly. But realistic?

Sam Peckinpah, determined to add his talents to those already squandered on the subject as the next step in his continuing artistic decline, executed for MGM (never much of a studio for Westerns) their third epic version of the saga, *Pat Garrett and Billy the Kid* (1973). "This is the real story," said Peckinpah, apparently with a straight face. "These are cats who ran out of territory and know it. But they don't bend, refuse to be diminished by it. They play out their string to the end."

Ho-hum. This basic concept doomed the movie from the start. Rudolf Wurlitzer's screenplay would have us believe that even back in 1881 the time for outlaws was over and the Wild West all but dried up. "Us old boys ought not to be doing this to each other," says a minor outlaw as he and sheriff Garrett stalk each other with six-guns around an old shack. "There aren't too many of us left." This touchingly ignorant thesis was not only historically wrong, but also at odds with some of Peckinpah's earlier work—notably *The Wild Bunch*, in which a group of aging, bestial killers "play out their string" during the 1910s. But the theme is continually emphasized so as to make of Billy (a clean-shaven, gruff-voiced Kris Kristofferson) a heroic, doomed symbol of the Last Frontier. This goes hand in hand with representing *everybody* in favor of law and order (getting rid of the Kid) as having sold out to corrupt business interests. At the time of his demise in 1881 the real Kid was, and had been for several years, nothing more idealistic than a cow thief, the passing of whose occupation is scarcely something to get choked up about. Peckinpah never shows the Kid doing anything so low as rustling a steer, allowing him to be simply a vague, glamorous Outlaw; it is never made clear just what, if anything, Billy is doing to overthrow the evil system engulfing the territory, but Peckinpah nevertheless wants us to think of him as some sort of noble rebel.

James Coburn's Garrett is rapidly nearing retirement age and in his desire to grow older without starving hires out to the Establishment to betray his former pal and (inevitably) fellow outlaw. Members of an endangered species not even the Auduborn Society could save, Pat and Billy wax nostalgic about the good old days when they used to ride together, though Billy's youth, as Vincent Canby observed, "raises questions about how old Billy was when they started riding together. Fourteen?" Garrett doesn't really want to plug Billy and advises him to leave the territory, adding that times have changed. "Times, maybe," says the die-hard Billy, "but not me."

Faced with such grit, Coburn naturally falls prey to guilt feelings worthy of the Macbeths. Stealing a line from *The Left-Handed Gun*, Pat's Mexican wife tells him that *he's* all dead inside, but Garrett summons up enough strength to beat information out of a luckless whore and find Billy out at the Maxwell ranch. So great is Peckinpah's loathing for Garrett that he even gives himself an appropriate cameo role as a coffin maker, who exists solely to shout abuse at Pat shortly before Garrett shoots first the Kid and then his own image in a mirror (self-hatred, you see). As if this didn't make his position clear enough, Peckinpah ends the movie like *Shane* in reverse: instead of little Brandon de Wilde shouting, "Come back, Shane!" as Alan Ladd's buckskinned Messiah

Betrayed and betrayer in *Pat Garrett and Billy the Kid*. (Museum of Modern Art / Film Stills Archive)

rides off into the mountains, a little boy, also shouting abuse, pelts the betrayer with clods of earth as he takes his leave.

Shameful, the way Garrett has been treated.

Reviews were mixed and *Pat Garrett* lost money, but the person most upset with the picture as released was doubtless Peckinpah himself. Bob Dylan had played a knife-throwing Bonney supporter named Alias ("Alias what?" "Alias anything you please") who skulked around the edges of the action with little to do save look ugly and remind one that those were his, *his* songs on the sound track. It had been Peckinpah's intention to use them sparingly, but MGM officialdom, keen on getting more mileage and an album out of Dylan's music, insisted on dubbing in his mediocre lyrics at inappropriate places. Not content with such musical rearrangement, former CBS president James Aubrey— otherwise known as "The Smiling Cobra"—belied his present company's motto of *Ars Gratia Artis* by snipping away some fifteen minutes of the completed film and adding to its confusion. Among the casualties were the character of John Chisum (nasty this time), which was considerably cut down, and a framing prologue and epilogue showing the assassination of Pat Garrett in 1908 and sandwiching in the body of the film as a giant flashback, which was completely eliminated. It hadn't happened that way (Garrett was shot in the back while urinating in the desert, the identity and motive of his killer being in dispute), but Peckinpah wanted him to die at the hands of a man who had ridden with him in pursuit of the Kid. This would bring everything full circle so that Garrett's killing of the Kid is seen as his own self-destruction, with Big Business triumphing over all for a nice pessimistic finish in which individualism is utterly crushed.

"My baby is maimed," wailed Peckinpah, and with good artistic reason, for had he himself not declared *Pat Garrett* to be "the definitive work on Billy the Kid"? As Dub Taylor, on the same location in Durango to act in the lamentable John Wayne vehicle *Cahill, U.S. Marshal*, insisted: "I'll tell you this. After Sam gets through nobody will ever make a pitchur about Billy the Kid again. *This is it!* They'll never touch Billy again."

Let me now flash forward to late 1977 and the periodical room in the library of a medium-sized East Coast university named after one of the nineteenth century's biggest crooks, where your humble narrator may be found leafing through that day's *New York Times*. Scanning the film section, he smiles slightly as he catches sight of a rather small advertisement.

HAND IN HAND FILMS

presents

JACK DEVEAU'S

WANTED:
BILLY THE KID

THE BIGGEST HUSTLER OF THEM ALL

Starring Mr. Bare America—Dennis Walsh

NOTES

1. The degree and extent of such glamorization, however, depends largely on the spirit of the age. In her forward to *The Omnibus of Crime*, Dorothy L. Sayers writes: "It will be noticed that, on the whole, the tendency in early crime-literature is to admire the cunning and astuteness of the criminal. This must be so while the law is arbitrary, oppressive, and brutally administered."

2. With a movieland disregard for truth admirable in its impartiality, Sam is a bad badman as played by fat Nestor Pavia in RKO's *Badman's Territory* (1946) and merely misunderstood as portrayed by Howard Duff in *Calamity Jane and Sam Bass*. Despite his popularity in Texas, Bass never figured in many films, doubtless because his name was too fishlike.

3. For 1941 these geniuses assigned Lang the direction of *Western Union*, a story of the laying of the transcontinental telegraph line which, Lang cheerfully admitted later, had nothing to do with the rather dull facts surrounding that event. Soon after the film was released, Lang was "tickled pink" to receive a letter from a society of old-time Arizona pioneers congratulating him on the authenticity of this Western and wondering how a mere foreigner was able to make it all so realistic. The movie was touted as "Zane Grey's *Western Union*," but there was no such novel: one was however, ghostwritten by arrangement with the Grey estate after the film stimulated interest in the nonbook. *Frank James*, Lang told reporters, had actually been his second Western, the first being a German silent he considered "one of the sins of my youth."

4. Bill Doolin, who took no part in the raid and was later glorified by Randolph Scott in *The Doolins of Oklahoma*, was killed four years later by marshal Heck Thomas; Thomas, Bill Tilghman, and Danish-born Chris Madsen were collectively known as Oklahoma's "Three Guardsmen."

5. Parker, the "Hanging Judge" who twice during his career arranged for an even half-dozen of desperadoes to be hanged simultaneously, was based at Fort Smith, Arkansas, but had jurisdiction over the entire Indian Territory. He is portrayed (sadly minus his "brown billy-goat beard" as mentioned by the Charles Portis novel) in *True Grit* and its 1975 sequel, *Rooster Cogburn*, and provided the model for the righteous Judge Fenton (Pat Hingle), who clashes with U.S. marshal Clint Eastwood in Ted Post's 1968 *Hang 'Em High*.

6. A hoked-up wanted poster used in the film and charging Sam and Belle with "Robbery, Murder, Treason and other acts against the peace and dignity of the U.S." has been reproduced and mistakenly identified as genuine in Horan and Sann's *Pictorial History of the Wild West* and *Mankind* magazine's paperback *Outlaws of the Old West*.

7. Hart's films were very different from the *Jesse James* type of whitewash in that, rather than playing a good man forced to turn bad, he usually *began* as a badman who finally reformed (or died nobly) thanks to the influence of a good woman. This permitted Hart to indulge his penchant for sentimentality while at the same time portraying a hero slightly more realistic than the clean-cut movie good guys who, never having been outlaws, couldn't get away with the things one might expect from even a good badman.

8. Of course many people are eager to believe in such lies and become angry at people who expose them. In 1960, for instance, Peter Lyon wrote for *American Heritage*, a scathing review of frontier heroes called "The Wild, Wild West" (expanded to short-book-length in 1969 and not to be confused with the gleefully anachronistic 1960s James-Bond-out-West TV series) which received considerable attention, especially from offended Hollywood screenwriters. In a letter to Lyon the eminent Texas historian J. Frank Dobie praised the article—which, perhaps, went a bit too far in condemning the Wild West as "an underworld, corrupt and rotten"—but added discouragingly: "You will not affect the public. The public wants to be fooled . . . concerning blackguards set up as heroes." The fact is that most people are indifferent to historical truth and many *writers*, having read corrected accounts of earlier lies, refuse to believe them. This provides the film industry no excuse, however, since the moviegoer is never asked before entering the theater whether he wants to be lied to or not or informed as to when the lies are forthcoming.

9. The climactic confrontation between John Wayne and Montgomery Clift in *Red River* so resembled a scene between Beutel and Huston in *The Outlaw* that Hughes brought suit against Hawks, and was only dissuaded by Wayne's entreaties from ordering the ending of Hawks's film changed.

10. "The filmmaker's only responsibility is to tell the truth," said Penn once, but what he meant by this I can't imagine. He is, of course, best known for his *Bonnie and Clyde* (1967), in which he canonized a pair of hideous mass murderers of the 1930s into two more manufactured folk heroes, while in lying fashion making a villain out of old-time Texas peace officer Frank Hamer, who adequately punished the couple by turning them into human sieves and was the sort of Western lawman that screenwriters dream of. (So much so that while he was on a tour of Hollywood screen cowboy Tom Mix urged him to stay on, saying he had the looks, the bearing, and the athletic ability to become a great Western star.) The motorized Midwestern bandits of the 1930s present a number of interesting parallels to the old-style horseback outlaws, and often consciously patterned their behavior on that of the mythic Jesse or other misnamed Robin Hoods.

5
Pretty Hollow
or Butch Cassidy and the Old West Punks

Wild Jack Crabb, Crabb's Last Stand—it just don't sound the
same.
—THOMAS BERGER,
Little Big Man

Some of the finest men I ever knew were horse thieves.
—AL JENNINGS.

Having already remarked upon the importance of the Name in the propagation
of certain Wild West "legends" (particularly by the electronic mass media),
we will look at some even more striking examples of its power—first at a top-
class badman whose name, with its objectionable connotations, seems to have
long delayed his coming of age as a Western movie hero, and then at some
small-timers who found it much easier to break into the movies in a positive
way.

Robert LeRoy Parker, alias Roy Parker, alias Ed Cassidy, alias Butch
Cassidy of the Wild Bunch, was one of the very first Western bandits to be
honored with a film. Percy Siebert was spending Christmas in New York
before sailing to South America and taking charge of a tin mine where the
outlaw and his sidekick were also destined to work. "By a strange
coincidence, I had wandered into a Coney Island movie and spent the
afternoon watching Butch Cassidy and the Sundance Kid ride across the

western plains after a robbery. Then a few weeks later I was shaking the same outlaw's hand!"

But between this forgotten nickelodeon flicker and the legend-making *Butch Cassidy and the Sundance Kid* some sixty-odd years later was a long dry spell during which few lenses were focused on Butch or his buddies. When they *were* portrayed, it was as heavies rather than heroes, as in *The Return of the Badmen*, with Robert Ryan as a particularly brutal Sundance who strangles the film's "bad" woman (she has to die so the hero can marry the good woman) before Randy Scott kills him, or the 1958 *Badman's Country*, in which Butch (Neville Brand) ranged his phalanx of outlaws against the likes of Pat Garrett and Wyatt Earp; Brand had earlier played Butch as a not unlikable rogue in *Three Badmen* (1949).

How *did* this come about, you say? I'm glad you asked. It's probably because "Butch" sounded too much like the nickname of some cheap urban hood and Cassidy was the same last name used from the mid-thirties to the early fifties by William Boyd, in his movie and TV role as Hopalong Cassidy, while a name such as "The Wild Bunch" (no relation to the gang in the Peckinpah film) may have carried overtones of menace, rowdiness, and confident numerical odds hostile to romance. Even though the real Butch had an enviable reputation among the citizens of his own region, his name—or so runs my own theory—prevented him from being exploited to his full potential. While other, less deserving bandits became well known to the modern-day public through the sheer catchiness of their handles or their whitewashed biopics—and thereby were counted as "legendary" in the Hollywood sense— Butch had to make do with being a mere local folk hero that few back East, save for readers of frontier criminal history, had ever heard of.

Born in Utah in 1866, Robert was one of thirteen children, and the only one who ever achieved any considerable fame except for a sister, Lula Parker Betenson, who in 1975 wrote a book—and even *that* was called *Butch Cassidy, My Brother*. In his formative years, Bob fell under the unwholesome influence of Mike Cassidy, a veteran rustler whose name he would later honor by adopting it as one of his aliases and a boyhood idol who taught him the finer points of handling guns and horses and of stealing cattle. (This last was an occupation looked upon rather indulgently by the local settlers, since many of them resented the overbearing behavior of big ranchers and were not above lifting the occasional stray themselves.)

In 1884 Bob left the family farm in Colorado and drifted up to Wyoming. Here he hung around with a number of badmen affiliated with the Wild Bunch, less an organized gang than a catchall term for those outlaws who hid out at Brown's Hole (or Brown's Park), a rocky area bestriding the Wyoming, Utah, and Colorado state lines. He was soon running with the notorious McCarty boys and joined them in several robberies.

As a bandit, Butch was not gratuitously violent, and claimed never to have killed a man during a holdup. Indeed, aside from plundering institutions such as banks and railroads—never a private citizen, this being a point of pride with a number of "high-class" bandits—he seems almost revolting in his documented good qualities, and was even said to rob from the rich so as to give to the poor. But as this seems contrary to all of Nature's laws, I, along with many other Western buffs, tend to doubt it. In the Betenson book, Edna Robison, an acquaintance of Butch, ungrammatically tells in a taped interview of "another interesting story that *I knew absolutely that it happened*." It was the ol' widder's-mortgage tale; the italicized words I found, in the Morris County Library's copy of the book, underlined in red pencil by some heartless wretch who at the bottom of the page had proclaimed in black-penciled caps: "BULLSHIT!—SAME TALE USED FOR JESSE JAMES AND OTHERS ALL THE WAY BACK TO ROBIN HOOD." There's just no faith anymore.

After breaking with the McCartys, Bob worked as a ranch hand and did a turn as a butcher's assistant—hence the nickname added to his current alias of Cassidy—but continued stealing livestock on the side. In 1894 "George Cassidy" was sentenced to two years in the Wyoming state pen, allegedly after a frame-up engineered by local cattlemen who couldn't get him for any of the crimes he *had* committed; he got out in a year and a half, supposedly by promising the governor not to rob any more banks or steal livestock in Wyoming and having sufficient presence of mind not to include trains in the agreement. In those days even outlaws (of the better sort) were expected to keep their word. But another version of the story simply has Butch promising to go straight and then neglecting to do so.

Teaming up with another ex-con, named Elzy (pronounced Elza) Lay, Cassidy rode for the natural mountain fortress of Hole-in-the-Wall, where gathered numerous owlhoots seeking refuge from an encroaching civilization. Butch and his gang, counting among its members such hardcases as Harvey "Kid Curry" Logan,[1] looted trains and banks in several states with a high degree of success. But such triumphs soon brought down upon their heads the Pinkerton detectives, and Butch realized that old-style banditry wasn't as easy as it used to be. In 1899, shortly after Elzy Lay was caught and imprisoned, Butch decided to go straight by becoming a Union Pacific railway guard in return for amnesty (and security against extradition) from the governor of Utah. A rendezvous was arranged, but the railroad representatives were, unbeknownst to Cassidy, delayed by a snowstorm, and a disenchanted Butch, leaving behind a quick note telling them to "go to hell," rode away.

Sometime in 1900 Cassidy went into partnership with Harry Longabaugh, the Sundance Kid. But since the lawless Wild West seemed to be falling away too quickly for comfort, Butch, Sundance, and the Kid's girl friend, Etta Place, took a tour of Gilded Age New York in 1901 and then sailed away to throw the detectives and find themselves a New Frontier.

After looking over various parts of South America, Butch secured some land in Argentina with his share of the gang's loot, but he and Sundance soon brought the Wild West to the continent to become *los bandidos Americanos*. They did do a spot of honest work now and again, as at the Concordia mine in

The Wild Bunch pose for a group photograph at Fort Worth, Texas. *Seated, left to right:* the Sundance Kid, Ben Kilpatrick ("The Tall Texan"), and Butch Cassidy. *Standing:* William Carver and Harvey Logan, alias Kid Curry. (Museum of Modern Art/Film Stills Archive)

Bolivia, where Butch was allowed to handle large sums of money even though the Americans in charge knew who he was. (An honest thief would never dream of robbing his employers, especially when they provided such a good hideout.) The two men supposedly met their end in 1909 at San Vicente, Bolivia, where they had been surrounded by a party of government troops.

We have, of course, the usual stories in which Butch survives to make his way back to the States, but they are more widely credited than most. In a 1970 interview, Mrs. Betenson even claimed that Butch came home in 1925 for a family reunion, and in her book he is quoted as reporting that he had traveled widely in Europe after leaving South America, while Etta and Sundance (who, in his opinion, "liked his liquor too much and was too quick on the trigger") settled in Mexico, where Butch encountered them by chance a few years later. He assured his fond relations that he'd refrained from killing in South America as he had back home, but that "some of my boys had itchy trigger fingers. I tried to control 'em. I feel real bad about some possemen who got shot." Not bad enough to stop, presumably.[2]

The returned prodigal, according to his sister, told a few other outlaw tales as well, notably the old chestnut about the widow's farm. "This was so successful that I paid off more than one mortgage in the same way. In fact, I wasn't the only outlaw who salved his conscience in that way." Judging from

Etta Place. A portrait taken in New York. (Museum of Modern Art/Film Stills Archive)

such expert testimony, the Old West must have been overrun with poor widows being kicked off their land and wealthy bankers just waiting to be held up by the nearest remorse-stricken badman.

In his *The Authentic Wild West: The Outlaws* (1977), James Horan points out errors in Mrs. Betenson's book and dismisses all stories of Cassidy's survival. But in his *In Search of Butch Cassidy*, published the same year, Larry Pointer (who contradicts Mrs. Betenson on several key points) makes a fair case for the theory that Butch, alias William T. Phillips, died in Spokane, Washington, of cancer in 1937.

Twentieth Century-Fox's *Butch Cassidy and the Sundance Kid* (1969) resembled the Grand Canyon in being pretty and hollow. But whereas the Grand Canyon is truly impressive in its own right, this truly awful film, inexplicably beloved by some critics, was worthy of notice only with regard to the "legend" it created, the money it grossed (almost $30 million, making it the most profitable Western of all time) and the undeserved Oscars reaped by William Goldman's incompetent screenplay, Burt Bacharach's atrocious score, and the same composer's trifling and wholly irrelevant song "Raindrops Keep Fallin' on My Head," which through repeated replayings on radio, on TV, and in doctors' offices began to beat on one's brain like the proverbial water torture.[3]

Why *did* this particular film prove so popular? Maybe it appealed to the public of the time because it was supposed to be antiestablishment or pro-youth or something, with rebel Paul Newman (somewhat old, it's true, for a "youth" film) getting off such hot lines as "I got vision and the rest of the world wears bifocals." In any event, the film has dated far more rapidly than do most Westerns, even with some who were originally enthusiastic about it.

One might almost be tempted to say that *Butch Cassidy* was one of the more "accurate" bandit biographies, following to a degree the very, very broad outlines of the outlaws' careers and including a few comparatively factual minor incidents, like their demolition of both a safe and the railway car surrounding it, scattering the cash inside. But I don't think I'll say that. In any case the prologue's claim that "most of what follows is true" is manifestly nonsense, and *not* simply because the film was largely fictitious or, as Mrs. Betenson pointed out, "most of the episodes in the movie involved Elzy Lay, instead of the Sundance Kid."* Even had everything in the movie actually happened it would have seemed fake. A glib, not particularly funny attempt at comedy, *Butch Cassidy* seemed to strain for cuteness at the expense of all else; Butch and Sundance may, despite the latter's quick trigger finger, have been the life of the party, but there was surely more to them than these shallow clowns, who are neither historically nor artistically "right." (Ford's Wyatt Earp, if false to the facts, was at least believable.) With its one-dimensional characters the film seems oddly *empty*, and when Goldman does try to get "serious" about the plight of the anachronistic horseback outlaw in a changing era, the results are typically clumsy and embarrassing.

The two heroes are anachronistic in more ways than one: among other offenses, Newman's Butch and Robert Redford's Sundance exchange wise-cracks with what John Simon recognized as "a language and humor that are half a century too early and half a continent too easterly for their historic time and place," and are backed up by a resolutely, intrusively antiperiod score, perhaps the most abominable moment coming when a chorus of what could have been eunuchs "cutely" sing a gay wordless bum-bum-bum-bum during an ostensibly amusing montage of Bolivian bank jobs and chases. Westerns have always been influenced by their dates of production more than other period films, but this time the "now" aspects almost seem calculated to assure true swingers that they weren't sullying their eyeballs with one of those nasty,

---

*One might argue that it would have been dramatically indefensible, or at least harmful, for Butch to change partners in mid-film, and as Mrs. Betenson herself shrewdly asked, "Who would go to a movie entitled *Butch Cassidy and Elzy Lay?*"

old-fashioned horse operas. "In fact," said director Hill, as though the two were incompatible, "it's not a Western at all. It's a character study." And a bad one. As if to compensate for this lack of period sense, we have the first scenes shot in unnecessary tinted monochrome and the bandits' tour of New York and voyage to South America shown by way of an annoying but labor-saving montage of sepia-tinted stills, some of them actual photos of the period with the actors' likenesses faked in.

The film makes no attempt to portray its heroes as Robin Hoods or victims, here parting company with all those films which exploit our admiration for the bandit's alleged lawless freedom[4] while frantically trying to pretend otherwise. Although the faceless possemen pursuing them ("Who *are* those guys?" the heroes keep asking—with deep symbolism, no doubt) are hired by the railroad, this concern is not shown either driving them to crime by blowing up their relatives or oppressing the local farmers, even if Butch does express the belief that the railway president has more money than he knows what to do with. Perhaps this type of fantasy is the less desirable, though more "modern": the implied message seems to be that it is better to be an outlaw than some stodgy bourgeois. Whitewashing is confined to ignoring the worst aspects of the Wild Bunch's holdups: their real record was far from bloodless, but since the movie gang never kills anybody during the two train robberies it pulls off in the U.S. (though in blowing open a boxcar they do seriously injure an

Butch, Etta, and Sundance find they dislike Bolivia in *Butch Cassidy and the Sundance Kid*. (Museum of Modern Art/Film Stills Archive)

express agent who bravely refuses to admit them and is, typically, portrayed as a comic figure), the audience could regard the charismatic twosome as the same sort of lovable rogues they would later play in Hill's *The Sting*.

But things get gorier after they make their way to what is intended as Bolivia, a fact Pauline Kael seems to have found particularly disturbing (although she hadn't when the victims were the policemen in *Bonnie and Clyde*, supposedly *Butch*'s inspiration): "Maybe we're supposed to be charmed with this affable, loquacious outlaw and his silent, 'dangerous' buddy Sundance blow up trains, but how are we supposed to feel when they go off to Bolivia, sneer at the country, and start shooting up poor Bolivians?" Since during that montage of "funny" South American bank holdups we are never forced to witness the bandits killing anyone (in contrast to the regrettable "I tried to control 'em" truth), the first chance to shoot some Bolivians comes with a fictional episode, during which Butch and Sundance try to go straight by becoming payroll guards for the tin mines and run up against local bandits. These bandits inhumanely murder the *Yanqui* payroll cashier before making off with the loot. Since they later refuse to give the money back when asked with a polite *por favor*, the two conscientious payroll guards must wipe them out in gory slow motion.

Viewing the destruction they've wrought, Butch and Sundance appear very upset and decide to become bandits again—because, it is absurdly implied, the occupation is somehow less bloody than that of payroll guard. But in the glorified final battle soon afterward, they inconsistently knock policemen and soldiers down like tenpins without turning a hair (this picture was not well received in Bolivia), and seem to have trouble taking even their own deaths seriously. Hopelessly outnumbered and surrounded, the two wounded comrades exchange some final banter about going to Australia next time before running out with guns blazing, the image first freezing them in midstride as we hear three crashing volleys and then slowly changing to the now-familiar antique sepia as the two are absorbed into legend and box-office history. This technique was doubtless chosen because actually showing death or bullet-torn bodies would have added a bit of grim honesty, and that would have been a downer, man. (Actually, the standard account of the duo's end which inspired Goldman has one of the wounded American bandits, trapped in the hacienda at San Vicente, simply blowing out his brains to avoid capture—even more depressing, unless you're Japanese.)

Lula Betenson, who went to visit the set while *Butch Cassidy* was being shot ("Hi, I'm Butch," said Newman. "Hi, I'm your sister," parried she) rather liked the film. It would be interesting to know whether she ever told the folks on location that the ending planned for Butch differed from her own version instead of waiting until the film's release—and if not, why not. Perhaps no one there would have cared had they been told, since lighthearted heroes such as Butch should die young, if at all. But the final siege did seem to cancel out any hope of making a sequel: it would have been just a bit much to have either bandit survive that storm of lead.

Newman and Redford shoot their way into our hearts as they dash toward certain death. (Museum of Modern Art/Film Stills Archive)

But Etta Place had survived—and her Pinkerton file had never been closed, opening up a vast field of speculation as to her fate. What luck!

In 1974 ABC televised *Mrs. Sundance* (a misnomer) with Elizabeth Montgomery as a blonde Etta hearing that Sundance is still alive and setting out to find him. The 1976 sequel to the sequel, *Wanted—The Sundance Woman* (retitled, for a later broadcast, *Mrs. Sundance Rides Again*) had Katharine Ross, the original film's brunette Etta, last seen leaving Bolivia for the U.S. so she won't have to see her boys die (she actually left to have an appendicitis operation), adventuring in Mexico—and *still* looking for Sundance. The good old-fashioned vulgarity of its ads ("SHE WAS A LOT OF WOMAN . . . TO A LOT OF MEN") reminded one of Cassidy's purported judgment of her character: "She was the best housekeeper in the Pampas, but she was a whore at heart." She seems to have been one professionally as well, rather than the thrill-seeking schoolteacher of legend and Hill's movie.

If you can't go forward, flash back: since Butch and Sundance have been recognized as hot mythic properties, William Goldman produced and Richard Lester directed for 1979 a presequel (sans Newman and Redford) entitled *Butch and Sundance: The Early Days*. There were no "early days."

Hollywood's curious neglect of Butch and his pards until 1969 seems all the more unusual when one considers that during the late forties and early fifties, the industry was apparently hard-pressed to meet its own demand for historical badmen. Besides remaking the well-worn sagas of the deadlier bandits—and even glorifying Jack McCall—the studios resorted to hitherto unused material concerning people like those we'll meet below.

Al Jennings, a small fry in everything but conceit and imagination, was a good liar but a poor outlaw. Formerly county attorney of El Reno, Oklahoma, the diminutive Al had decided to become a bandit for the gratification of his purse and ego, but he and the other hapless members of the "Jennings Gang" reaped little profit and less glory. In one train robbery the gang got $400, a gallon of whiskey, and a bunch of bananas, but managed to blow up an entire boxcar without even denting the two safes they had tried to open; Jennings participated in one brief, bloodless posse-vs.-outlaws shoot-out, during which he panicked and, after firing once, kept shucking good shells out of his lever-action rifle without remembering to pull the trigger, one of the many bits of Oklahoma bandit history Charles Portis was to use in his *True Grit*. Marshal Bud Ledbetter finally arrested Al and two other bandits single-handed and without a fight, having first bet Bill Tilghman that he could do that very thing.

After serving his time, Jennings ran for governor, wrote of prison life and the outlaw career he had dreamed up for himself, and took a bit part in the 1908 Western *The Bank Robbery,* ineptly directed by none other than Bill Tilghman (who also produced a few other films, including one depicting the destruction of the Doolin and Jennings gangs by himself and other U.S. marshals). This finally led to Al's starring in and directing a number of silent films himself, several of them guaranteed to be true and factual re-creations of incidents in his own action-packed career; Jennings's Westerns, oddly enough, tended to be unusually downbeat and realistic, and he expressed ₌ contempt for the makers of the more patently phony dramas.[5]

In California, Jennings floated among the stars—buddying around with Bill Hart, telling lies about himself, and boasting that he could hit a thrown can in midair at 100 yards without ever missing. In truth Jennings could barely hit a barn from the inside with the doors closed, but, in his occasional role of technical director, he nevertheless took it upon himself to instruct Tex Ritter in the art of the fast draw for the 1936 *Song of the Gringo,* in which he also acted.

In 1948 a kindred soul, "J. Frank Dalton," claimed that he was the unkilled Jesse James and all of 101 years old, so the 85-year-old Jennings went to see him, took a good look, and confirmed his claim. "It was a touching scene and the tears flowed," reported the Associated Press man on the spot. "Boys, there isn't a bit of doubt on earth," said Al, who neglected to inform the watchdogs of the press that he had never met Jesse James and that Dalton had somehow contrived to grow a new tip for a left-hand finger to replace one shot off during the Rebellion; when asked by James biographer Homer Croy (who knew a lot about Jesse but somehow liked him anyway) about this deficiency, or surplus, Dalton merely offered Croy a doughnut. This last of the bogus Jameses carried on nobly despite such skepticism and, predictably, found many believers; in 1950 he even asked a Missouri court to change his name legally to Jesse James.

That year Columbia fittingly honored his fellow imposter—a man who epitomized every decent mogul's attitude toward the bygone West—with *Al Jennings of Oklahoma*; true, Jennings's name was rather bland as outlaw names go, but he was very well known in Hollywood. Al was played by Dan Duryea, who carried on a private war against the capitalists of the territory.

Jennings, inexplicably, failed to see its value and publicly damned it as "a disgrace to the Old West." The old ingrate died in 1961, aged ninety-eight.

Black Jack Ketchum, Desperado (1956) concerned a reformed badman's

Black Jack Ketchum achieves immortality. (Western History Collections, University of Oklahoma Library)

attempt to clean up a lawless Western town. It had Howard Duff and Victor Jory in it. Now, travel back in time with me.

Peer over the shoulder of Thomas B. "Black Jack" Ketchum as he reads a letter from his gal, describing how her secret paramour had watched Black Jack kiss her good-bye before cowboy Ketchum rode off on a cattle drive. "No more than you got out of sight," she wrote, "than we went to Stanton and got married."

It was our hero's custom, when he found that he had committed an error in judgment, to pound himself on the hand with the butt of his trusty six-shooter, saying to himself meanwhile, "You will, will you? Now take that! And that!" This time Black Jack Ketchum, desperado-to-be, took out his twisted saddle rope and went down to the bank of the Perico River, his friends watching open-mouthed as he administered a severe flogging to himself while cursing all womankind.

A rather unimaginative train robber and killer,* Ketchum led his New Mexico associates in holding up the same train at almost the same spot four times during 1898–99. He was finally caught and sentenced to hang, and even the *New York Times* found room for his story after it was reported that outlaw bands were preparing to storm the jail and effect a rescue. But there was no rescue. According to the *Times*, Ketchum fairly "leaped" up the gallows steps and helped the hangman to adjust the noose. "I'll be in hell before you start breakfast, boys!" he shouted. "Let 'er go!" He was taken at his word: the executioner pulled the trap and the rope, which had been stretched too much by a 200-pound weight used to test it and left attached all the previous night, tore off Ketchum's head. On the bright side, a cameraman was on hand to record both the prologue and grisly aftermath of this event.

The pictures sold very well.

The present-day fame of Black Bart, one badman about whom the general public knows absolutely nothing, magnificently illustrates the power of the Name. What nickname more notorious? What moniker more menacing?

Black Bart!

It was in July of 1875 that the frightening figure in long linen duster and flour-sack mask held up his first California stagecoach. "Throw down the box!" he cried in a strange, hollow voice, and the driver complied; this done, the mysterious road agent ordered him to move on, and after the coach had rattled off, removed the gold from the express box and vanished into the brush on foot. The same masked marauder struck twice in 1876, using the same *modus operandi*; but after he held up the Point Area stage on August 3, 1877, he changed his pattern by leaving behind this bit of doggerel:

---

*"I've got outlaw blood in me," boasts Gary Busey, star of the recent *The Buddy Holley Story* and Ketchum relative.

A scene from *Black Bart*. (Cinemabilia)

Black Bart.

> I've labored long and hard for bread
> For honor and for riches
> But on my corns too long you've tred
> You fine-haired sons of bitches

It was some time before anxious Wells Fargo detectives realized that the signature "Black Bart, the Po8" meant that the author considered himself a maker of rhyme. After his next robbery, the mysterious Bart left another scrap of Po8ry at the scene of the crime, with his previous effort sandwiched in between the first and last stanzas.

> Here I lay me down to sleep
> To wait the coming morrow
> Perhaps success, perhaps defeat
> And everlasting sorrow
> . . . .
> Yet come what will, I'll try it on
> My condition can't be worse
> And if there's money in that Box
> 'Tis munny in my purse.

Bart, who never went so far as to actually use his gun in a robbery, left no more verse behind, but after the last of his twenty-eight holdups, in 1883, he did leave behind a number of clues. These led to the arrest of one Charles E. Bolton, obstensibly a prosperous mining man then living in San Francisco. When confronted, Bolton, an impeccably dressed, middle-aged swell, at first declined to admit anything ("I am a gentleman," said he); a detective noticed the name Charles E. Boles on the flyleaf of a Bible in his apartment, but on being arraigned, the suspect gave his name as T. Z. Spaulding. When asked what sort of education he had received, he grandly replied, "Liberal!" At last he confessed that he had taken the name Black Bart from a story published in the *Sacramento Union* back in 1871. Lightly sentenced and a model prisoner, he was released in 1888, at which time one of the reporters present dared to ask Bart if he contemplated writing any more poetry. This was a question the ex-bandit viewed as wholly unnecessary: hadn't he already *said* that he would commit no more crimes?

They made a movie about him in 1948, with Dan Duryea. And did it, you ask, portray him as the lovable rogue he really was? As the bloodless, poetic bandit who charmed a nation with his verse, and whose name would later be appropriated for the Negro sheriff of Mel Brooks's *Blazing Saddles?*

Don't be silly.

NOTES

1. A vicious killer, Logan once found himself lodged in jail and so deluged by "respectable" women bearing gifts that the sheriff had to call a halt to their visits. He shot himself after a chase following a 1904 train robbery in Colorado that left him wounded and unable to elude capture. A girlfriend, Catherine Cross, was later killed by an unbalanced citizen after she insisted on singing a song commemorating Logan's exploits, which included at least eight murders.

2. Percy Siebert reported that the bandits' "Robin Hood quality had been tarnished when they killed some people—one of them an innocent bank official—during a holdup. Both Clement Glass and I denounced Cassidy for the killings one night when we were sharing a glass, and Cassidy seemed surprised. 'He had a gun and was about to use it,' he protested. 'What could we do?' I guess this was the usual warped philosophy of the outlaw: no man has a right to protect himself or the property he is responsible for."

3. Conrad Hall also got an Oscar for his professional, but misused cinematography, while George Roy Hill was nominated for his doomed-by-the-material direction.

4. Regarding such admiration: "I know I'm guilty of it," admitted Robert Redford, who wrote the introduction to the Betenson book (though it might have been more appropriate for Newman to do so) and named a ski resort he owned "Sundance." Redford has recently written a big picture book called *The Outlaw Trail* and narrated a somewhat fuzzy-minded documentary of the same name, in which the notion was put forth that old-time badmen were recognized in their day as just doing their thing, so to speak. To which one British critic (in the *New Statesman*, if I recall correctly) nastily suggested that, had Redford been discussing World War II, he might have defended the SS's right to be the SS, if that was what they really felt like doing.

5. The transition from badman to screen actor was made more abruptly by the notorious bank robber Henry Starr, a nephew of Belle whose criminal career spanned twenty-eight years, though interrupted by periodic jail terms. On being released once again in 1919, he took the advice of friends who told him that "there's more money in the moving picture business than there is in bank robbery" and acquired a quarter interest in a Tulsa picture company. His first production was *Debtor to the Law*, the story of a 1915 raid in which his gang became the first to rob two banks at the same time, though Starr himself was wounded and captured; the film was made on location and the boy who had shot Starr also played himself. Henry starred in several subsequent pictures, but in 1921 was killed by the elderly president of a bank he had attempted to rob. It was claimed that Starr had returned to crime because he had been cheated by his business associates; if true, it was the only case in history of the motion-picture industry causing the death of a noted Western badman. The early silents, requiring large numbers of real cowboys, usually had a more beneficial effect on contemporary horseback outlaws, who could hide out in the crowd while getting paid for it.

6
Never a Last Stand
or Custer Died for Your Cash

> Oh, could you but have seen some of the charges that were made! While thinking of them I cannot but exclaim "Glorious War!"
> —GEORGE ARMSTRONG CUSTER, 1863

> She could never be a saint, but she thought she could be a martyr if they killed her quick.
> —FLANNERY O'CONNOR,
> "A Temple of the Holy Ghost"

On the last day of his life George Armstrong Custer, commander of the fabled Seventh Cavalry, stands resplendent in fringed buckskins, his long locks blowing in the wind, his face grim. About him on the grassless desert lies a myriad of the slain, feathered shafts protruding from blue-coated bodies. The fighting Seventh, charging with sabers drawn, had been suddenly surrounded by hordes of mounted Indians under the Sioux chief Crazy Horse, and had dismounted to fight on foot. The Indians had charged—hand-to-hand fighting!—and been driven off each time. But now only one or two soldiers remain alive to stand with Custer.

He snatches up a saber stuck into the bone-dry earth and, as his remaining comrades fall pierced by bullets, stoically waits, alone, one man against the hundreds of painted savages who now gallop toward him in one last wild charge.

A feathered chieftain—the great Crazy Horse himself—raises his Winchester to his shoulder as his pony plunges on toward the yellow-haired soldier. He fires, and Custer sinks to the ground. The chief grabs up the proud guidon of the Seventh and leads his victorious braves past the gallant dead to vanish into the distant hills.

A few minutes later the lights in the Warner Brothers projection room go on. Studio chief Jack Warner turns to director Raoul Walsh and says, "That is one of Flynn's best. If Custer really died like that, history should applaud him."

Custer hadn't exactly died like that, but of course one could scarcely expect Jack Warner to bother finding out about such things. The film under discussion was 1941's *They Died with Their Boots On*, only the most ambitious and expensive of those films dealing with that most famous personality of the West's Indian wars, whose last fight at the Battle of the Little Bighorn in

The Boy General in 1872, displaying his full-dress uniform complete with horsehair-plumed helmet. When left to his own devices, Custer adopted a more individualistic approach toward clothing. (National Park Service, Department of Interior, Custer Battlefield National Monument)

Montana immortalized both the commander and his regiment. It is an immortality which many feel the commander, at least, does not deserve.

After a career as a West Point cadet which he later cited as an example to be avoided, the Ohio-born, Michigan-raised Custer graduated with his classmates one year early, the newly erupted Civil War having created a great demand for commissioned cannon fodder. His subsequent rise from second lieutenant was spectacular: a born horse soldier who loved combat and won the confidence of generals in key positions, he gained a brigadier's star at the age of twenty-three just in time for the great cavalry fight east of Gettysburg, where his badly outnumbered Michigan Brigade played a crucial role in preventing J. E. B. Stuart's gray horsemen from flanking the Union Army. Although not quite the youngest such officer, Custer was soon dubbed "the Boy General" by a lionizing press which fed on his vain sense of showmanship and romantic gallantry; flaunting his long blond locks and often clad in a black velvet costume that, in the words of one eyewitness, made him resemble "a circus rider gone mad," he charged home to glory in dozens of mounted actions—polishing up the glory with sometimes exaggerated reports of his troopers' actions. Much of Custer's writing, both public and private, was marked by this feature; according to his friend Captain William Ludlow, "He was apt to exaggerate in statement, not from any wilful disregard for the truth, but because he saw things bigger than they really were."

Custer emerged from the war a major-general of U.S. Volunteers in command of a cavalry division, and a popular hero who had received the first flag of truce at Appomattox. But while comparable heroes of that day no longer live in the public memory, Custer endures, thanks to his death in a disastrous Indian fight at which he commanded only a regiment; more successful Indian fighters, such as Crook, Miles, and Mackenzie, bear names unfamiliar to the average American.

After a period of duty in Reconstruction Texas during which he was criticized for the ruthless measures employed in disciplining his troops (actions documented and defended in John M. Carroll's *Custer in Texas*), Custer secured a lieutenant-colonelcy in the shrunken postwar Regular Army and was given command of the newly formed Seventh U.S. Cavalry, while retaining the "brevet" or honorary title of major-general. Custer drove his men relentlessly and was a ferocious disciplinarian, which may have accounted for the nickname of "Hard Ass" which some of the Seventh's troopers came to use in referring to their commander. ("He is the most complete example of a petty tyrant that I have ever seen," complained Captain Albert Barnitz in a letter to his wife.) His first Indian campaign, General Winfield Scott Hancock's unproductive expedition of 1867, ended in Custer's court-martial for, among other things, summarily shooting deserters and going AWOL to visit his wife. Much of Custer's behavior on this campaign was certainly irresponsible, but it is felt by some partisans that the court-martial was an attempt by high officials to make Custer a scapegoat for the campaign's failure, in response to what grandnephew Colonel Brice C. W. Custer has termed "the public's cry for a victim."

The rather light sentence—one year's suspension of rank and pay—was cut short at the behest of several high-ranking officers, including Custer's old Civil War commander Phil Sheridan, who planned a winter campaign against the southern Plains tribes in response to attacks on white settlers by far-ranging war parties. In order to avoid being attacked by mistake, peaceful tribesmen in the same area were to seek sanctuary at Fort Cobb, Indian Territory.

Custer as he appeared during Sheridan's winter campaign. (National Park Service, Department of Interior, Custer Battlefield National Monument)

Custer led his Seventh deep into the territory, and on November 26, 1868, his Osage scouts discovered a large Indian village on the banks of the Washita River. Custer resolved to attack at dawn and the next morning signaled the regimental band, which he had thoughtfully brought along through the deep snow, to play "Garryowen," the Boy General's favorite march and the tune always to be associated with the Seventh Cavalry; the instruments soon froze up as the men charged into the village, firing. During the fight a small detachment under Major Joel Elliott, who had broken away from the main command, was cut off, surrounded, and destroyed.

After the torching of the village and the selection of mounts for the fifty-odd women and children taken prisoner, over 800 ponies were slaughtered to prevent their recapture and the Seventh marched back to its base camp. General Sheridan, his risky plan of campaign vindicated, tendered "special congratulations" to the Boy General, while his superior, William T. Sherman, professed himself "well satisfied with Custer's attack."

Criticism came from other quarters. From the very beginning the Seventh's officer corps, like those of other regiments, had tended toward factionalism—in this case, division into those for and against Custer—and his conduct at the Washita deepened the rift. Some officers, notably Captain Frederick Benteen (who was "only too glad" to say that he despised Custer) considered him to have abandoned Major Elliott when his command was known to be missing. Defenders argued that a search would have risked the safety of the entire command, threatened by swarms of Indians from nearby villages whose proximity was unsuspected prior to the attack.

Even more damaging to Custer's reputation as a *beau sabreur* were the charges of massacre. After his officers had compared notes on the action (no formal body count was made) Custer claimed 103 warriors slain, also stating: "In the excitement of the fight, as well as in self-defense, it so happened that some of the squaws and a few of the children were killed and wounded. The latter I have brought with me, and they received all the needed attention the circumstances of the case permit. Many of the squaws were taken with arms in their hands, and several of my command are known to have been wounded by them."* The deaths of women and children gave rise to charges, persisting to this day, that Custer had purposefully executed a slaughter of noncombatants, but although individual atrocities may have been committed by men of his regiment there is nothing to indicate that Custer should be held responsible for such acts or that there was any deliberate mass killing of noncombatants. In his memoirs he states: "Orders had been given to prevent the killing of any but the fighting strength of the village; but in a struggle of this character it is

*Other sources insist on varyingly lower totals of slain; the Cheyenne half-breed George Bent came up with perhaps the lowest (probably too low), saying that 11 men, 12 women, and 6 children were killed. For *Bury My Heart at Wounded Knee* Dee Brown apparently cross-pollinated Bent's and Custer's figures and came up with a queer bastard set: he says that 103 Indians were killed but that only 11 were men. Brown's figures for Major Eugene Baker's 1870 action on the Marias are equally unreliable.

"Attack at Dawn," commonly used to illustrate the Washita fight. Veterans of the action praised its accuracy, but the troopers are dressed and equipped in the style of the late 1880s, and few of the Indians were given time to mount up during the initial storming of the village. (National Park Service, Department of Interior, Custer Battlefield National Monument)

impossible at all times to discriminate."[1] Many women and children had in fact participated in the village defense; fear, the confusion of battle, and the sheer volume of fire undoubtedly had more to do with the outcome than any white bloodlust—which situation was scarcely unique to the Washita attack in Indian warfare.

Whether the attack itself was justified remains one of those unresolved questions that keep historians busy; there is no easy answer. Custer's victims had been Cheyenne under chief Black Kettle, and this led to the charge that he had attacked a camp of innocent, peaceful Indians. Black Kettle, who with his wife was killed in the assault, had possessed quite a reputation as a "peace chief"; just four years earlier he had seen his people, thinking themselves under military protection and flying the American flag, ruthlessly butchered by Colonel John M. Chivington's Third Colorado Cavalry (militiamen enlisted for a 100-day period) in what became notorious as the Sand Creek Massacre. Ugly parallels were drawn. But fortunately for himself, Custer could point to the presence in the village of several white captives and other proofs that residents had engaged in depredations, regardless of what Black Kettle's wishes may have been. (In most tribes an Indian chief's power was simply advisory.) Prior to Custer's attack Black Kettle, who had confessed an inability to control his warriors, had discussed coming into Fort Cobb with General William Hazen. Fearing that Cobb would also become a refuge for those warlike Cheyenne seeking to evade punishment, Hazen had refused and merely warned Black Kettle that Sheridan's troopers were in the field, with the result that the village was located in the combat zone when Custer's Indian scouts discovered it. In using large-scale military force to punish transgressing Indians, it was often difficult to distinguish innocent from guilty, especially since it was rare for an entire tribe to take the warpath against whites; a workable police-action or civil-law solution, on the other hand, was usually possible only with Indians already permanently placed on a reservation.

Following the Washita fight, Custer directed his awesome energies toward gathering in other Indian villages without bloodshed, a task accomplished only after great haredship and risk and one which has earned him praise even from some, though by no means all, of his severest critics. He saw no further

Custer on the Black Hills expedition of 1874. Pointing to the map is his hunting companion and favorite Indian scout, the Arikara Bloody Knife; according to one Arikara, Custer "had a heart like an Indian." (National Park Service, Department of Interior, Custer Battlefield National Monument)

action until the 1873 Yellowstone Expedition, during which he had several successful brushes with the Sioux and was briefly placed under arrest by his superior for going on an unauthorized scout. In 1874 Custer led an exploratory expedition into the Black Hills of the Dakotas, previously guaranteed the Sioux by treaty; gold was discovered and the undermanned frontier army made only a token attempt to halt the subsequent stampede of miners, another addition to the list of grievances held by the Sioux. That same year saw some of Custer's articles for *The Galaxy* magazine collected and published in book form as *My Life on the Plains, or Personal Experiences with Indians*.

Perhaps the most interesting sections of this highly readable account, which exemplified the author's rose-colored, romantic way of viewing life and glossing over its less pleasant realities, are those in which the Indian fighter gives us his own views on the Indians. These range from racist condescension to admiration—a common phenomenon among nineteenth-century whites and perhaps especially among members of the Indian-fighting army. Anxious to refute the view of the red man as a pure child of nature, Custer nevertheless reflected the white man's characteristically ambivalent attitude. On the one hand, he could proclaim the Indian "a *savage* in every sense of the word; not worse, perhaps, than his white brother would be similarly born and bred, but one whose cruel and ferocious nature far exceeds that of any wild beast of the desert"; on the other hand, Custer could confess himself impressed by many facets of Indian life and bemoan the fate of the reservation Indian: "If I were an Indian, I often think I would greatly prefer to cast my lot among those of my people who adhered to the free open plains rather than submit to the confined limits of a reservation, there to be the recipient of the blessed benefits of civilization, with its vices thrown in without stint or measure."

Custer added by way of disagreement with those who would exterminate the Indian that the idealized Noble Red Man view was "equally erroneous with that which regards the Indian as a creature possessing the human form but divested of all other attributes of humanity, and whose traits of character, habits, modes of life, disposition, and savage customs, disqualify him from the exercise of all rights and privileges, even those pertaining to life itself."* But the reluctance about fighting Indian wars which Custer occasionally expressed, whatever its authenticity, did not, of course, prevent him from ruthlessly pursuing and savoring his victories, any more than his sympathies for the South had prevented him from becoming an enthusiastic, successful, and ambitious Union general. To Custer, as to most other whites, "civilization" was without question the superior way of life.

In March of 1876 Custer was summoned to testify before a congressional committee probing corruption in the administration of Indian traderships, and implicated not only Secretary of War Rufus Belknap, but also President

*In his 1968 *The New Indians*, Stan Steiner slyly cuts this short to read, "equally erroneous with that which regards the Indian as a creature possessing the human form," thus making it appear that Custer regarded the red men as positively subhuman: Dick Gregory subsequently reprinted this in his America-the-rotten *No More Lies*, which purported to tell the "real" story of American history.

Grant's crooked brother Orvil as parties to the extensive graft. Unfortunately his evidence was mostly hearsay, and its success lay chiefly in angering the president, who decided to refuse Custer a part in the upcoming Sioux campaign. When General Alfred Terry interceded on Custer's behalf and antiadministration newspapers played up his plight as a martyr to the cause of reform, Grant finally relented—in part. Rather than command the entire expedition, Custer would lead only his own regiment, marching in the Dakota column under Terry's personal command. It is probable that his humiliation strengthened Custer's determination to win a victory over the "hostiles"; even a small success would go far in wiping away the stain of Grant's rebuke.

Custer's actions, once he and his regiment were turned loose from the main column, have led to accusations that he had disobeyed certain of Terry's orders. But these orders were sufficiently vague as to inspire endless controversy. (Custer had never been the type to let mere orders stand in his way in any event, even if he did demand strict obedience from his own subordinates—but, of course, none of this would have mattered had Custer emerged victorious.)

On the morning of June 25 Custer's Indian scouts informed him that a large hostile village was some fifteen miles away; told that the hostiles knew or would soon know of his presence, Custer decided to attack immediately rather than wait until the morning of the 26th as he had originally planned. His primary concern was that the Indians would escape him, since they usually chose to avoid fights with large bodies of soldiers.

At about noon the Seventh started into the valley of the Little Bighorn, and here Custer made his fateful decision to divide the command in the face of an unknown number of hostiles, so as to envelop the Indians if possible. Captain Benteen was sent with three companies on a fruitless scouting mission to the left, with orders to strike whatever hostiles he might come across. Major Marcus A. Reno, also with three companies, was to cross the Little Bighorn River and attack the village, while one company was assigned to guard the pack train and Custer remained in direct command of the remaining five companies. With him were approximately 215 men, including his brothers Tom and Boston—serving as, respectively, a captain in the Seventh and a civilian employee—his brother-in-law Lieutenant James Calhoun, and his teenage nephew Autie Reed.

Reno charged with his three companies toward part of what turned out to be one of the largest assemblies of Plains Indians ever to gather, including perhaps as many as 3,000 warriors. (For various reasons, these were many more than anyone had been led to expect.) The attack came as a complete surprise to the Indians and resistance does not appear to have been particularly strong, but the very size of the village and the amount of dust kicked up by the hostiles apparently convinced Reno that it would be suicidal to continue the charge, which ground to a halt. Reno first formed a skirmish line and then retreated in disorder.

The Indians failed to press their advantage and Captain Benteen's

Custer's last portrait. (National Park Service, Department of Interior, Custer Battlefield National Monument)

detachment soon arrived to reinforce Reno. But Benteen had actually been on his way toward Custer, who had sent back a courier with a message telling him to come quickly and bring the packs. Reno had the captain halt and aid his own command instead. In the meantime Custer had attacked, and his men were soon wiped out by many times their own number of Sioux and Cheyenne; the Boy General's corpse, naked, as were most of the others, and shot in the temple and breast, was later found within a small group of dead men and cavalry mounts on the slope of what is now known as Custer Hill. Pressure on the survivors under Reno continued for the rest of that day and for most of the twenty-sixth; on the morning of the twenty-seventh they were relieved by troops under General Terry.

The defeat and death of "the American Murat" at the hands of mere aborigines shocked the U.S. in the year of its Centennial celebrations and created a near-instant heroic legend in the tradition of Thermopylae, the Alamo, and other battles in which a small, beleaguered band had fought the good fight only to be overwhelmed by barbarian hordes.[2] Already a figure of glamor to many, Custer swiftly became one of America's greatest heroes and myth figures. The poets were inspired, Walt Whitman and Longfellow adding their efforts to those of lesser talents; likewise the illustrators, whose generally unimpressive versions of Custer's last battle number in the hundreds, the most famous being an 1886 Anheuser Busch lithograph prominent in saloons for generations afterward. Like many of the other "Custer's Last Stand" or "Last fight" or "Last Charge" pictures, it featured an idealized, Olympian hero— a clean-shaven Custer flaunting those famous golden locks in the face of his scalp-hungry foes while slicing them up with a romantic saber, although the general was actually wearing his hair short when the campaign began,[3] had let his beard grow for some weeks before his death, and had ordered all sabers left behind as being of little use against Indians.

The story of the Little Bighorn battle quickly came to fit the archetypal pattern of the heroic Last Stand, not, in most cases, because writers of the time consciously restructured the facts to fit a known, preconceived model, but simply because people's minds have always worked that way where last stands—and the sort of life-upholding death that Whitman called "the old, old legend of our race"—are concerned. Civil War veteran Frederick Whittaker,

"Custer Hill," where the buckskinned general and a small group of whites apparently made their stand. Each marker is intended to indicate a fallen combatant. Photograph by Mary Minton. (National Park Service, Department of Interior, Custer Battlefield National Monument)

Custer's first biographer, probably had a keener mythic awareness than most, and his shoddy, semifictional *A Complete Life of Gen. George A. Custer*, though rushed into print just six months after the debacle, poured the Boy General expertly into the mold. It was Whittaker who was responsible for the fantasy which had the "only survivor," a Crow scout named Curly who in fact was not present at the actual stand, offer Custer—or "Son of the Morning Star," as he was known to the admiring Crows—a chance to escape with him so that Custer can refuse and prove his nobility by riding back to die with his men.

In the immediate wake of Custer's defeat, the Boy General's own rash nature was sometimes blamed, but betrayal, an important ingredient in such quasi-historical Last Stand myths as that of Roland at Roncesvalles, soon proved a more popular explanation. The history of the fight was accordingly interpreted or twisted to fit the theory. Custer had been betrayed by his Indian scouts; by white renegades leading the redskins against their racial kinsmen; by Reno and Benteen; even by Grant. In Whittaker's hands Custer became the young god (an 1861 binge, after which Custer took the pledge—he didn't smoke either—is termed "the one fault in a perfect life") who would surely have won the day had he not been deliberately "abandoned" by his subordinates. Since the indisputably courageous Benteen was the lower-ranking officer, Whittaker and other Custer partisans tended to concentrate their fire on Reno—so much so that in 1879 a court of inquiry was convened at the major's own request. The court cleared Reno of any wrongdoing, although some have disagreed with the verdict; Whittaker charged whitewash and continued his campaign of vituperation against the Seventh's surviving officers. (In fact there apparently was considerable covering-up done.)

Criticism of Custer himself was largely muted for the first half century or so due to rampant Victorian sentimentality, a natural reluctance to "kick a dead lion," and sympathy for Mrs. Elizabeth Bacon Custer, who recorded her life with the general in three idealizing books and did everything in her power to defend his reputation. Such gentlemanly restraint did little to hurt the heroic legend—particularly as Mrs. Custer outlived all those Seventh Cavalry officers who felt hostile toward her "Autie," dying in 1933.

In 1934 Frederic F. Van de Water came up with his *Glory-Hunter;* seemingly anxious to make up for lost time, he portrayed Custer as a fool, egoist, and sadist. His work, which revealed more thorough research than that of any previous biographer, made some valid points, but was ultimately less productive of light than of heat in its vindictive tone and its presentation of the author's pet psychoanalytical theories as indisputable fact. Despite the obvious bias, *Glory-Hunter* quickly became the most influential of Custer biographies, many authors simply echoing Van de Water's interpretation.

Turning Custer into an utter villain proved particularly popular among those writers who made a point of being "pro-Indian," as distinct from those who simply hated the man. In the 1948 *Fighting Indians of the West*, an illustrated history by Martin F. Schmitt and Dee Brown, Custer, out of all frontier regular army officers, is singled out for special vilification. He is presented as

Mrs. Elizabeth Custer. (National Park Service, Department of Interior, Custer Battlefield National Monument)

fiendishly plotting a strike against peaceful Indian villages purely for his own, glory-hunting benefit, even though it was Sheridan who had thought up the winter campaign and recalled Custer from Michigan exile to help execute it. Dee Brown's disregard for the truth is less relevant here than a need to shift the blame for the *entire* 1868 campaign onto a subordinate officer. Thanks to his spectacular end, Custer had come to personify the Indian-fighting soldier, and to pro-Indian writers he could be a useful symbol of all that was least attractive in the Western cavalryman, especially as he had commanded at what some have termed a massacre. Actually John M. Chivington, who, though not a professional soldier, did fit the stereotype of the blue-coated butcher, would have personified anti-Indian villainy in more convincing fashion, and all this symbolism (which reached its climax in the Nixon era with Vine Deloria's raving best-seller *Custer Died for Your Sins* and bumper stickers insisting that "Custer Had It Coming") was sadly misplaced. But the Boy General was the only Indian-fighting commander that most people *remembered*.

Custer literature continues to be dominated by violent partisanship, perhaps, as Robert M. Utley suggests, because Custer's own personality made him a mass of contradictions. Van de Water, one of the malady's chief victims, was not far wrong when he wrote that Custer was "impossible to regard with balance. . . . Custerphobe and Custerphile strive with the heat of the man's actual intimates." At present the Custerphobes appear to have succeeded in dominating the more popular Western writings, but the Custerphiles refuse to concede defeat and include in their ranks many diligent scholars, as well as the expected quota of hapless romantics. (As late as 1968 the part-Sioux D. A. Kinsley produced the second half of a hefty, worthless biography whose author seemed unable to decide whether he was writing a work of history or a two-volume dime novel; so far no really satisfactory biography has appeared, and all Custer literature should be approached with caution.) Many Custer buffs have banded together into the Little Big Horn Associates, whose professed goal is to "seek and preserve the truth about the Battle of the Little Bighorn and all of Custeriana." Argument still rages over what *really* happened during the Last Stand; whether Custer did indeed violate orders; whether Reno could have put the Indians to flight and won the battle had he continued his charge. Much more ink than blood, as the cliché would have it, has been split over the controversy.

But controversy has rarely interested makers of historical Westerns, where heroes of purest white and villains of darkest dye are preferred: although Custer has proved a popular subject ever since William Selig's 1909 *Custer's Last Stand*, his story has never been told with any accuracy. There sometimes seems a positive *compulsion* to lie, possibly rooted in a screenwriter's need to demonstrate his own "creativity." And perhaps their fabrications should be considered creative in at least one sense: unlike certain of those which appear in Wyatt Earp or Billy the Kid films, they are usually original lies and scholarship, or the lack of it, has comparatively little influence on them, except perhaps insofar as an author's attitude toward Custer may influence the screenwriter to invent fictitious derring-do rather than fictitious villainy. Whatever its purpose, most of the falsification was unnecessary since, as the historians have so graciously shown us, the same basic facts can be used to shape either a laudatory or a debunking narrative.

As often happens, the distortion began long before all the participants had died or even faded away. Among those present at the New York premiere of

1925's *The Flaming Frontier*, featuring some contrived white shysters whose machinations bring about both the death of Custer and their own downfall, was Little Bighorn veteran Edward S. Godfrey. Prior to the actual screening, General Godfrey was introduced amid grand applause, but unfortunately the old soldier's opinion of the film seems to have gone unrecorded. Several Seventh Cavalrymen present at the battle survived into the late 1940s, while the last Indian participant, a Sioux warrior named Dewey Beard, died in 1955.

Until 1941 a sixteen-part serial called *Custer's Last Stand* (also released as an extremely low-budget feature), with an overcomplicated plot and a long-awaited climax consisting of a few soldiers shooting at a veritable handful of redskins, was the only sound film professing to use Custer or his final fight as its main subject. Usually Long Hair just did guest shots like those in *Wyoming* (1940) and *Badlands of Dakota* (1941); toward the end of the first film Custer, after he and the Seventh have fulfilled the famous cavalry function of arriving just in time to save the embattled whites, casually mentions that he's bound for the Little Bighorn to put down "a little Indian trouble." In *The Plainsman* a no-nonsense Custer (John Miljan) had a few scenes with Gary Cooper and is granted the extraordinary honor of appearing with him in the final allegorical shot. But his last stand, seen in flashback, is more or less dragged in by the ears, gleefully narrated to Bill Hickok and Cody by a captive Cheyenne. The Indian was played by an unknown bit player named Anthony Quinn, who later said he'd passed himself off as a genuine brave to future father-in-law De Mille by making up his Cheyenne dialogue as he went along.

In 1940 *Santa Fe Trail*, directed by Michael *(Casablanca)* Curtiz and produced by Hal Wallis, became Errol Flynn's first contact with the Custer myth, but instead of playing old Hard Ass himself, he "portrayed" Custer's equally flamboyant adversary, Confederate cavalier Jeb Stuart—complete with refined Australian accent.[4] It was the hideously undashing, second-string lead Ronald Reagan who got to be Custer this time, graduating from West Point in 1854 along with Stuart and some other Civil War "names" and going to Kansas with Flynn to fight crazy old John Brown (Raymond Massey) and what seems like his small army of abolitionist renegades. The real Custer was antiabolition until he saw slavery's effects first-hand while on duty in the South. But Reagan's Custer, planted by hack writer Robert Buckner to represent the presumed Northern point of view, gripes mildly about slavery not being especially nice only to be told by Stuart that Brown is going about things the wrong way and that the South will take care of the problem "in its own time and in its own way." This exceedingly polite way of saying "we'll run the nigger ourselves" is followed by an astounding revelation: the South is just about to get rid of slavery anyway and would do it a lot faster if those pesky Northerners would just leave well enough alone.[5] By such boot-licking hocus-pocus Wallis and Buckner doubtless hoped to ease whatever guilt their Dixie audience might have over slavery (probably none to begin with) and succeed ın once again blaming everything on the damnyankees, who were not so sensitive since their side hadn't lost the Civil War.

This thoroughly loathsome film did stop just short of advocating black slavery as a positive good, but almost the only authentic chattels we are allowed to meet are a pop-eyed family of stereotypes led by Hattie McDaniel; after gallant Southron Stuart saves the darkies from a burning abolitionist stronghold, they announce their firm intention of returning to the ole plantation where their massa can watch over them. The climax comes with Brown's famous 1859 raid on the Harper's Ferry arsenal (in which Lieutenant Jeb Stuart actually did play a part); after Flynn personally vanquishes Brown at sword's point as though still playing Captain Blood, the abolitionist leader is hanged, but lest the audience file out depressed, we quickly dissolve to a happy ending, namely Flynn's marriage to Olivia de Havilland. (Stuart's death in 1864, from a bullet fired by one of Custer's troopers, is decidedly not foreshadowed.) Brown's body lay a-molderin,' but the lies went marching on.[6]

They Died with Their Boots On—subsequently and with some understatement described by Raoul Walsh as "a romanticized biography"—was the first movie pretending to illustrate Custer's adult life from cadet days to apotheosis. Now Flynn would have a chance to impose his accent on Jeb Stuart's Michigan adversary, who, of course, hadn't looked quite so handsome as Flynn, but did share with the actor the boyishness, recklessness, panache, and charisma that made both men appealing figures to their contemporaries. With such a star insuring a worthwhile return, the spectacle lacked only Technicolor, but the money might better have been spent on some of the Bugs Bunny cartoons Warners made so well.

After Flynn, despite his charming penchant for disobeying orders, manages to graduate one year early from the Point,[7] he becomes a general when a harried War Department clerk sends him a brigadier's commission by mistake, and immediately sets about trouncing Jeb Stuart (not played by Ronald Reagan) at Gettysburg. The Rebels surrendering, Custer finds peace just too dull; "he's been drinking—much more than he knows," says wife Libbie (Olivia De Havilland). Soon Ned Sharp (Arthur Kennedy), earlier seen annoying Flynn as a fictitious fellow cadet and cavalry officer and now a fictitious representative of the "Western Railroad and Mining Company," approaches Custer and urges him to lend his name to some dubious business enterprises—this because, as Custer mutters and as any screenwriter could tell you, that name "means something." Declining this offer, Custer is saved from the DTs only when he gets command of the Seventh and teaches it to sing "Garryowen." The controversial Washita fight is not shown.

Who should then turn up but that scoundrel Sharp? His father highly placed in The Company, Sharp peddles guns to the redskins and whiskey to Custer's men; the general responds by beating him up for the third or fourth time in the movie (Ah! What a man!), afterwards telling him that glory is better than mere money because "you can take it with you." Sharp is unrepentent.

At a horseback summit conference with the great chief Crazy Horse (Anthony Quinn, having jumped from the Cheyenne to the Sioux tribe), Custer listens as the chief generously offers to give up *all* Sioux lands, save for the sacred Black Hills. Custer gives his word and an unusually responsive Congress passes the treaty pronto. But Custer has reckoned without the dastards of The Company, who start a (false) rumor of a gold strike so that miners will pour in and force the government to annex the Hills for exploitation purposes. Custer testifies as to their dark plotting, but it's all hearsay, which, he is told, is acceptable only in the case of a "dying declaration." After bursting into President Grant's office to complain, Custer goes reluctantly out West to fight the hostile Plains tribes, including the Shoshone—who actually fought *with* the Army against the hostiles in 1876. (Walsh later said he wanted *Boots* to treat the red men favorably, but, like many another, he ends up tossing tribal names around like so many Indian clubs.)

Custer marches out with the regiment after first kidnapping Sharp, who had hoped that the Company-provoked Indians would get rid of the Boy General for him; realizing that the redskins will wipe out Terry's column unless lured away, he leads a suicidal saber charge. During a lavishly financed battle, with Flynn flipping Indians over his shoulder like a judo expert, Sharp is shot and has a change of the heart he's apparently just been plugged through. "Maybe you were right," he gasps, ". . . about glory." The Indians gallop forward in their final charge, Crazy Horse personally shoots Custer, and the hostiles ride off without even bothering to loot the dead. Have the white heavies triumphed over our golden boy?

Perish the thought; as we soon learn, Custer had left behind a letter revealing all, and even though the evidence is still hearsay, it naturally counts as a dying declaration and therefore indisputable proof of everyone's guilt. Mrs. Custer intimidates chief villains Sharp, Sr. and Mr. Romulus "Taipe" (Belknap) into throwing in the towel and then says that the Grant administration must protect the Indians' right to exist in their own country. Responds General Sheridan conveniently, "I have the authority to answer that from the administration—from the president himself." So everything works out just swell in approximately thirty-seven seconds of dialogue, and (as with other Last Stand myths) a greater good comes out of the hero's sacrifice, even ignoring the salvation of Terry's column.[8] "Come, my dear," says Sheridan, as the music swells. "Your soldier won his last fight, after all."

In his commentary for the Raoul Walsh segment of his 1973 series *The Men Who Made the Movies* (narrated by Cliff Robertson), critic Richard Schickel defended such cleaning and pressing on the grounds that "it is not history as it was, but history as it should have been. It is all honor and glory." Tempting, but carrying this argument to its logical conclusion one might find Custer winning at the Little Bighorn: even the most tolerant would probably cavil, but how far does one go? And please, no more nonsense about "myth" and "legend"; such Western tales frequently tell us much about ourselves, but

Flynn achieves his apotheosis in *They Died with Their Boots On*. (Museum of Modern Art/Film Stills Archive)

even from the entertainment standpoint are usually inferior to the truth. Custer, like MacArthur or Patton, is more interesting with the warts on, and in any case the story would have proved equally exciting and absurd had the names been changed—something Bosley Crowther suggested the moviegoer do for himself, muttering "John Doe" every time a historical personage was mentioned.

Revisionist influence was evident in the four page spread of period photos and publicity stills *Life* headed "Custer's Last Stand—'They Died with Their Boots On' Glorifies a Rash General": "George Armstrong Custer, who was not one of America's best generals, was cut out to be a swashbuckling movie hero. . . . It all makes for a good show, except it is a half hour too long. Custer himself was enough of a showman to cut his life dramatically short."

Custer lay mercifully dormant during World War II, when Hollywood was more concerned with slaughtering Germans and Japanese than redskins. *Boots* had fit in very well with the prewar industry's period of emphasis on patriotism and the military services, but now you could simply go ahead and show our boys fighting the present-day Axis threat rather than glorify them with peacetime service films or historical epics.

After the war, he was back, but with a difference: the last of the cavaliers was almost washed up and a new villain had emerged. This was partly attributable to the adoption of a revisionist viewpoint and partly to the fact that Custer, as the only Indian Wars general known to the public, had a symbolic and presumably monetary value even when presented negatively. In, for instance, Sidney Salkow's 1954 *Sitting Bull*, Douglas Kennedy's Custer was the Injun hater who tried to stop Injun-loving Army officer Dale Robertson from effecting a treaty with the Sioux; after war is provoked, he rides to a well-deserved death and gets an arrow in his chest. Other films employed the same Custer-as-devil formula with no attempt at either historical reality or subtlety—and even Walt Disney, staunch defender of the blandly wholesome, got into the act. The former hero must have been a very safe target indeed.

Disney's 1958 *Tonka*, subsequently shown on the Disney TV show as *A Horse Called Comanche*, was supposed to be the true story of Comanche, a horse belonging to the Seventh's Captain Miles Keogh and the well-known "only survivor" of the Last Stand. (He was actually the only horse left alive on the field, since the Indians captured many of the cavalry's mounts.) As the horse didn't really have much of a story—one shot and one subtitle had sufficed for Francis Ford's 1912 *Custer's Last Stand*, which mistakenly showed the horse fleeing the battlefield entirely—an invented narrative was presented as fact. Though Custer did die with his hair cut short, Sal Mineo played the Indian youth White Bull, who captures the horse wild before the cavalry capture it from the Sioux; attempting to retrieve it, White Bull gets captured, too and is hauled before Custer (Britt Lomond), a thorough heavy who calls him a "dirty redskin," personally manhandles him, and threatens to torture him if he doesn't tell all he knows. But White Bull and Comanche are finally united in a rather queasy Happy Ending right after the massacre. Fun for the whole family.

Not content with one attack on Custer, Sidney Salkow struck again in 1965, using stock footage from his previous cheapie to make an even shoddier film he called, with fine deference to Indian sensibilities, *The Great Sioux Massacre*. It begins during Major Reno's "court martial" [*sic*], the narrative unfolding through flashbacks by Darrin McGavin as Captain "Benton"; somebody must have been too lazy to write "ee." This time Custer (Phil Carey) starts out as an okay guy, but then has a conversation with a shyster in a business suit who hints that if Custer were to slaughter some Sioux in a new Indian war, he could be a big hero and become the Great White Father in Washington. A swell idea, thinks Custer, and deliberately provokes the hostilities that end with his being shot with another arrow.

In 1967, Twentieth Century-Fox planned a $10 million Custer epic, to be Fred Zinnemann's first Western since he had won an Oscar for *High Noon*. "Our concept," he told Richard Zanuck, "is of a newsreel of the period," and, on hearing that Zanuck was considering filming in Mexico, remarked, with the true fervor of a naturalized citizen, "It's outrageous, shooting a great American folk legend in a foreign country." But he still had some rather strange ideas about casting. For one thing, he wanted to use English actors to "raise the whole tone of the acting and break up the clichés of Western acting." For another, having already won assent from Fox to have Japanese superstar Toshiro Mifune play Crazy Horse, he wanted another Oriental to play Sitting Bull, explaining, "It'll maintain an ethnic balance, Dick." According to John Gregory Dunne's *The Studio:*

> A stricken look crossed Zanuck's face. "Jesus, Freddy," he said, "you want us ostracized by the American Indian Association? [*sic*] Those are the two biggest heroes in the history of Indians. And you want Japs to play both of them?"

Despite Zinnemann's talk of newsreels, his "folk legend" reference somehow makes it seem doubtful that the movie would have been more than another piece of fictitious "legendry." In any event his zeal came to naught, and all that Fox produced for 1967 was an ABC-TV series which, even before its premiere, was loudly decried by Indian organizations who felt that Custer was not at all a suitable subject for a weekly adventure show. "If the network felt it was doing something detrimental to the Indians of America," said one ABC flak-catcher sweetly, "obviously the show would never be put on the air." Obviously. ABC producer Frank Glicksman carefully explained that Custer "lends himself to the TV medium" (meaning that he had a name likely to make money for Glicksman and his associates) and that the general was a "much maligned man," which was certainly true.

A. A. Hopkins-Duke, Kiowa director of the Tribal Indian Land Rights Association, got so steamed up that he just had to malign Custer some more. "General Custer was the Indian's worst enemy," he raged. "Custer endorsed a policy of genocide and massacred village after village of Indians." This, of course, was not true, but it sounded good. ABC went ahead anyway (in a misguided attempt to grab the youth market, Custer's long hair and rebellious ways were made selling points), and was defeated not by offended pressure groups but by poor ratings, which sent the series into the discard and its previously unknown star, Wayne Maunder—one of the better screen Custers—back to the ranks, though he would later star in the film of Irving Wallace's *The Seven Minutes* (1971). Perhaps just to show how little it cared for the feelings of the Indian population (despite Richard Zanuck's sensitive comments about "Japs"), Fox had three episodes tacked together for theatrical release as *The Legend of Custer* (1968), which for obvious reasons was one Custer movie lacking a big Last Stand sequence.

One that did have one was Robert Siodmak's 1968 *Custer of the West;* filmed on the plains of Spain and patriotically premiered on July 4, it was originally a 146-minute Cinerama epic, pared down to 120 minutes for theatrical release and only restored to full length for broadcast on ABC ten years later. Despite its close resemblance to nothing in history, this is probably my own favorite Custer movie, if only for its slightly more "adult" approach. Robert Shaw, putting in a vivid performance and making a partly successful attempt to suppress his English accent, begins his post-Appomattox career as a stern, unboyish Boy General and rather unsympathetic figure who, in obedience to General Sheridan's (Lawrence Tierney) dictum that "the only good Indian is a dead Indian,"[9] does his bit toward conquering the West for the benefit of materialistic white expansionists; even Sheridan himself, however, ends by having doubts about the course of empire and expressing sympathy for its victims. Clearly writers Bernard Gordon and Julian Halevy were not afraid to grant Custer a dash of complexity and less than sterling moral stature, without reducing him to a secondary role and setting up some other white character as protagonist. It is unfortunate that they did not explore his personality within the framework of historical events instead of constructing a ramshackle, unchronological structure out of the Black Hills gold rush, the Washita and some other wrongly portrayed events tacked together with sundry fictions.

The movie really starts going soft when Custer embarks on a one-man crusade before Congress to denounce not only corrupt traders, but also the general trend of westward expansion, and goes even softer when he is turned into Mr. Anachronism. This is an almost sure-fire way of gaining audience sympathy, whether the man who's outlived his time is a boy general, a gunfighter, or an Indian in the process of becoming a Vanishing American: the Western, dealing with a frontier that starts dying as soon as it feels the tread of a white explorer, is naturally the most elegiac of all genres. After Custer has fallen out of favor by dropping brother Orvil's name at the hearings, his wife (Mary Ure) arranges an opportunity to get some favorable headlines by endorsing an armored, Gatling-armed railway car destined to be adopted by the War Department anyway. But he refuses even after being told that it will replace the horse and that "cavalry is dead." (What if the Indians just keep clear of the tracks?) Shaw's response, inconsistent with his behavior earlier in the film, would be unlikely even for a romantic like Custer, who actually considered dragging Gatlings along to the Little Bighorn before deciding they would slow his march: "War isn't just killin'," he growls. "It's a contest, a man against a man. . . . If this is the future I don't want any part of it." When Elizabeth asks where that leaves him, he replies, "With the Indians."

Prior to the Last Stand, Custer rides ahead with his detachment and tries to talk the Indians out of it by telling them that their day of independence and glorious war is past. But the Sioux chief decides to have a last fling for old times sake. The redskins ride in a tight merry-go-round circle around the soldiers and soon only Custer himself, saber in hand, is left standing in the ring of dead, à la Flynn. The chief offers to let him go free, but Custer, perhaps remembering what Sheridan had told him about dead men making better legends, existentially forces them to kill him.

Custer is left unsupported since Major Reno (Ty Hardin), whose detach- ment is safely in reserve, refuses to go to his aid, telling Benteen (Jeffrey Hunter) that Custer got "just what he wanted" by charging to his doom, and adding: "You might say he's luckier than you or me." (Western characters are sometimes suffocatingly self-conscious concerning their own legend.) It is not exactly clear whether Reno, a somewhat unsavory character as represented here, refuses to fight because he knows that Custer's plan is doomed or because he is a disloyal poltroon; the ads seemed to favor the latter view, describing him as "behind Custer all the way—knife in hand!" Either way, Reno's closest male relative, grandnephew Charles Reno, charged in a suit filed with the New York State Supreme Court that *Custer of the West* had depicted his Uncle Marcus as "a coward, as a drunkard, as an immoral person, as an incompetent officer, as a traitor, as a criminal, and as a murderer" and thus brought him "into public scorn, scandal, infamy, contempt, and obloquy among his friends, neighbors, employers and acquaintances." Reno sought damages from Cinerama and Security Pictures Inc. to the tune of $25 million, which, of course, he didn't get.[10]

Thomas Berger's *Little Big Man*, published in 1964, was a picaresque epic novel of the Old West "introduced" by an effete Western buff, who identifies what follows as the taped memoirs of one Jack Crabb—a very old man who, dismissing the claims of all those "nuts or plain liars" who sought the honor for themselves,[11] insists that *he* is the only white survivor of Custer's Last Stand. Berger's thrust was broadly comic, but the novel's settings and chronology both seemed reasonably authentic once one had accepted the presence of the hero and the essential looniness of the conceit: "I can certify," says Jack's imaginary Boswell, "that whenever Mr. Crabb has given precise dates, places and names, I have gone to the available references and found him frighteningly accurate—when he can be checked at all." When he can't be checked, anything goes, whether it be Crabb outwitting Bill Hickok in a showdown or a carefully caricatured Custer going mad during his last fight, and the self-proclaimed Man of Letters is finally unable to decide whether Jack Crabb was "the most neglected hero in the history of this country or a liar of insane proportions."

In 1970 Arthur Penn tried to turn this unlikely material into a message picture after the manner of Stanley Kramer, with lamentable results.

"It challenges the notion that the heroes of America are the ones you read about in the history books," proclaimed Penn righteously. "It challenges the glorification of the gunfighter and the simple proposition that the cavalry was the good guys and the Indians the bad guys. It exposes the rotten morality of commercialism." Since any number of Westerns had already done this (see *The Man Who Shot Liberty Valance*, *The Gunfighter*, and yes, even *Sitting Bull*), one might assume that there was no point in making the movie and that Penn was "challenging" nonexistent windmills to mortal combat. But one would be wrong, for he had a greater goal: he wanted white America to know just how evil it was and had always been, and most of all, how evil George Custer and his Seventh Cavalry were.

Penn's basic error lay in trying to fashion from Berger's novel a didactic propaganda piece not about some burning social issue, but about some historic injustices of the previous century presumed to have allegorical value. Screenwriter Calder Willingham compounded the offense by grossly distorting all the real-life events depicted in the novel so that the whole "historical" aspect of the film—supposedly the project's *raison d'être*—lost any limited meaning it may otherwise have had.

Rejecting the simple proposition that the cavalry was the good guys and the Indians the bad guys, Penn substitutes the deep and complex proposition that the Indians were the good guys and the cavalry the bad guys. The snotty young "historian" who interrogates the makeup-aged Dustin Hoffman in the prologue uses the word "genocide" to describe U.S. policy toward the Indians. When Crabb registers bewilderment at this new-fangled word, he quickly explains to the old buzzard (and to us) that genocide means "the near-extermination of a people. That's practically what we did to the Indians."[12]

Although Penn and Willingham might have wished that it were so, and despite the fashionable use of the term by those who are ignorant of (or simply ignore) the realities of Indian warfare, that's not what "we" did to the Indians. Had it even attempted to exterminate the red men, the army would logically have forced almost every Indian in the country into war, and as Western enthusiast and scholar Don Russell has written: "Had that been so, the U.S. Army, limited to 25,000 enlisted men during most of the period of wars in the Far West, should have had a Custer massacre a day in opposing the 250,000 Indians of Indian Bureau count." One authority gives the number of army-Indian fights from 1789 to 1898 (excluding 21 during the War of 1812, 1 during the Mexican War, and 295 during the Civil War) as 1,240, with army casualties 2,125 killed; examining the most reliable estimates of enemy dead available, Russell thought it "improbable that more than 3,000 Indians were killed in all of the U.S. Army's fights. Even if all the wildest claims be taken at face value, the total would not exceed 6,000." But having floored us with his *j'accuse*, Penn must try to prove it—first by showing us the dead women and children resulting from an unnamed and fictitious attack on a Cheyenne village early in the film (this serves no real plot function), and then, halfway through *Little Big Man*, with the first of his big action sequences.

Some time after we have been introduced to Richard Mulligan's buffoonish Custer, a sergeant at a Seventh Cavalry encampment, having received word that a small band of Cheyenne is located conveniently "down the river" (terribly obliging, these victims), rides off with some mangy, subhuman troopers to wipe out everyone there, the sergeant giving orders that women and children be spared "if possible" and then charging in to be among the first in slaughtering the innocent. No such massacre was ever committed by the Seventh; the scene's inspiration was apparently the novel's description of a Cheyenne attack on the encroaching U.P. railway, foiled by Major Frank North and his famous Pawnee scouts, who chase the Cheyenne back to where their women and children are fleeing with their camp baggage and kill a few noncombatants "despite what North could do to stop it." This obviously wouldn't have made us feel all that guilty, so Penn merely has a few Pawnee

Little Big Man: **the Washita attack.** *(Movie Star News)*

(never employed by Custer) guide the soldiers to their prey and assist them in their bloody work—not that they need much help, since the Cheyenne just run aimlessly about and never think of shooting back. At no time are we enlightened as to just *why* the soldiers are intent on committing "genocide" against the Cheyenne and not the Pawnee, nor why the latter are acting as the soldiers' allies; what makes things especially confusing is that early in the film we are shown a massacred settlers' wagon train and told that some Pawnee were responsible. To Penn, apparently, the sheer nastiness was more important than any question of motivation or logic.

Little Big Man: a less than heroic Last Stand. (Museum of Modern Art/Film Stills Archive)

Having established the malevolent nature of the cavalry with a massacre that never occurred, Penn pounds his point home with sledgehammer finesse some fifteen minutes later by way of an artistic "re-creation" of the fight on the Washita. Berger's description of that event (which, I should add, is inaccurate in some details and never adequately explains the circumstances resulting in the attack; he erred greatly in saying that the Indians were on their "reservation" at the time) and his comments elsewhere in the novel reveal some awareness of the nature of village attacks. But said description surely held few charms for Penn and Willingham: it just didn't make the cavalry come out *badly* enough. So they went ahead and faked their own version.

After Custer's troopers, who appear to number seventeen or so, ride leisurely into the peaceful, snowbound village to the music of the regimental band, they again find killing everyone in sight a remarkably easy job. Any notion of "battle," even a one-sided one, can be safely discarded since once again the Indians are too scared and/or stupid to do anything but dash about like decapitated hens. The bluecoats can therefore take their own sweet time about riding by the tipis torch in hand and setting them on fire with the Indians inside. (One woman runs out with clothes aflame, ripping them off before she's shot and adding a dash of nudity to the violence). The slaughter draws to a close as the camera cuts from one dead Cheyenne face to another in extreme closeup and "Garryowen"—music to massacre by?—swells ironically on the sound track.

Presiding over the butchery is, of course, Custer, growling in improbable and un-Custerian fashion that the Indian women are of the utmost importance because "they breed like rats!" His motive unexplained to animal lovers, Custer then orders the slaughter of the Indian ponies, handily stored in a regular log corral.

If Penn were really so intent on educating us as to the atrocity of the Washita attack, he might have shown it as it really happened instead of palming this lurid set piece off on an unsuspecting public. A filmmaker wishing to condemn Harry Truman for the Hiroshima or Nagasaki bombings might easily do so by dramatizing the facts; it would not be necessary to show Truman operating a Nazi death camp while clad in the black uniform of the Schutzstaffel. In his 1975 dual biography *Crazy Horse and Custer* (one of the more objective books on the Boy General, if sometimes falling prey to easily avoided errors of fact), Stephen E. Ambrose refused even to pass judgment on the Washita incident:

> Despite the hundreds of books by Indian lovers denouncing the government and making whites ashamed of their ancestors, and despite the equally prolific literary effort on the part of the defenders of the Army, here if anywhere is a case where it is impossible to tell right from wrong.
>
> But we can tell truth from falsehood. . . . Custer was many things, but he was no Nazi SS guard shooting down innocent people at every opportunity.
>
> History is not black or white nor is it propaganda. History is ambiguous, if told honestly. It is hard enough to figure out exactly what happened and why; it is impossible to play God and judge the right and wrong of a given action, even the Washita.

One may easily disagree with Mr. Ambrose's belief that we should refrain from making moral judgments on such controversial events; the filmmaker may feel *obliged* to proclaim his stand for or against. But I do think that, if a film does depict such an event with intent to "educate" us, it *should* try to show "exactly what happened" insofar as possible, whether the deed in question is condemned or upheld. As things stand it's hard to get upset over an "historic wrong" that exists only in the minds of a writer and director— unless, of course, you don't know any better.

Penn was reasonably successful in conning the general public as well as an assortment of critics, some of whom were acquainted with histories which condemned the Washita attack and thus satisfied themselves that Penn had indeed revealed the truth of history. After witnessing the conduct of the sadistic Seventh, the well-conditioned audience usually cheered lustily as the Indians rushed forth to wipe out Custer's men—certainly not the reaction of one reading Berger's Little Bighorn section, in which most of the doomed characters are treated sympathetically (even Custer has a *few* good points), but clearly what the bloodthirsty Penn intended. No doubt he thought of the Last Stand as a proper comeuppance for the Washita and thus an event to be applauded. But unless you believe the only good trooper's a dead one, this view has its drawback when applied to those who died with Custer, since only a handful had actually been at that action eight years before—and none, of course, in Penn's invented down-the-river bloodbath.

While caricaturing Custer as blind, arrogant, and finally quite mad, Berger was careful to keep his major activities "historical" up until the actual battle begins; the accuracy is a vital part of the joke. Only during the Last Stand does Custer go absolutely bonkers, talking to dead men and quoting at length from his memoirs as arrows darken the sky. Before the end comes Custer recovers (more or less) and assumes a pose worthy of the finest military martyr, firing at the Indians with studied coolness while clutching his personal guidon; then he is hit and falls with arms outflung as though crucified. The cynical Crabb, who'd previously thought to kill the "son of a bitch" in revenge for the Washita, recalls: "I had finally accepted that fact that he was great—and he sure was, don't let anybody ever tell you different, and if you don't agree, then maybe something is queer about your definition of greatness. . . . He had impressed me, dying the way he did. He had worked out a style and he stuck to it."

Although Penn had in his wisdom pronounced the real Custer to have been "right out of his gourd" for attacking so many Indians (presumably all of Custer's defenders must be crazy too), he was not content to have him follow his historic battle plan. Instead, Custer uses Jack Crabb, whom he regards as a renegade, as his "reverse barometer": when Crabb tells him the proper course of action, Custer does precisely the opposite. (For his part the suicidal Crabb, making further voice-over reference to Custer's nonexistent "hatred of Indians," *wants* to kill all of Custer's men, even if he has to die with them.) The resultant fight, with a few bluecoats standing off scattered horseback Indians, resembles Custer's Last Skirmish more than anything else.

The nonhistorical aspects of Berger's Little Bighorn are also changed in accordance with someone's strange ideology; the novel's Last Stand scene, which weirdly glorified Custer's death even as it was satirized, was obviously too subtle for all those unenlightened lowbrows in the movie houses. Penn has Custer rave wildly, but denies him Berger's "legendary" death and doesn't let him impress anyone, least of all Crabb: while trying to kill Jack, he is interrupted by two arrows (sigh) entering his back in gory, unromantic close-up. While Berger's Crabb (who, if you're wondering, is saved by a Cheyenne acquaintance after shooting several Indians, something he's not allowed to do in the movie) is at pains to say that "there wasn't no cowards," Penn shows the evil sergeant cowering in fear as a righteous red man prepares to kill him. A truly happy climax.

The one-hundredth anniversary of the Last Stand, almost as though Custer himself had planned it, happened to coincide with the year of our

Bicentennial. But it received surprisingly little publicity, possibly because the National Park Service, in evident fear of Indian trouble, took steps to minimize attendance at the actual commemorative ceremonies. Several important factual works on Custer were published that year, as well as Colonel Gordon C. Jones's inadequately researched and pathetically written novel *The Court-Martial of George Armstrong Custer*. "This is a fantasy which needs no apology," ran the author's prologue. But he was wrong.

Jones's ostensible purpose was to dramatize what might have happened had Custer survived his wounds, but all the events he fantasized seem among those least likely to have happened. The promising trial format serves only as a dreary soapbox from which the author can abuse Custer with just about every charge ever made against him (whether they are true or believable doesn't seem to matter) and include a mass of defamatory testimony both irrelevant and immaterial as well as suspect. One might expect Custer to be a major player in these Perry Masonic doings, but he is reduced instead to a minor cartoon figure barely more credible than the caricature of a caricature in Penn's *Little Big Man*, with whom he shares a common madness. Jones's frenzied swipes at Custer fell upon his immediate family as well: Libbie Custer is unchivalrously termed a "bitch," and even the couple's love letters are dragged in and criticized. At the end Custer is irrelevantly revealed to have been impotent, in explanation, I presume, of the fact that he and Libbie had no children. (Or did Jones see Custer's saber solely as a phallic symbol? Hmmm . . .) The whole enterprise was as silly, trashy, and tawdry as could be—perfect for prime-time television.

NBC's 1977 *Hallmark Hall of Fame* production exceeded my most sanguine expectations, reducing its subject matter to the same level of titillating idiocy (though not social irresponsibility) as had ABC's *The Trial of Lee Harvey Oswald* earlier that year. The controversy over the Little Bighorn fight—which, of course, cannot be adequately discussed in only part of a two-hour drama—is easily resolved by having the waxy Custer (James Olsen) go stark raving mad during the trial, which nevertheless ends in acquittal. Few of the other characters behave like human beings either, least of all Mrs. Custer (a well-cast Blythe Danner), who casually and for no rational reason reveals her husband's impotence to the officer who had prosecuted him! The Sioux and Cheyenne were more merciful: they merely killed Custer, while it was left for TV to publicly castrate him.

A hell of a way to sell Christmas cards.

Probably the best movie dealing with Custer is one in which he's never mentioned—Ford's 1948 *Fort Apache*, adapted by former critic Frank S. Nugent from Frank Warner Bellah's story "Massacre."[13] The icy martinet Colonel Thursday (Henry Fonda) disregards the advice of subordinate Captain York (John Wayne) by ordering an insane mounted saber charge in column of fours into a canyon full of waiting Apaches, who—inflicting losses rather excessive for an Indian fight—wipe out most of his regiment, save for a small detachment left to guard the supply train. Thursday has a chance to save his own neck during the fight, but instead, like the Custer of the Whittaker saga, chooses to ride into the valley of death and perish with his men in a gallant last stand.

The film then leaps ahead some years and we see York, who had not participated in "Thursday's Charge," defending the lie of the glorious Thursday to some newspapermen because the now reorganized regiment should have a hero in its recent past. But, more importantly, York has himself come to respect Thursday for his deed and even resemble him in some ways.[14] Instead of simply recycling the myth, *Fort Apache* shows us how it works, though of course Ford intensifies the myth's power, as had Whittaker, by making the death a deliberate sacrifice. A valiant demise atones for a multitude of sins, and the hero's faults are forgotten, forgiven, or swept under the rug as he is transformed into a legendary figure possessing—at least for the time being—glory in defeat. As Bruce Rosenberg wrote in his study of the Little Bighorn's relation to other mythic Last Stands:

> I think that most Americans feel that Custer is, in some way, however vague, a hero; and this feeling will persist because of the circumstances of his death, despite what we think we now know about the man, despite our compassion for and guilt over the Indians, because the story of the Last Stand seems to reach imperceptibly deep into some profound and impalpable region of our psyche, and there it is united with those impulses that aroused our grandparents, and theirs before them.

Perhaps that's why so many have worked so diligently at portraying Custer as fool and villain: this particular Western mystique is indeed a powerful one. Logic rarely enters the picture, of course, but what do you expect from a legend that goes so much deeper?

WHY SOLDIER BLUE?

Fort Apache was the first film of an unofficial trilogy, directed by Ford, inspired by Bellah's stories of the U.S. Cavalry, and starring John Wayne, the next two being *She Wore a Yellow Ribbon* and *Rio Grande*. In spite of some historical errors, the films were not particularly "unrealistic," and there was even some talk about the dog's life of a trooper. But the treatment, especially in the sentimental, lushly Technicolored *Ribbon*, was deeply romantic, with a decided emphasis on the more glorious side of Indian campaigning. This picture of army life as seen through a nostalgic haze was, of course, incomplete, but at least Ford never claimed to be giving us a comprehensive history lesson instead of telling a story with a frontier setting. In later films he tended to concentrate on the less appealing aspects of the West's conquest, culminating in *Cheyenne Autumn*, which featured several villainous horse

John Wayne and ruggedly romantic cavalrymen prepare to charge in *She Wore a Yellow Ribbon*, John Ford's best-loved tribute to the Western horse soldier. (Museum of Modern Art/Film Stills Archive)

soldiers as well as sympathetic ones. At one point the fur-hatted cavalrymen are compared by a Polish sergeant to the Cossacks who ravaged his homeland, while a German-born captain (Karl Malden) conjures up in crude fashion memories of Nazi atrocities with his talk of "only following orders" in pursuing harsh policies toward Cheyenne prisoners. These prisoners later break out only to be shot down by soldiers killing brave and noncombatant alike.

In doing all this Ford was reflecting not only what might be taken as his own increasing pessimism concerning white civilization, but also the industry's growing tendency to inject an element of moral uncertainty into the Indian Wars film—an element which, I should add, had never been completely absent. Any movement toward "sympathetic" treatment for the red man, as in the 1950s, was bound to blur things: if the Indians are justified in their struggle the cavalry must inevitably appear in a less heroic light. The chief military character in such films, glib and superficial as most of them were, was nevertheless likely to have uncomfortable reservations about his job.

In an era during which many white Americans reveled in antimilitary sentiment and masochistically wallowed in self-hating guilt over the racial wrongs done by their ancestors, it was predictable that a new stereotype of the frontier soldier would emerge—that of the brass-buttoned sadist gleefully slaughtering the downtrodden aborigine. This stereotype, though popular in guilt-mongering literature of the period, never figured in many films at the time since the late sixties and early seventies were simply not prolific years when it came to movies about Indian fighting. But the prevailing ideological climate of 1970 did result in both *Little Big Man* and what was apparently intended as the last word in anti-Army films.

WHY

Why does 'SOLDIER BLUE' show, in the most graphic way
imaginable, the rape and savage
slaughter of American Indians by
American soldiers?
Why did Ralph Nelson, after
'Lilies of the Field' and 'Charly,'*
turn to a shockingly
different kind of story?

BECAUSE

it's true . . . and now, more
than ever, is the time
for the truth.

*Not to mention (and they were careful not to) his 1966 *Duel at Diablo*, a well-made action picture with heroes James Garner and Sidney Poitier helping more or less sympathetically portrayed cavalrymen kill Apaches.

More massacring in *Soldier Blue*: white liberal Candice Bergen is dragged away to safety so the evil soldiers can pour fire into the Cheyenne women and children. *(Movie Star News)*

That "now more than ever" jazz had something to do with "relevance" and with Vietnam. In accordance with Sam Peckinpah's dictum that "the Western is a universal frame within which it is possible to comment on today," what Nelson wanted to do was make an anti-Vietnam movie set in the Old West— much more profitable at the time than doing something *silly*, like making an anti-Vietnam war movie set in Vietnam. The message was roughly that of *Little Big Man*, the sole reason that then red-hot-radical Dotson Rader clutched it to his indignantly heaving bosom; one of the nicest things about the West is that it has myths for everybody, no matter what their politics.

Starting out what may be termed a guest review in the *New York Times* with a paragraph on the Sand Creek Massacre, the film's inspiration, Rader followed it with a description of the 1890 fight at Wounded Knee and managed to incorporate into its short length of eighty-nine words no less than ten serious errors of fact. After this scholarly dissertation, Rader told a waiting world that *Soldier Blue* had to be considered "among the most significant, the most brutal and liberating, the most honest American films ever made . . . a movie of great art and courage," adding that it attempted to "confront and break with the indecent complicity of the American film industry in a racist falsification of history; to destroy at last the phony myth of Cowboys and Indians, Good Guys and Bad Guys, which Hollywood has gleefully been embellishing and profiting from for half a century."*

Nelson and screenwriter John Gay *might* simply have told the true story of the events leading up to Sand Creek—possibly using as the basis for a screenplay Michael Straight's 1963 novel *A Very Small Remnant*, in its author's own opinion a work of fiction "not in opposition to fact"—and so come up with a historically valid and perhaps even interesting film. Instead, they took the perverse step of lifting the plot and main characters from Theodore V. Olsen's undistinguished Western novel *Arrow in the Sun* (in which the soldiers are the *good* guys), sticking a few antiarmy pronouncements into the dialogue and tacking onto the end a Sand-Creekish massacree by the fictitious "Eleventh Colorado Cavalry."

After the movie starts with a Cheyenne attack on a detachment of the aforesaid regiment, the only survivors are a white woman returned from living among the Indians, Cresta Lee (Candice Bergen), and young trooper Honus Gant (Peter Strauss). This is unfortunate since they are one of the least appealing couples ever to infest the screen: Bergen is a foul-mouthed flower child who's supposed to be from New York (Boston in the novel, but maybe New York's more "progressive") and really doesn't seem to be from anywhere, while Strauss is a dolt.

Soldier Blue is very informative. Upon first surveying the dismembered bodies of his late comrades, Strauss understandably goes into an emotional

---

*Curiously, nonguest *Times* critic Roger Greenspun seemed unaware that it had destroyed any such thing, concluding that "critics who admire the Western for its clear-cut moral values, for its firm distinction between good and evil, will no doubt applaud *Soldier Blue*." The rest of us, he added, might have some doubts.

"Murdering savages!" routine, but Bergen—a thoroughly callous and repulsive young lady—brushes off the deaths of twenty-one men as "a drop in the old bucket," and then proceeds to rave about white soldiers regularly sticking babies on their "long knives" (sabers) issued by the "bloodthirsty Army." Anyway, says she, the whites taught Indians to scalp and mutilate the dead, though the red men at least refrain from making tobacco pouches out of body parts. "You're lying," Private Gant keeps repeating—and in real life he'd be right. But in the movie he's just a dupe of the military-industrial complex refusing to face the grim facts.

Since Nelson's film was entirely devoid of art, courage, and much, much more, what we were left with was a tedious Wild West history lesson—which might have been a shade more endurable had the history been accurate. It seems to have had a poweful effect on Rader, however; he testified that "our kneejerk loyalty to the white troops dissipates into ambivalence and then into outrage, as we learn that it was the whites who taught the Indians to scalp . . . that it was the whites who dismembered bodies to make tobacco pouches from their parts."

Some people just can't believe that an Indian could think up *anything* on his own. The truth was that numerous tribes had been merrily scalping each other for hundreds of years before the white men arrived to corrupt the innocent natives; scalping was unknown to contemporary Europeans (though it had apparently been practiced by the ancient Scythians, among others), and it was the Indians who taught the whites to take hair. Some of them learned very well, and the scalping of Indians by white frontiersmen and soldiers was by no means uncommon. [15]

I am not sure just why Rader was so joyfully "outraged" over whites mutilating Indians; he would seem to be implying that it was all right for the red men to commit such acts, but that the whites ought to feel guilty. Perhaps the belief that the Indians learned such tricks from the whites had something to do with this. But I think that Rader and Gay and Nelson—much as the thought would have horrified them—were also expressing a philosophical outlook vaguely akin to that of Texas Ranger Jim Gillett, who wrote that it was common practice for his fellow Rangers and other whites to ply the knife in what was sometimes thought of as retaliation for Indian atrocities:

> Yet, notwithstanding all the crimes committed by Indians, it must be remembered that they were savages, and [that] is no reason why an enlightened nation or white people should mutilate the bodies of their fallen foes. To scalp a dead Indian is a barbarous and inhuman act and I am ashamed now to admit that I helped to scalp an Indian we rangers had killed. I sewed a part of his scalp onto my revolver holster and with the long hair hanging down almost to my knees, wore it around over the frontier. Now isn't that almost like a savage? Yet we thought nothing of it at the time, but as we grow old we grow in grace, and I have many times knelt down and prayed to God for his forgiveness.

The fact that scalping and other mutilations were universally applauded among, say, the Cheyenne (whereas many whites frowned on the practice despite its frontier popularity) would, of course, place a greater share of individual moral responsibility on the white scalper or mutilator than on the Indian brought up to think it natural. As Hoxie Neale Fairchild writes in his *The Noble Savage*, this was a premise accepted by some fiction writers as far back as Colonial times: "The Indian can be forgiven his cruelty, since he knows no better; but the European, who knows the right and chooses the wrong, is to be condemned."

Nelson rejects such intriguing moral questions for some more "now" melodrama of the most old-fashioned sort. At last Gant makes it back to his regiment and Cresta rides to the Cheyenne encampment, where she is reunited with the handsome, virile chief Spotted Wolf, played by Jorge Rivero. (All historical characters are conspicuous by their absence, as if someone were afraid that Chivington might sue.) Thus both white lovers manage to witness the big massacre.

The trusting Spotted Wolf rides out to parley bearing both a flag of truce and the national colors, which he promptly drops when the soldiers open fire; Old Glory is shortly thereafter churned into the dirt by the cavalry's hooves in an unpleasant countercultural or possibly symbolic image. What follows shows up Arthur Penn as positively squeamish; in the eloquent words of *Newsweek*'s S. K. Oberbeck: "The obsessive blood bath drips, squirts and splashes enough sadistic, slow-motion gore (children's heads and occasional limbs come whizzing by) to make Clint Eastwood chew his serape in envy." This fascination with the mechanical details of killing and dismemberment gave the special-effects men work and must have drawn in numerous Yahoos anxious to see the blood flow.[16] But its own excesses worked against its impact and failed to compensate for the superficial treatment given the murderers, one-dimensional villains whose pompous colonel regales the intended generation-gap audience with hard words about "young people today." They are utter *outsiders*, with whom the white viewer feels little connection, and guilt is converted into "outrage" requiring a scapegoat.

After the massacre, radicalized peacenik Gant, who's had some uncomplimentary things to say about the operation, is hauled off to an unspecified fate, while Cresta accompanies the few surviving noncombatant captives to an equally nebulous destiny. A spoken epilogue briefly describes the Sand Creek Massacre as though the preceding film had been a historical reproduction, gives the casualties as over 500 dead (an inflated figure derived from Chivington's own boastful reports, though 130 seems a more reasonable estimate) and repeats General Nelson A. Miles's characterization of the incident as "perhaps the foulest and most unjustifiable crime in the annals of America."

This would seem to undermine the film's theme of army bloodlust: if massacres such as Sand Creek were as common as *Soldier Blue* implied, why should Miles—who was, after all, a high-ranking general—single this one out for special denunciation? (Sand Creek was also denounced by three governmental investigatory bodies, two congressional and one military.) Nelson's inability to reconcile his view of history with the facts was to blame here, but Dotson Rader guessed that the epilogue was part of a foul plot by the film's backers to deprive the public of its guilt—through enabling them to see Sand Creek as exceptional, "a horrible mistake acknowledged as such by its perpetrators [sic]. It is there to allow them to dismiss Sand Creek, to forget that it was a forerunner in a line of American-directed massacres running from before the Civil War . . . through Dresden and Hiroshima into Vietnam. It is to make them forget that very little has been learned by us." The reader should try to remember that in referring to "us" Rader really meant all of (white) America with the exception of himself and whoever happened to agree with him.

Since the General Miles quote was authentic, though somewhat out of place in this fictional film, it would seem that to Rader some truths were more important than others, assuming, of course, that he was aware of its truth, which seems doubtful. Sand Creek became so infamous precisely because it *was* something of an exception, and to suggest otherwise in a cheap commercial ripoff begging acceptance as some sort of sociopolitical tract (or "excellent essay on historical truth," as George Fenin has inanely termed it) was to advance a countermyth as silly as it is revealing.

The massacre which inspired the film was, of course, not typical of U.S. military operations against American Indians before, during, or after the Civil War; indeed, although some commanders were overly aggressive, Western settlers often criticized the army for not being tough enough on the redskins. Taking into consideration instances in which noncombatants were deliberately or carelessly killed, it seems safe to say that most officers attempted to spare them and that most such deaths were accidental.[17] (This was of course small comfort to the victims.)

The worst atrocities against Western Indians were generally the work of civilians or short-term volunteers such as the men of the Third Colorado Cavalry who struck the Cheyenne at Sand Creek; hatred for the Indian was naturally greatest among those with the biggest stake in crowding him off his land and the most to fear from Indian raiders. Fortunately those who advocated the extermination of the red man (or some particular tribe thought to be troublesome or simply inconvenient) were often too busy to bother making the effort themselves instead of leaving the "Indian problem" in the army's lap and too inefficient to kill many Indians when they actually tried; their greatest success came in California, where the hapless natives often fell easy prey to murderous whites. In his thoroughly depressing *The Destruction of California Indians*, Robert H. Heizer informs us that though the national government did make some ineffectual efforts to protect the Indians and federal troops seemed "on the whole" to have acted with discipline and restraint, indiscriminate massacres by citizens of the Golden State and future movie capital, with attendant scalpings and mutilation, were "common." It seems a shame for the movies to pin so much blame on the soldiers; but I guess there's plenty to go around.

NOTES

1. In his 1976 *The Battle of the Washita*, Stan Hoig fails to mention Custer's statement even for purposes of refutation, instead making the odd charge, unsustained by any documentation, that Custer's men had orders "to kill anyone and everyone before them."

2. There was no evidence: it was simply *known* that Custer's men had died fighting "like tigers"; most Indian participants interviewed in subsequent years, though varying wildly in their stories, tended to comfort those who desired to believe in a stout struggle. In the 1931 *A Warrior Who Fought Custer*, translated by Dr. Thomas Marquis, the Cheyenne veteran Wooden Leg claimed that nearly all the soldiers had "gone crazy" and shot themselves or each other (presumably to avoid torture), but that the Indians had kept mum because they knew their white interrogators would be displeased. The late Cheyenne historian John Stands in Timber, who talked with many Indian veterans, discounts this in his *Cheyenne Memories* and says that Wooden Leg later "took back" his suicide stories. Marquis's challenge to the heroic Last Stand image was so shocking that the good doctor could not find a publisher for his own analysis of the battle during his lifetime, and *Keep the Last Bullet for Yourself*, which acquits Custer himself of all responsibility for the defeat, was finally published only in 1976.

3. Perhaps this was the reason Custer wasn't scalped, or perhaps it was pure chance. The most romantic explanation, which does have some Indian support, has it that the hostiles refrained from mutilating the remains because they respected him as a great chief and warrior, although most of them were unfamiliar with the soldier the Sioux called Long Hair. Take your choice.

4. Flynn ultimately made eight Warner Westerns and, unable to understand such casting, mockingly dubbed himself "the rich man's Roy Rogers." In only two films was his accent explained away: *Dodge City* (1939) had him as an Anglo-Irish adventurer who cleans up the town in 1872, and *Montana* (1950) as an Aussie sheepherder troubled by narrow-minded cattlemen.

5. This might have happened at one time, before radical abolitionists had helped drive the South into defending slavery as a positive good instead of apologizing for it. But by John Brown's heyday it was much too late. One might have expected Warners to duck such a "dangerous" topic altogether and send Custer and Stuart after some other foe.

6. You may wonder what the movie had to do with the Santa Fe Trail to the Southwest. Nothing, actually—but two comic-relief characters do lead a male chorus in a ditty called "Along the Santa Fe Trail," which justified both the title and a costly publicity excursion to Santa Fe, New Mexico, organized by Warners and the Santa Fe Railroad. A *New York Times* reporter noted that the local Indians were forced to "limit their conversation to 'ugh' and to 'Paleface wantum buy blanket?' . . . for fear of disillusioning Hollywood."

7. This, of course, contradicted completely *Santa Fe Trail*, made only a year previously and produced by the same man. Hal Wallis does not appear to have had a very high opinion of the public's memory, let alone its intelligence.

8. The Japanese heroic tradition, as opposed to its Occidental counterpart, more frequently celebrates the defeated hero whose death proves wholly useless, or even counterproductive, since as Ivan Morris writes in his *The Nobility of Failure*, his "single-minded sincerity will not allow him to make the manoeuvres and compromises that are so often needed for mundane success."

9. There is some doubt as to whether Sheridan actually made this statement—or, rather, "The only good Indians I ever saw were dead," which he allegedly made at a conference with some chiefs in 1869, after which it was honed down into the more familiar and serviceable form of the aphorism (also credited to General Sherman). Sheridan's brother Michael once denied that Little Phil had ever said such a thing. Maybe he did say it and was only kidding, since the remark certainly did not reflect his own philosophy or policy, hard-liner though he was.

10. In 1967 Charles Reno had been responsible for having the major's 1880 dishonorable discharge (the offense was "conduct unbecoming an officer") changed to an honorable one by the army's Board for Correction of Military Records; unfortunately the proceedings of this board produced mostly muddled testimony as to the facts of this case. Charges included drunken brawling and Peeping Tommery.

11. Some seventy-odd such gentlemen eventually cropped up. Curiously, the late Custer authority Dr. Charles Kuhlman believed that one of these, Frank Finkle, was a bona fide survivor.

12. Penn at least refrained from debasing this word (as was so common in that day) to signify any unpleasant thing that might happen to members of a minority group.

13. Another no-names derivation of the story was Arnold Laven's 1965 *The Glory Guys*, written by Sam Peckinpah, in which actual events in Custer's career were more closely paralleled.

14. Ford approved of covering up for such celebrities because it was "good for the country to have heroes to look up to." I of course disagree, particularly as we have so many heroes, sung and unsung, who need no whitewashing.

15. The posting of bounties for Indian scalps by various governments (like that of New York) during the Colonial period has led careless historians and others to claim without any proof that such commercial inducements were the origin of the custom. But further research would have revealed their error; the most convincing proofs are various pre-Columbian skulls bearing the unambiguous mark of the scalping knife. (On a few of these the bone had begun to heal, proving that the victim had been scalped while still alive; the loss of one's topknot was not always fatal and many victims survived, to go about thereafter with large areas of skin or skull exposed as mute testimony to their hair-raising experience—a facet of frontier life briefly depicted with grisly humor in *Western Union*.) From books the we-taught-the-Indians myth has passed into a number of movie and TV productions whose characters always talk as though they'd done research at their local library. James Fenimore Cooper's backwoods hero Natty Bumppo, variously known as Hawkeye, Deerslayer, Pathfinder, and Leatherstocking, always refused to take hair on the ground that God had intended the custom for "another race" and not for whites like himself. But in a 1977 TV version of *The Last of the Mohicans*, Hawkeye (Steve Forrest) assures the British Major Heywood in un-Cooperian fashion that scalping started in Europe. "Bone up on your history, Major," counsels he. The acting in such relevatory scenes is usually quite bad.

16. Nelson naturally defended his extravagance on the grounds of historical accuracy (even though the massacre had been wrenched from its true historical context) and insisted that his film had been a "moral lesson," presumably since he had bravely exposed massacres of innocent people as Bad Things and messy besides. Fortunately no one thus far has found it necessary to depict Indians slaughtering whites in such a voyeuristic manner, and I'd hate to think about what would be said of someone who tried.

17. One might reject this assessment by holding up the example of the Wounded Knee Tragedy, about which much balderdash has been written. But even James Mooney, a contemporary student of the battle who termed most of the many noncombatant deaths "unnecessary and inexcusable," wrote that the number of women and children slain was "no reflection on the officer in charge" since he had taken specific measures to guard *against* such an occurrence and had issued strict orders against the killing of noncombatants: "The butchery was the work of infuriated soldiers whose comrades had just been shot down without cause or warning." (In *The Last Days of the Sioux Nation* Robert Utley offers a reconstruction more favorable to the troopers.) General Miles convened a court of inquiry to probe both the killings and the regimental commander's behavior, but its criticism was confined to chiding him for improperly deploying his unit while attempting to disarm the Sioux.

ADDENDUM

A. I feel obliged to note that the more popular view of Sand Creek as an unforgivable slaughter has always been challenged by a minority of writers, who dispute the degree of "protection" offered the Cheyenne, the peacefulness of the Black Kettle's village, and the atrocities committed by soldiery. Evidence at the hearings was often contradictory, and even Chivington (a former Indian missionary!) does not appear to have been a complete Indian hater. Don Russell comments simply that "there is no proof that Chivington said or did anything to encourage atrocities—or to stop them."

B. One eyewitness to the Washita, scout Ben Clark, did testify that some women and children were deliberately killed—but also reported that Custer personally stopped this upon learning of it.

C. Recently examined evidence indicates that Custer may have had arrows through the testicles, along with a finger or two severed and a punctured eardrum. A curious anomaly presents itself here: if, as is theorized, eyewitnesses were moved to conceal these out of consideration for Mrs. Custer, they might have refrained from their total frankness concerning the condition of Tom Custer's body, recognizable only by a tattoo. Despite the finding of Custer's body on the hill, some believe he may have been killed or critically wounded early in the fight and then carried to the hill.

7
Diatribal Legends
or The Red and the Green

Hey, didn't I kill you twelve pictures ago?

JOHN WAYNE to Navajo chiefs
on the set of *McLintock* (1963)

At one time I did try to pin him to a category—"With which
people were you most at home?" He only shouted at me: "With
the warriors of the Silver Screen! Apaches in feathers, bathing
trunks under their breechclouts, Sioux in sneakers. Tonto, him
my brother!"

JOANNA GREENBERG,
"The Supremacy of the Hunza"

The supreme moment of the 1973 Academy Awards ceremony came when
Marlon Brando, rather than accept the Oscar he had won for *The Godfather,*
sent in his place one "Sasheen Littlefeather," otherwise known as Maria Cruze
and Miss Vampire, U.S.A. Miss Vampire appeared in colorful tribal regalia to
read Brando's written statement, which explained that he had refused his
award in protest against "the treatment of Indians by the film industry, on TV
and in movie reruns." Audience response was not enthusiastic.

Some of those who did not actually question using the Academy's ceremony
as a personal soapbox felt that Brando should have delivered his message in
person, instead of leaving somebody else to face the music. But it was
doubtless better than applauding the fall of Saigon or that old semi-Stalinist
Lillian Hellman, as later winners were to do. In denouncing the portrayal of
Indians by the white man's cinema, Brando was simply following the trail

blazed by such pioneers as that determined delegation of Shoshone, Arapahoe, Cheyenne, and Chippewa who, in 1911, demonstrated on the steps of the Capitol building in protest against the image of their race presented by silent films. That this particular trail ultimately leads nowhere should not be held against him.

Badly handled in Westerns generally, physical detail becomes especially suspect where real or alleged Indians are concerned. The usual attitude taken, consciously or not, has it that all Indians are pretty much the same despite whatever vast tribal differences may actually exist. The Hollywood concept of the well-dressed redskin, like the popular stereotype, resembles in the case of the man a painted warrior from one of the nomadic, buffalo-hunting Plains tribes such as the Sioux, Cheyenne, or Crow—beaded, buckskinned, and befeathered.

The feathered warbonnet is the item of Plains-culture costume which seems to turn up most frequently among other tribes, as in Walsh's *A Distant Trumpet* (1964); here they are worn, with other Plains items, by alleged Southwestern "Apaches," who never really went in for such display and dressed quite drably on the warpath.[1] Such mistakes might be attributed to the homogenizing tendency, but other items of "Indian" dress seem simple fabrications, like the skinny little headband that Sioux Sal Mineo sports in *Tonka:* this particular

A band of Sioux warriors, the best known of the Great Plains tribes, in garb that fits the usual conception of "Indian." Some have modified tribal costume with conspicuous items of white man's clothing. (Western History Collections, University of Oklahoma Library)

type of band appears to have been developed by nineteenth-century theater folk and adopted by the movies as a method by which Indian fright wigs could be kept in place or fake braids secured. They're good to stick feathers in, too.

The tribal grab bag includes hairstyles as well as headdress, and going below the neck would open up an even greater field for error spotting. But lack of space forbids. Suffice it to say that all such errors could be prevented with a minimum of effort. Infrequently, Indians with knowledge of the old days and/or portraying members of their own tribes have been permitted to inject some authenticity into the proceedings. But more often they have simply gone along with the pretense, if only because of economic need. On the rare occasions when technical advisors on Indian subjects have been employed, they have sometimes been ignored when their historical expertise failed to meet the movie Indian's peculiar requirements. Members of one tribe playing those of another may add to the confusion: in *The Searchers* some of the Comanches wear anachronistic bits of Navajo jewelry and all were in fact Navajos from Monument Valley, John Ford's favorite Western location.[2]

Less amusing than the outfits of movie Indians are the misuse and desecration of Indian customs, traditions, and ceremonies. Since this is another vast subject, I shall confine myself to a few of the more stupid and malicious examples.

The term "ghost dance" sounds just as dramatic as can be to the screenwriter, and so the ritual, or rather its name, has been exploited in several films. Historically, it was largely inspired by the Christian faith and widely adopted in the late 1880s by desperate reservation Indians, dancing to hasten the coming of a Messiah who would return to his red children their vanished way of life. White fears of an uprising among the Sioux ultimately resulted in the death of Chief Sitting Bull, several minor actions, and the carnage at Wounded Knee.

In Charles Marquis Warren's *Arrowhead* (1953) the term "ghost dance" is anachronistically dragged into the early 1880s, with the Apache Torriano (Jack Palance) bringing it to his people from somewhere in the East, where he's been educated white-style. It is, of course, presented as a dance of violent Indian rebellion. (The film was adapted from a novel by W. R. Burnett, who also wrote *Sergeants 3*, one of Frank Sinatra and Friends' expensive home movies, in which the ceremony is referred to as a dance of death and its participants gambol about a skull-covered altar.) Like a good many other Westerns, such as *The Outlaw Josey Wales*, this one also throws in a pseudo-aboriginal "blood brother" ceremony, of the type practiced by some African tribes and European secret societies, but by no American Indians with which I am familiar. Warren has the fearless white scout Bannion (Charlton Heston) force Torriano at gunpoint to mix his blood with Bannion's so that Torranio can let no other Indian but himself kill the paleface. But Heston finally breaks the Apache's red neck in a Homeric brawl and tells the other Injuns to vamoose back to their reservations.[3]

Hollywood Indians, not only with feathered bonnets, but also a fabricated "native" beaded headband for the young eyebrow-pencilled maiden. From *Oklahoma Jim*, a typically cheap Monogram programmer of the thirties. *(Movie Star News)*

Any Indian ritual seen in a film, such as the imaginary one from which writer-director Samuel Fuller's 1957 *Run of the Arrow* took its name, is likely to be either hoked-up or wholly fictitious. What made Elliot *(Cat Ballou)* Silverstein's *A Man Called Horse* (1970) the biggest such Indian hoax to date were the loud claims to authenticity made by its producers, who were extremely anxious to ballyhoo this aspect of the film even though both the costumes and the customs of the Sioux depicted (such as their alleged casting-out of useless old people to starve or freeze to death in confetti snowstorms) were mostly phony. Richard Harris, who was to repeat his role in *The Return of a Man Called Horse* (1976), played a captured English nobleman who, prior to marrying a Sioux "princess" and improbably becoming chief of the band,[4] undergoes their grueling sun dance (or Sun Vow, as the film terms it), which ritual was tastelessly exploited as the film's main selling point. Based, the prologue said, on descriptions by "George Catlin, Carl Bodmer and other eyewitnesses of the period," the ceremony had Harris pierced through the pectorals with rods to which cords were attached. He is then hauled up to hang suspended from the ceiling of an Indian earth lodge, spinning about while bathed in a shaft of light entering through the hole in the lodge roof. Picturesque to be sure, but about as much a Sioux ceremony as Harris's plastic pectorals were human flesh; it was, regrettably, nothing but a sacrilegious fraud.

While it does resemble in certain respects the most extreme form of the Sioux sun dance, "Gazing at the Sun Suspended," the ritual was actually patterned after the Mandan "O-ki-pa" ceremony—aimed partly at attracting buffalo to the land of the sedentary Mandan—and takes place in a Mandan earth lodge impractical for the nomadic Sioux. George Catlin, for one, had witnessed this ceremony, painted it, and described it in some detail, but the people at Fox ignored his words and saw only The Indian when they looked at his paintings.* Thus the Sioux in *Horse*, presenting a refreshing visual contrast to the usual movie routine, do dress more like "authentic" Indians— but not, for the most part, like the Indians of their own tribe.

Since just talking to some of the Sioux supposedly being represented in the film might have enlightened Silverstein and his associates as to this sacred, and by no means defunct, ritual (which, incidentally, was not undertaken as a tribal initiation ceremony, as shown in *Horse*), one is left with the unavoidable impression that they were striving less for authenticity than for a king-sized ripoff: all ya gotta do is take the most dramatic ritual you can find (or concoct) and exploit it as part of a "good show," all the while making your concoction *seem* authentic. If these people really did intend to portray the Sioux Indians as they were, they can only be described as bumblers on an epic scale. Nevertheless, the film's publicity managed to convince almost everyone. The *New York Daily News* praised *Horse* for its "unflinching realism," while *Film Quarterly* remarked: "The attention to carefully researched details of setting, costume, and ceremony produces some extraordinarily beautiful images . . . almost like an anthropological document from another time." A bit more skepticism might have been in order here.

If critics can, with the help of the ad men, find authenticity where none exists, we can expect still less from the general public. In *Jeremiah Johnson* (1972), Robert Redford attacks a small Crow war party single-handed and ends by chasing the last survivor, a rather stout personage, down into a snowy ravine.[5] The unarmed Crow then begins to sing his "death song" to ward off his demise—this provoked a few titters from the audience in a theater where I viewed it, the man in front of me muttering, "First time I ever saw a fat Indian." (I resisted the temptation to kick him in the back of the head.) How many of those who were amused by a man singing when in dire peril had been entranced by Silverstein's ersatz, packaged blood ritual only a few years before?

The military tactics employed by Hollywood Indians bear much the same resemblance to reality as their "customs" and "ceremonies," and frequently exhibit a combination of courage and stupidity ideally suited to the white actors trying to mow down red extras in large numbers. The most conspicuous

---

*Special dishonor should go to "technical advisor" Clyde Dollar, who boasted: "There are still mistakes in it, but I'd defy anyone but an expert to detect the factual errors. Some schools have already made the film required viewing in their anthropology classes."

In the earth lodge of *A Man Called Horse*. *(Movie Star News)*

victims of this cretinizing process have been the Apaches, who can often be seen throwing their lives away in mounted charges against riflemen in prepared positions. Their historical counterparts were, of course, masters of concealment and ambush, who rarely fought mounted unless in pursuit of fleeing enemies and wouldn't fight at all unless they thought victory would be sure and inexpensive or had no choice in the matter.[6] The Apaches' martial style, usually involving far more running than fighting for the troopers chasing him, was perhaps best portrayed by Aldrich's *Ulzana's Raid* (1972), in which a cavalry detachment is run ragged by a small band of Apaches who wreak considerable havoc before they are wiped out.

As a rule not even the fierce horsemen of the Great Plains, who lived for war and often made spectacular (if sometimes quite pointless) displays of individual bravery, would accept heavy casualties if they could possibly avoid it. The familiar image of movie Indians riding in tight circles around wagons drawn up in a smaller circle and being shot down by the pioneers within is probably derived from the actual Plains harassing method of circling (at a considerable distance) around the foe while the Indians trusted to their superb horsemanship to make them difficult targets; as far as the record shows, Indians almost never attacked a wagon train so big and so well prepared as to be drawn into a neat circle.

Occasionally movie Indians provide a challenge by fighting *more* efficiently than they should, at least in the sense of adopting European-style military tactics and discipline.[7] In Gordon Douglas's *Chuka* (1967), the Arapahoe provide what would ordinarily be a standard climax by mounting an assault on a frontier fort (something which happened perhaps half a dozen times during the nineteenth century, when many Western forts weren't forts at all in the architectural sense and looked nothing like the wooden-stockaded affairs commonest in films). But the Arapahoe supply some novelty here by using civilized wall-scaling techniques, which they can execute precisely because their chief has been training them on a mockup of the fort wall. Gunfighter-hero Rod Taylor, who also produced the film because he thought it a "realistic" story, at least has perception enough to point out that "these aren't ordinary Indians."

The red men of movieland, whatever their tactics, are usually fated to lose by the last reel—a pattern which, I suppose, conforms in a grim sort of way to historical truth as well as the demands of melodrama. "All books and movies about the Indians are the same," complained radio comic Fred Allen long ago. "The redskins invariably get it in the end." Until the apparent rise in Hollywood's ethnic consciousness in the 1950s, not too many people besides the Indians themselves really seemed to care how often this happened on the screen. It was not necessary to be a racial bigot in order to enjoy the mock killings of Indians; they were simply the necessary mass enemy, to be shot down in heaps to provide action. In his review of the 1944 *Buffalo Bill*, Bosley Crowther enthused guiltlessly that "the redskins are knocked off like pigeons. . . . The consequent slaughter of Indians is beautiful and terrible to see."

A suitably drab Apache dismounting in *Stagecoach*. Why don't the Injuns shoot the horses? (Museum of Modern Art / Film Stills Archive)

The blurred memories retained by the casual moviegoer or TV-watching child may lead him to think, if he should chance to ponder over the matter, that the red men are almost invariably presented as out-and-out villains prior to their inevitable trouncing by the whites. But very often this is simply not the case: it just *seems* that way. A film might deal at some length with the Indians' grievances, or the writer can merely provide some token justification for the mayhem to follow. Sometimes said "justification" seems tossed in as an afterthought: in *The Gatling Gun* a cavalry officer denounces as a murderer the Apache chief Two Knife, who is somewhat given to mutilating the dead and burning helpless prisoners alive. "But who made him that way?" shouts an open-minded rancher—most unconvincingly. (This was, of course, during the enlightened 1970s, when one was supposed to feel reasonably guilty over the Indians' sad fate; it comes as a slight surprise to find that, in Tom Gries's enjoyably unpretentious filming of Alistair McLean's *Breakheart Pass*, [1976], the Paiutes are conniving with white renegades and fighting Charles Bronson and the U.S. Cavalry without any discernible moral purpose.) The big Indian fight in *Buffalo Bill* that Crowther found so beautiful and terrible is in like fashion preceded and followed by much solemn meditation on the plight of the red man; so is it really appropriate that we enjoy it when they're "knocked off like pigeons"?

Not at all—but it's natural. In the end it usually doesn't matter whether the Indians' motives are explained at length or whether, as in *Stagecoach*, we are never told (and don't care) just why they are at war. Either type of film, crippled by an essentially adventure-movie format scarcely suited to a tragic portrayal of Indian subjugation, may result in the oft-observed spectacle of Indian children joining white tots (who might be expected to view with concern the prospect of people much like themselves being attacked by strangely dressed, whooping tribesmen) in cheering on the cavalry and settlers threatened by their racial kinsmen.[8] One might best avoid this problem by making a movie about white mistreatment of Old Western Indians which contained little or no fighting, often of secondary importance in considering their plight (especially as many tribes never fought the whites at all). But in that case the filmmakers might more usefully, if less profitably, detail the contemporary Indian's woes, about which something can presumably be done.

If the nonviolent approach is rejected, one might avoid having the Indians serve as a threat to sympathetic characters. Even better would be for their white victims to be dehumanized outright, as in *Little Big Man*, so as to negate our "knee-jerk loyalty," although this would probably involve cheating since most of those whites killed by Indians were never involved in whatever wrongs had produced their hostility.

There might be no problem if the Indian could be the authentic hero so that the audience could in some way identify with him; having him kill nonvilified whites might still leave a bad taste, but perhaps it should in a "serious" film rather than a melodrama where killing can, very properly, be more enjoyable. But although many attempts at Indian heroes have been made, Hollywood has had too much trouble simply portraying the Indian as a *person* to be very successful. The typical Noble Savage can only strike a statuesque pose and go through the motions of being a hero, while speaking a sort of neutral English both grammatically perfect and stilted.[9] Not really the sort of guy on which to hang an entire film. Even the most accomplished director can have trouble breathing life into such "heroic" figures, and some never make the effort. Concerning Ford's failure in his last and most pro-Indian Western, Richard Whitehall complained in *Film Quarterly* that "*Cheyenne Autumn*, that most magnificent of nullities, never once looks at its Indians as human beings, but sees them only as splendid picturesques." Primitive man has rarely been the subject of believable dramatic characterization, and I can't imagine what the remedy might be.

It was Darryl Zanuck's expressed opinion that he who desires his audience to favor the Indians should secure a "great Indian lead." But although a white actor (the kind usually assigned any Indian role of consequence) may succeed in putting some power, if not complete credibility, into a "heroic" role, the Hollywood Indian is, sadly, at his most impressive playing the villain, like Jack Palance in *Arrowhead* or Henry Brandon in *The Searchers, Two Rode Together* (1961), and *Comanche* (1956). All of which helps explain the preference for white heroes; even in those "courageous" anti-white movies *Soldier Blue* and *Little Big Man*, the main characters are "good" whites, as distinguished from the more common scoundrelly variety.[10]

Despite the necessary presence of Dustin Hoffman, Penn's *Little Big Man* did manage to portray some of its Indians (played by Indians) as relatively believable people instead of the usual copper-colored stick figures, largely because it retained much of the novel's humor. Portraying a joke-homosexual Cheyenne, for instance, was certainly a change from the grim Fenimore Cooper mold, though perhaps not a wholly welcome change. (In 1970 homosexuals had not quite become a fashionable minority group in their own right, and Penn did not follow Berger's lead in explaining the *heemenah*'s role in Cheyenne society.)

All the more regrettable, then, that Penn and Calder Willingham should have so diluted Berger's portrait of the Cheyenne. In the novel, which had no particular axe to grind, the Cheyenne who adopt young Jack Crabb are the very warriors who had killed off his fellow pioneers in the first place, but who reason that they shouldn't be held responsible for their murders or rapes since they were drunk at the time. In the film the Cheyenne arrive helpfully on the scene after the whites have been massacred by the Pawnee.* Milk-and-water braves, they do nothing more abhorrent to white sensibilities than eat puppy

*Later, of course, we see Pawnee scouts helping the whites massacre the Cheyenne; I wonder what the Pawnees thought of this particular "pro-Indian" film, since they get it from both directions. (The Pawnee also took quite a pen-lashing from Dee Brown in the early 1970s because they perversely insisted on allying themselves with the Army against their red "brothers" of the Sioux and Cheyenne tribes—tribes which had been shoving the Pawnees around for years and shown no inclination to stop.)

dog, steal a few ·horses from the Crow, and—finally—defend themselves against Custer, although at one point man of wisdom Old Lodge Skins (Chief Dan George) is permitted to fondle a human scalp, which in the novel is long, blond, and female, but here appears as dark, short, and fairly ratty-looking. Nineteenth-century white society is, of course, shown at its worst in what is Penn's notion of a courageous exposé.

In speaking of (other people's) Westerns, Penn hinted that some deep, dark conspiracy was at work, systematically degrading the noble red man to justify the white man's Manifest Destiny. "If it was necessary, they changed the nature of the character who lost—they changed him from a good man to an evil man in order to prove that the good must always win. That's what used to happen to the Indian. He was converted in films from his pacific and sublime nature to a man who was a bloodthirsty savage."

Penn had termed Berger's novel "a marvelous book," but after absorbing such poppycock, I must wonder whether he simply skipped over the gorier bits of the work or conveniently forgot about them. For Berger's Cheyenne *are* what someone like Penn might consider "bloodthirsty savages"—a great bunch of guys once you get to know them, sure, but still given to certain rough aboriginal habits, with the gentler sex and those of tender years joining in the fun of dispatching the enemy wounded and mutilating the dead: "This was a real treat for them. . . . Buffalo Wallow Woman was sort of my Ma, just a fine soul. . . . But now what'd you think when you saw that sweet person ripping open some helpless Crow with her knife and unwinding his guts?"

Penn would understandably prefer not to think of such things at all, and including them in his film might have led people to accuse him of doing something *wicked*—of perpetuating the objectionable movie image of the savage Indian fiendishly torturing helpless captives, killing noncombatants, and raping damsels fair and otherwise. This is an image which Indians and their friends do not like. In a shrill book completely devoted to Hollywood's mistreatment of the red man, 1972's *The Only Good Indian*, authors Ralph and Natasha Friar (who seemed to have some rather quaint notions concerning real Indians[11]) complained about it. They complained about it some more while plugging their book on NBC's "Today" program, displaying to the camera a still from *Duel at Diablo* which showed Dennis Weaver tortured with fire by Apaches. This, of course, was a vicious slur on the Native American, as they rather tiresomely insisted on calling the real Indian to distinguish him from the Hollywood product.

Alas, burning captives to death was considered rather good sport by a number of Indian tribes, and there is nothing that you or I or the Friars can do about it. Since torture and other distasteful practices were looked upon by the Apaches and various other Indians as legitimate aspects of warfare, it seems rather unfair to criticize a picture for showing such things—*except* on the grounds that it gives the public a negative impression of Indians as a *race*, the more so since when one sees an Indian in a motion picture or on television he is usually participating in an Indian war. Today's Indians are often heard to complain not that these films damage the image of their ancestors, but that they damage the image of Indians, period.

Thus the Friars and others find themselves in the position of railing against films that simply depict Indian violence as it occurred—condemning John Ford for "blatant" racism because he depicted Comanche captivity as an unpleasant experience for white women in *The Searchers* (a work they rather simplistically misread), laughing off gruesome narratives of Indian atrocities as the product of bigoted minds, and praising as "realism" the amazing behavior of adventuress Shelley Winters in *The Scalphunters* (1968): offering the leader of some hostile braves a bottle of whiskey (not a wise move), she happily informs him that he's about to get "the damnedest white squaw in the whole Kiowa nation." In such a picaresque comedy-adventure this did not seem terribly out of place, but more characteristic of the era was the same actress's behavior in *Winchester '73*, where she is prepared to commit suicide rather than face capture by the Sioux and the traditional fate worse than death.[12]

Covering up for Indian atrocities is hardly confined to filmmakers such as Arthur Penn. Writers of Indian or Indian wars history have also been guilty: among the shortcomings of Mari Sandoz (these included citing reference sources which, on investigation by later researchers, were discovered to be fictitious), displayed in such works as her semifactual novel *Cheyenne Autumn*, was a tendency to whitewash such Native American misdeeds as the murders and gang-rapes inflicted upon members of the German family in 1874. At this point I shall reproduce an Army officer's report concerning Cheyenne mayhem from the 1860s, not because it is in any way remarkable— it is not—but because of the volume in which I found it.

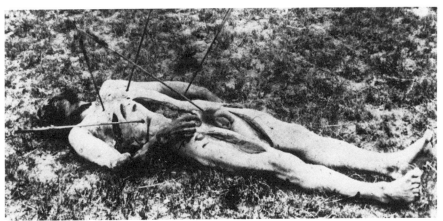

The body of Sergeant Frederick Wyllyams, Seventh Cavalry, killed in 1867 by Cheyenne warriors during the first noteworthy action of the newly organized regiment. (Western History Collections, University of Oklahoma Library)

The body of one lay in front of the ranch, stripped of all clothing, and from his chest protruded more than twenty arrows. . . . Not far away lay another, also nude, his body pierced with many arrows, his tongue cut out, and he was otherwise namelessly mutilated. In the rear of the ranch a still more sickening sight met our view. Here the fiends had made a fire . . . and across the yet smoldering embers lay the body of a man half consumed from the knees to the shoulders. The arms were drawn to the chest, the hands clenched, and every feature of the face indicated that the man had died in agony. Without doubt he had been burned alive.

The above account was not reprinted by some Gilded Age sensationalist of the "Horrors of Indian Warfare" school. Instead it is reproduced, along with others equally gruesome, in a fairly sober history called *The Galvanized Yankees*, published in 1963 and written by none other than Dee Brown. Mr. Brown is best known for his subsequent *Bury My Heart at Wounded Knee*, an "Indian History of the American West" worth mentioning here since as of 1971 it has become a mammoth best-seller and is widely accepted as the "real story" of the Indian Wars. This is unfortunate, since its artful mixture of half-truth, omission, and outright fiction easily makes Brown the equal of such historical giants as Burns and Lake.

We are concerned chiefly with omission. When writing about "galvanized Yankees" (Confederate prisoners enlisted into federal Indian-fighting units during the Rebellion) Brown could safely tell of as many such incidents as he desired. But in a volume solely devoted to glorifying the Indian and slinging mud at the white man, it is safer to omit most of the best-known atrocities and blame those reluctantly included on the evil Caucasian tribe. In describing Colonel Henry Carrington's reaction to the dismemberment of dead soldiers by the Sioux and Cheyenne after the Fetterman fight of 1866, Brown sneers at Carrington's contention that the Indians were moved by their pagan beliefs to do such things, claiming instead that they were only imitating Chivington's men at Sand Creek. But this was, as far as I can tell, a deliberate lie. Carrington had merely stated that the Indians mutilated dead foemen largely so that they would be similarly maimed in the spirit world—which is true, and exactly what Brown himself had said (agreeing with Carrington) in his earlier *Fort Phil Kearny: An American Saga*. We are thus presented with an allegedly pro-Indian author not only failing to describe an important Plains Indian belief, but also denying that such a belief even existed, and contradicting one of his own books into the bargain.

The reason? Brown's public had a hard time accepting the Indians as they were, so he handed them scrubbed-up Noble Savages whose morals and customs would meet with instant approval ("Number One Bestseller!") in white suburbia. We learn surprisingly little about the Indians themselves in his book, but that hardly matters; his Indians are not people, but victims. As anthropologist Edmund Carpenter wrote a few years later:

I cannot find Indians anywhere in the great mass of recent books on them. . . . The only identity they are permitted comes from their response to white men.

The popularity of *Bury My Heart at Wounded Knee* didn't derive from any interest in Indians, but from concern over My Lai, over genocide, but genocide hidden in the safe past. . . .

Today's Indian exploiters say they write in opposition to genocide. But one cause of genocide is the absence of self-respect based on respect for the identity and integrity of others.

We honor Indian life for that life itself, not for its destruction. It needs no retouching.

The Brown method of retouching, in both films and pop books, seems necessary simply because it is hard to accept the nineteenth-century Indian as someone with a different set of values and judge his actions accordingly (though quite a few contemporary white observers managed to do just that). For a "favorable" portrayal the Indian must be transformed into an imitation white man, and a rather idealized white man at that. Only "civilized" natives, who know their Geneva Convention, can be suitable victims or possess honor; faced with the bare fact of "barbaric" behavior, the viewer may not respond well to explanations. Only a few films have succeeded in presenting Indians as both cruel and honorable, savage and worthy of respect.

Nice people simply don't *do* such things. Since modern white standards—standards which, I might add, have caused many contemporary Indian spokesmen, corrupted by imported European notions of martial morality, to deny part of their proud heritage—are used to judge the movie warrior, it is helpful to look at the rather small percentage of films in which white people, presumably brought up to respect those same standards, commit certain bloody deeds. Their souls or minds usually bear some sort of taint. In *The Searchers*, John Wayne mutilates a dead Comanche so he'll be blind in the next world and scalps the Comanche chief who had killed his family years before. These acts seem to link the obsessed revenge killer with the Indians themselves, and the sinister chief he finally scalps appears as both enemy and alter ego. The mercenaries of *The Scalphunters'* title and the mutilating cavalrymen in *Soldier Blue* are unadulterated villains. In *A Man Called Horse* Richard Harris reluctantly scalps a dead Shoshone, but we don't think too badly of him since he is in a "do as the Romans do" situation and has a pained expression on his face as he cuts away. For *Jeremiah Johnson* screenwriter John Milius, who thinks that white people shouldn't hide their own barbarism under a bushel ("I tend to like the savagery") wanted Robert Redford not only to scalp his Crow enemies but also cut out their livers and eat them, something the original "Liver-Eating" Johnson apparently only pretended to do. But during the script's revision by Edward Anhalt these idiocyncrasies were dropped, and in the film Johnson delicately declines a jolly if somewhat rough-hewn companion's invitation to scalp some Blackfeet the two whites have killed.

In *Ulzana's Raid*, one of the more unsparing Westerns where savagery is concerned, a young cavalry lieutenant (Bruce Davidson) expresses anger and dismay after learning that some of his men are capable of mutilating dead Indians, only to be told by veteran scout Burt Lancaster the real reason for his discomfiture: he doesn't like to think of white men behaving "like Indians" because it confuses things. In like fashion, the pro-Indian filmmaker does not want to think of his red men, oppressed or not, behaving like Chivington's men at Sand Creek.

Among the practices which tend to cast doubt on the sincerity of those making "sympathetic" Indian pictures is the self-conscious use of the Indian as a subject when you're really talking about something else. This is nothing new; the Noble Savage, defined in 1928 by Hoxie Neale Fairchild as "any free and wild being who draws directly from nature virtues which raise doubt as to the values of civilization," has long been used by social critics—like Voltaire, with his "Huron" or the Roman historian Tacitus with his Germanic tribesmen—to show up their own countrymen. (Of course, it has never been necessary that the person attacking the ills of society actually *believe* in his Noble Savage.) Until the 1950s sympathetic movie Indians were usually just supposed to be Indians; it would have been particularly ludicrous during the teens or twenties to "draw parallels" using a people who had so recently been subjugated. After 1950 it seemed that Indians in liberal Westerns often stood in for blacks. Michael Wood, in his 1975 *America in the Movies*, commented that "as if it weren't enough that lands and lives should be stolen from them, we even stole the Indians' problems." But the Hollywood Indian is nothing if not versatile.

The unfortunate Cheyenne featured in the three major "sympathetic" films made from 1964 to 1970. In *Cheyenne Autumn*, they are probably supposed to be real Indians, but toward the end they do seem a bit like substitute Jews as they are persecuted by that German-American captain. In *Soldier Blue* they were simply expendable ersatz Vietnamese set up so as to be knocked down by the spiritual ancestors of Lieutenant Calley; even though the subject was white guilt rather than white derring-do, Ralph Nelson still preferred dead Indians to live ones.[13] Many people were under the impression that the Cheyenne in *Little Big Man* were also supposed to be Indo-Chinese, but Arthur Penn would never do anything so sneaky. What they were *really* supposed to be were American blacks—or so Penn said back in 1968, when he explained why he couldn't make a movie about *real* blacks with some typically silly statements about historical "perspective." Of course, they are just as obviously red-skinned *Alice's Restaurant* hippies exuding peace, love, and respect for the ecology.

Even more suspicious than setting up the Indian as a symbolic figure—the results might be all right if you don't make things too blatant and avoid distorting nineteenth-century people into twentieth-century puppets—is the continued use by the "pro-Indian" filmmaker of non-Indian actors rather than the real thing. The practice is objectionable not so much on narrowly racial grounds, perhaps, as because they are rarely convincing, particularly if they have blue or gray eyes. Whatever the reasons behind it, the custom has been followed by even the most high-minded and "liberal" of directors. Listen to Abraham Polonsky babble on about his casting of Robert Blake in *Tell Them Willie Boy Is Here* (1969).

> You must accept Blake as an Indian in 1909. I think any first-rate actor can handle most roles, but to look like it, too, is the hardest thing to accomplish. And I think he made it: he actually seems to look like that person, and he certainly is that person as an actor. Toughest part in the picture.
> Ross had the same problem. I mean, how does one become an Indian girl? I tried to overcome that difficulty by making her an Indian girl who wanted to be a white girl. So, whenever she's not really Indian, you say, "Well, that's because she's trying to make it with the whites." . . . It works out kind of nicely, I think.

Very nicely—except for poor Robert Blake attempting to transform his protoplasm by sheer force of will so as to "look" Indian, and poor Katharine Ross playing (badly) an Indian girl who *really* wants to be a white girl, perhaps so that she can launch a silent-movie career and put on some brown pancake and play Indian girls who, perhaps, *really* want to be . . .

It seems never to have occurred to Mr. Polonsky that he might actually have used real Indians in these roles. Robert Redford, who played the sheriff destined to dispatch the persecuted Willie Boy (and named, in accordance with somebody's idea of irony, Coop), had been offered the Blake role but had heretically suggested instead that an Indian play it, only to be told, according to his own account, that "they couldn't find one." It was as though some genocidal white man had indeed had his way and destroyed every Indian on the continent—or at least all those with any acting talent. Said producer Phillip Waxman: "Willie didn't want to be a 'Yassuh, boss' Indian on the reservation; he fights for his identity. Katharine Ross fights for her identity. We're saying that second-class citizens all over the world are fighting for their identity." And with good reason. Waxman's pious clichés almost rivaled in absurdity Fox producer Sandy Howard's claim that *A Man Called Horse* was "not just another Hollywood version of the Indian legend but the Indians' own statement."

The real Indians in *A Man Called Horse* were restricted to being extras or minor players, while all Indian roles worth mentioning were taken by white thespians such as Dame Judith Anderson—but for *Horse* this common policy seemed even loonier than usual since they had to speak *all* their lines in Old Sioux, none of which they could understand without the translations provided them by the studio. (There were no subtitles and director Silverstein relied on the device of a mixed-blood, French-accented captive to provide paraphrases; oddly enough, Richard Harris manages to become a Sioux chief without ever

Chief Dan George as the Cheyenne sage Old Lodge Skins in *Little Big Man*. (Museum of Modern Art / Film Stills Archive)

bothering to learn the language.) The big Indian performance of that year was left to Chief Dan George, who received considerable acclaim for his performance as Old Lodge Skins in *Little Big Man*, though his was a last-minute piece of casting: Penn had originally wanted someone like Sir Laurence Olivier or Paul Scofield and was once on the point of having Richard Boone play the Cheyenne wise man. Subsequently to steal the show as Clint Eastwood's sidekick in *The Outlaw Josey Wales*, the chief received an Academy Award nomination for Best Supporting Actor in recognition of his fine performance—and partly, I suspect, because he looked and sounded so thoroughly *Indian*.

Since Hollywood exploits all worthwhile names known to it without regard to race, color, or national origin, the great Indian leaders have played before the cameras in more than their share of "biographies" and "historical" Westerns. Sitting Bull, Crazy Horse, Cochise, Geronimo . . . Ah! Who has not heard these famous names? And who, out of all the paying public, knows a damned thing about the men who owned them?

An insignificant portion, thinks the screenwriter, and chuckles grimly as he pounds his typewriter—or at least that's what he *should* do, if only for dramatic effect. So industrious has Hollywood been in fabricating lies about famous Indians that we shall confine our attentions to two Apache war leaders and a Nez Percé chief whose exploits have been approached with a respectable degree of accuracy.

Geronimo has been filmed twice, and as you might expect the two films have only their title in common. Paramount's 1940 version, with a plot partly borrowed from the same studio's *Lives of a Bengal Lancer*, consisted largely of stock footage from films such as De Mille's *Plainsman*, hastily glued together with new dramatic footage in the evident hope of cashing in on the success of *Stagecoach* (which had employed him as the oft-mentioned threat to the coach's passengers, seen only at the outset of the big chase and given no dialogue). In Paramount's version Geronimo (Chief Thunder Cloud) is supposedly the main attraction, but he gets no dialogue here either—he simply glares ferociously and kills people.[14] The red devil is finally captured by cavalry officer Preston Foster (whose mother Geronimo had slain), and a grateful President Grant, out of office ten years when Geronimo surrendered in 1886, and dead to boot, pins an award to the regimental colors. Some unexpected criticism came from Joseph Kinchen Griffis, who claimed to be a quarter-breed Osage and natural son of Custer scout "California Joe" Milner as well as an acquaintance of Geronimo; originally secured by the studio for the purposes of publicity, Mr. Griffis soon got out of hand, and when a *New York Times* reporter asked him who had the role of the Apache leader, "the old man sniffed contemptuously. 'Somebody that can't play him,' he remarked, stubbornly, with two press agents sitting there listening."

For good measure Griffis added that Jesse James, whom the ancient one claimed to have once held up at gunpoint, did not look anything like Tyrone Power.

While the first *Geronimo* was more obviously distorted and childish, Arnold Laven's 1962 drama easily excelled it in hypocrisy, its preface telling us what a swell guy Geronimo had been and then adding by way of excuse that the following combined "fact and legend" in order to tell his story. Legend, as usual in such cases, meant not something found in a compendium of folklore or sung by a back-country balladeer, but instead whatever original lies the writer could think up. Chuck Connors, grim-faced and blue-eyed throughout, along with such convincing Apache buddies as Ross Martin (whose bug-eyed performance is one of the most embarrassing jobs of Indian-acting ever recorded on film), suffers mightily from white persecution before heading out for the wide-open spaces and a faked happy ending with justice for all. In real life there was no happy ending, which adds to the problem of making good, uplifting escapist fare out of the Indian Wars.

When the facts are examined objectively, Geronimo's credentials as a great Apache leader and freedom fighter are dubious; possessing only a small following (which nevertheless managed to tie up some 5,000 troops during the final Geronimo campaign of 1886), he was unpopular among his own people, and many of his contemporaries, red and white, would have concurred with the judgment of Apache scout leader Lieutenant Britton Davis, who in his *The Truth about Geronimo* termed him "a thoroughly vicious, intractable, and treacherous man. His only redeeming traits were courage and determination. His word, no matter how earnestly pledged, was worthless." Geronimo seems to have reached the pinnacle of fame largely by virtue of his memorable name, the huge effort required to run him down, and his good timing in being the last Apache of any importance to defy the white military; it was the latter fact which has helped him to achieve status as a patriot,[15] though in the Hollywood of the 1950s his belligerence was viewed rather differently and he was portrayed in films such as *Broken Arrow* and *Taza, Son of Cochise* as the evil malcontent, preventing everybody else from living in peaceful coexistence.

Chuck Connors plays Indian in *Geronimo*. It was originally planned that Connors use brown contact lenses, but these were discarded because they gave his blue eyes a less fiery appearance. *(Movie Star News)*

Pancho Villa has General Pascal at his questionable mercy in *Viva Villa!* The Mexican government periodically found it necessary to ban (or edit) such films to eliminate negative portrayals of Mexican characters. (Museum of Modern Art/Film Stills Archive)

The latest word on Geronimo comes from William Goldman, who again demonstrated his inability to write a decent Western screenplay with 1979's *Mr. Horn*, a four-hour TV fiction bearing some coincidental resemblance to the career of army scout and hired killer Tom Horn (David Carradine). Goldman gave Horn entirely too much credit for the surrender of Geronimo, but then so did Horn himself; his false claims concerning his own role, published after he was hanged for murder in 1904 (innocent, some still insist) have long been discredited. Geronimo himself appears very briefly, but this must be counted a blessing after hearing the execrable mock-solemn dialogue he is given; General George Crook also shows up, inexplicably portrayed as a drunken has-been: "A lot of people think I'm dead," he confides to Horn in 1904, and small wonder, since he *had* been dead for fourteen years.

The Apache chief Cochise probably appears at his best in *Fort Apache*, which shows the Apaches driven to the warpath by a typically crooked agent; but his nonhistorical participation in Colonel Thursday's fictional defeat apparently did little to make that particular chieftain a movie favorite.[16] It was Delmer Daves's highly successful *Broken Arrow* (1950), seemingly the film which touched off the pro-Indian film cycle of the 1950s, which made Cochise a kind of movie star in his own right. Ostensibly concerned with the career of real-life frontiersman Tom Jeffords and a screaming historical farce, it detailed Jimmy Stewart's efforts at maintaining peace with Cochise, played by Jeff Chandler.[17] (Cochise's grandson Niño Cochise had tried out for the part and was dismissed as not being the type.)

It seemed as though Chandler was *always* playing Cochise, perhaps encouraged by the Oscar nomination he'd received for the Daves film. He played him again in *Battle at Apache Pass* and yet again in the 1954 *Taza, Son of Cochise,* which title hints at just how popular the old chief was thought to be; *Taza* director Douglas Sirk stated that it was to be called something else until Chandler was signed on for a considerable fee. This was his shortest appearance as Cochise, since he soon dies and leaves the reins of government in the hands of Taza (Rock Hudson in a black fright wig), here falsely given credit for thwarting the evil Geronimo and bringing about everlasting peace.

Since Chandler, having become a star, was too busy to play in the "Broken Arrow" TV series, Michael Ansara was found to serve. In his 1959 *I Fought with Geronimo*, Apache ex-warrior and U.S. Army scout Jason Betzinez (who himself once appeared on the "I've Got a Secret" program) refers to "Cochise, whose fame is preserved even today through a television serial," and describes a run-in with its star down on the Fort Sill reservation:

> At the post I found that an actor was there, who takes the part of Cochise on a television program. They wanted me to pose for a picture with him and Mrs. Birdsong, one of [Comanche] Chief Quanah Parker's daughters. I was glad to do so, though I told this young man, "You are a good actor, and you take the part of Cochise almost as well as if you were an Apache. But there are a few incidents in the film that are not entirely the way things happened." Everybody laughed....

To date the most accurate filmed account of an Indian chief's losing struggle (not all *that* accurate, mind you, but as accurate a one as we're ever likely to get) is doubtless ABC's 1975 TV production of *I Will Fight No More Forever*. Indian actor Ned Romero portrayed Chief Joseph of the Nez Percé, who with his followers strived vainly to reach Canada from Idaho in a spectacular fighting retreat, only to be thwarted when a few miles from his goal. The actual production was mediocre and low budget, but did at least stick to the *major* facts, perhaps the most significant warping of reality providing an illustration of the Dee Brown syndrome: after the film opens with a white settler killing a Nez Percé brave, we see the avenging of the murder and the just death of the Indian-killer in a saloon at the hands of some painted braves, who then go on to smash up, Carrie Nation–like, the saloon's stock of firewater. The actual retaliation consisted of parties of young braves, some of them drunk, killing not only several whites guilty of anti-Indian acts, but also some more or less innocent settlers.

This omission smacked of cowardice. But the incorporation of these killings into the film need not have marred Joseph's deservedly heroic image, since he did not condone them and with few exceptions his people exercised admirable restraint during the campaign; this, together with their unusual military prowess, led General Sherman to term the flight of the Nez Percés "one of the most extraordinary Indian wars of which there is any record." The film cuts short Joseph's story with his eloquent speech of surrender (which, according to Mark H. Brown's excellent study of the campaign, was not given at the moment of surrender commemorated by most histories and the film). This ends the show on a appropriately dramatic note, but unfortunately fails to tell us of the shoddy manner in which the government dealt with the Indians *after* their surrender.

In 1971 the Jicarilla Apache tribe spent two million dollars to produce the first full-length Western film financed entirely by members of their race. It was called *A Gunfight*, and contains no Indians.

NOTES

1. In modern times this type of headgear has been adopted by some formerly nonbonnet tribes as part of ceremonial or, more typically, tourist-pleasing dress in demonstration of what the late Oliver La Farge termed "Pan-Indian" culture

2. The Navajos last played for Ford in *Cheyenne Autumn*, Monument Valley's stark grandeur being singularly unsuited to the reality of the Northern Plains country, where the story was supposed to take place.

3. *Arrowhead* broke sharply with contemporary trends in being one of the most ferociously anti-Indian films ever made. Hero Heston, an unpleasant character who today would make a good reactionary villain, regards the Apaches as subhumans unworthy of treatment as human beings, and the film not only endorses this view but in effect takes it as its theme. (It was banned in India by the people the first Americans were mistakenly named after, ostensibly due to excessive violence.) A closing scrawl claims that the character was based on that of Al Sieber, a famous scout of the Apache wars who did not in fact have an anti-Indian fixation.

4. Harris's wife was played by Corinna Tsopei, who is shown bare-breasted as she undergoes a premarital sweat lodge purification ceremony which wasn't actually the custom among the Sioux but did help to display whatever it was that had helped her become Miss Greece and Miss Universe of 1964; along with her unborn child, she is eventually killed off by the Shoshone. Something similar has happened to most other Indian brides of white heroes, a practice that might be attributed to racial jitters when considering a film like *Broken Arrow* but that has persisted into more permissive times; race aside, celibacy has often been a cherished virtue of the untrammeled Western hero. On occasion, as in Sturges's *Last Train from Gun Hill* (1959), the wife's death actually has something to do with the movie's plot.

5. With its exciting story of a mountain man fleeing civilization and becoming a living legend through his Indian-fighting exploits, *Jeremiah Johnson* evidently succeeded in convincing many that he was a real person: he was so referred to in the narration to a 1976 TV version of *How the West Was Won* and in a blurb on a paperback edition of Blevins's *Give Your Heart to the Hawks: A Tribute to the Mountain Men*. In reality the character was *based* on John "Liver-Eating" Johnson, who carried on a vendetta against the Crows (normally friends and allies of the white men) and managed to out-Indian them at their own game. Superstar Redford, oddly enough, said that his goal was to "deromanticize" life in the wilderness.

6. It is the Apaches who figure in the most famous of all contrived Indian fights, the climactic pursuit in Ford's *Stagecoach*. When asked why the Indians didn't simply shoot the horses pulling the stage, Ford usually replied that, if they had done that, it would have meant the end of the picture. But in 1968 he finally said that the "real truth" was that the Indians were more interested in the horses than in the white men, and that they were poor shots. (The latter was generally true, but of no concern in this case since the Indians get too close for even a nearsighted man with the shakes to miss.) I like his first explanation better.

7. The farthest the Plains Indians ever got along this line was, apparently, at Second Adobe Walls, where the besieged buffalo hunters were amazed to find the movements of the Kiowa, Comanche and Cheyenne controlled by bugle. Unfortunately, many of the hunters were also familiar with the standard Army calls blown and were thus forewarned of each Indian charge.

8. Let's hope the kids take Hollywood Indians a little less seriously than they apparently have movies and TV shows set in World War II; as late as 1963, a study found that third-grade schoolchildren still believed the major enemies of the United States to be Germany and Japan.

9. The usual alternative, broken English, is more realistic but less heroic, and cannot, of course, be used for conversations supposed to be carried on in an Indian tongue. (In a few films, such as *A Distant Trumpet* and *Soldier Blue*, some sub-titles were used for these.) Perhaps the dialogue problem was one reason why films with Indian heroes, as well as all-Indian stories, were far more frequent during the days of silents; not only were there a few Indian stars, but even an Indian director, James Young Deer (or Youngdeer, as he was to call himself) of the Winnebago, who also wrote scenarios and served as a leading man.

10. In *Cheyenne Autumn* the good white main characters were Richard Widmark and Carroll Baker as a fictitious cavalry officer and Quaker schoolmistress, who busy themselves with another of those irrelevant Indian-movie love stories. This romance was apparently put in at the insistence of Warners muck-a-mucks; as Ford told it, "the woman who did go with the Indians was a middle-aged spinster. . . . But you couldn't do that—you had to have a young, beautiful girl." Ford appears to have been misinformed: there was no white woman on the Cheyennes' great trek, beautiful or otherwise. But I suppose that a horrible Indian tragedy full of starvation, disease, and frozen, bloody corpses *is* always more palatable when dressed up with a little feminine grace, hubba-hubba.

11. It is to the Friars that we owe the assertion that Plains Indians never wore feathered warbonnets into combat because doing so would prevent hiding ungallantly behind bushes; but, of course, many Indians *did* wear them, so there. In their anxiety to be pro-Indian, the Friars also go so far as to equate TV commercials using Indians with "genocide" and insist that all non-Indian Americans in this country are "trespassers," almost as silly as the action of those Indians who picketed *Cahill, U.S. Marshal* because they thought John Wayne had killed too many movie Indians.

12. *Winchester '73* was another of those movies wherein the hero is sure that the Sioux won't attack at night because of a fear that they won't reach paradise if they are killed. Some believe, however, that the chief reason Plains Indians chose not to fight at night was that they didn't enjoy it.

13. I wonder how the moviegoer who was, say, one-eighth Indian was supposed to react to the film, intended solely to arouse white guilt. Should he have felt only seven-eights guilty over what his white ancestors did to his red ancestors? Even more inconsiderate is the apparent implication that the Cheyenne were somehow to be seen as substitutes for Indo-Chinese Communists—which, in view of the latter's universally bestial conduct, is an insult to any self-respecting savage, and seems particularly ironic when one considers the ways in which these Marxist conquerors have since dealt with the various primitive tribes resisting them (like dropping poison gas on the Hmong tribesmen in Laos). Surely Marlon Brando was not betraying his Indian friends when, in *Apocalypse Now* (1979), he told his story of Vietcong terrorists cutting off the arms of children vaccinated against polio by U.S. Special Forces—a story which, it seems, was a true one, despite the doubts expressed by various reviewers. Candice Bergen had her own lofty motive for appearing in *Soldier Blue*, remarking that she wanted to make a movie in which the Indians didn't say "How." It was a fairly dumb reason since the Cheyenne, and other Plains tribesmen, really did greet each other in this fashion.

14. Thunder Cloud, who had futilely suggested some changes in the scenario to show that Geronimo wasn't all bad (and spent some time under a sunlamp to meet Paramount's rigid standards for redskin pigmentation) repeated his bad-Injun characterization for the 1951 *I Killed Geronimo*, the very *title* of which contained an impressive lie since Geronimo died on an Oklahoma reservation in 1909. During the 1930s Thunder Cloud attempted to form those Indians regularly working in Hollywood into the "DeMille Indians" and have this new tribe recognized by the government.

15. An even more dubious Apache hero was Masai, who, as played by blue-eyed Burt Lancaster in Robert Aldrich's *Apache* (1954), was made a heroic symbol of one-man resistance to white oppression. In truth he was a thief, rapist, and murderer who preyed chiefly on his own people following Geronimo's surrender. Aldrich had originally shot a tragic (though wholly fictitious) ending for the picture, but producers Harold Hecht and Lancaster finally forced him to shoot a second, quite ludicrous conclusion insuring that Burt and blue-eyed Indian maiden Jean Peters will live happily, happily, happily ever after.

16. Since all white characters were supplied with fictitious names despite any resemblance they might have borne to real people, this name-dropping by writer Frank Nugent seems somewhat out of place. Perhaps he felt that only so famous a warrior as Cochise (plus such lieutenants as Geronimo) should have the privilege of destroying Henry Fonda's command with his somewhat oversized war party—or perhaps it was simply an unfamiliarity with Apache names that made the creation of a fictitious war chief difficult. Alan Sharp's screenplay for *Ulzana's Raid* likewise makes no pretense of dramatizing the real Ulzana's famous raid (which, unlike the ultimately disastrous one of the film, was wildly successful), and simply appropriates the name for a fictitious warrior.

17. Delmer Daves went on to direct and write *Drum Beat* (1954), a disgraceful parody of the 1869 Modoc War which masqueraded as pro-Indian while with rank lies covering up the white provocation responsible for the war and blaming the whole mess on Modoc leader "Captain Jack" (Charles Bronson), whose hanging supplies the happy ending. The film's "message," if it can be dignified by that name, was that there are good Injuns and bad Injuns, and as the unctuous narrator concludes: "Among the Indians, as among our own people, the good outnumber the bad." Daves must have written the script in crayon.

8
Inedible Preserves
or Chili con Carnage

Hell, look at all the people.
—CHEROKEE BILL, at his hanging

Get out, Yellowskins, get out!
OLD FOLK SONG

Having disposed of red men noble and otherwise, we are prepared to treat of three other minority groups in the Western, beginning with Mexicans and Mexican-Americans. We shall not discuss at length the stereotypes of passive peon, grinning bean-eater, and sneering *bandido*, except to note that they must possess a strange attractive power, judging by some of the offbeat places in which we may find them.[1] Nor shall we speak of those two perennial Mexican movie heroes, the aristocratic Robin Hooding blueblood Zorro and the roguish Cisco Kid—the latter character, who also broke into TV, having his bizarre origin (in O. Henry's story "The Cabellero's Way") as an Anglo bandit, one of whose pastimes was shooting Mexicans "to see them kick." Neither shall we discuss the occasional one-shot Hispanic hero such as Burt Lancaster in *Valdez Is Coming*, who through antagonizing the villain in his search for justice finds himself tied to a cross of poles—something symbolic here—and left to wander through the wilderness.[2] Let us instead concentrate on the overly kind treatment given certain individual "heroes" of history and legend.

The first film dealing with Mexican revolutionary leader Francisco

"Pancho" Villa was ostensibly documentary in nature, much of it taken during the teens by intrepid Yankee cameraman; at one point Villa signed an exclusive $25,000 contract with the Mutual Film Corporation forbidding him to let other cameramen on the battlefield, and was not above delaying one of his battles so as to allow the film men to reach the scene (incidentally permitting his opponents to secure additional ammunition and supplies). The great D. W. Griffith despatched young Raoul Walsh to film location and action footage which would be combined with staged scenes upon Walsh's return to the U.S.; although the difficulty of filming the actual battles inspired extensive faking, Walsh did get Villa to delay some of the authentic executions he used to hold "at four or five in the morning, when there was no light." At a meeting with the general himself, Walsh assured Villa that he would give him a good, nonbandit image in the United States and told him one of several fictitious plot lines he had previously thought up. Walsh himself played young Villa in the film, which was variously titled *The Life of Villa, The Tragedy in the Career of General Villa*, and *The Tragic Early Life of General Villa*.

Born Doroteo Arango in the state of Durango, Walsh's future co-star changed his name early in life upon becoming a bandit; the abnormally long-lived Diaz dictatorship put a price on his head, but Villa remained at large. He was finally pardoned after participating in the revolution of 1910 on the side of the victorious liberal Francisco Madero, only to be condemned by the new government for disobeying orders and refusing to give up a desirable horse he'd "liberated."* Villa learned of his pardon by Madero just as he was being placed against the wall to be shot, then "escaped" to the United States.

After General Huerta murdered Madero in 1913, Villa allied himself with General Carranza against Huerta, then threw in with the forces of Emiliano Zapata and others in their fight against the new Carranzista regime. Apparently piqued because President Wilson chose to recognize Carranza's government, Villa first slaughtered a group of American railway workers in Mexico and then sent a large force across the border into Columbus, New Mexico, on the night of March 9, 1916. There his men began a massacre of the inhabitants (Pancho liked mixing politics with banditry and murder and was always massacring *somebody*; for some reason he especially liked killing Chinese), but fortunately didn't get very far in that enterprise before being driven off by the Thirteenth Cavalry garrison with heavy losses. A massive punitive expedition was subsequently sent into Mexico under the command of General John Pershing.

The primary object of the expedition was not simply to "get Villa," as George M. Cohan urged in a ditty of the time, but to break up his bands of raiders, since the disadvantages of making war on one man, who could always take a boat for another country or simply go into hiding, were obvious. Villa's

*Villa never did quite master the ways of respectability. On one occasion he bet another general that he could use his six-gun to clip a Spanish comb from a café waitress's head without hurting her. Unfortunately he aimed too low. But Villa took his loss in stride, both men laughing uproariously.

forces were indeed defeated, but since Villa himself narrowly escaped, the popular myth arose that the expedition had been a ludicrous flop, with the wily peasant guerrilla leader slipping easily away from the slow-moving gringo cavalry.

Carranza managed to stay in power and Villa took to the hills to await developments. When Carranza, in the swift-moving political style of the day, was ousted and killed in 1920, Villa remained a potential threat to what passed for stability, so he was bought off with a large estate. In 1923 he and five companions were murdered by gunmen under somewhat murky circumstances.

Barely a decade later, David O. Selznick and Louis B. Mayer decided that Villa was worthy of, or perhaps just worth, a sweeping historical "epic." Ben Hecht was hired to write the screenplay, which he allegedly polished off in two weeks and which was suggested by a silly book by Edcumb Pinchon and O. B. Stade: Howard Hawks was originally chosen to direct, but was eventually replaced by Jack Convoy.

Since *Viva Villa!* was to be shot in Mexico, MGM naturally desired the government's cooperation, and sent an emissary across the border to assure powerful politician Plutarco Elías Calles—deceitfully, one must assume—that the film would be faithful to history. But that, as it happened, was not a pressing concern of *El Jefe Máximo* (the big boss); having a dislike for Villa, he desired that the film show him as a virtually mindless peon, arrogant in victory but later groveling in defeat before his captors. Accordingly, Hecht, who claimed not to like writing with "less" than he had, but never really took the movies very seriously, did a rapid rewrite and the president of Mexico, under Calles's control, affixed his mark of approval to the cover.

Unleashed upon the world in 1934, the film showed Villa as a fat, fun-loving Wallace Beery, who robs from the rich while marrying a woman or two wherever he goes and consorting with his gringo pal Johnny Sykes (Stuart Erwin), a typical wisecracking Hollywood-style reporter. Though given to occasional brutality, Villa is represented throughout as brave, noble-hearted, likable, and more than unusually stupid—about as mindless, in fact, as Señor Calles could ever have hoped for. His "whitewashing" more like that of a Frankenstein film than of a good-badman saga, Villa does wrong not because he is evil, but mainly because he is just too *dumb* to know better. Pancho also has to do a little groveling when captured by the sinister Huerta figure and killer of Madero, "General Pascal" (Joseph Schildkraut), but subsequently gets revenge by burying him up to his neck and covering him with honey for the ants to devour.

Villa's violence does not include the Columbus raid or any conflict with U.S. soldiers or civilians. Finally becoming ruler of Mexico, he is too stupid to rule effectively (one wonders why even the most suicidal revolutionary would willingly fight under such a pea brain) and so resigns, only to be picked off in the street shortly thereafter by the brother of an aristocratic Spanish bitch (Fay Wray) for whose death he had been indirectly responsible. In a memorable closing scene which appears almost like a secret gibe at the falsifications of the preceding screenplay, the ubiquitous Johnny Sykes rushes to Villa's side, promising that he will tell the world of the great man's immortal last words—and, since Villa is too dumb to think of any, making them up himself. As stolid peons look on, the noble but tragically flawed *enchilada* passes to his reward.

Villa's nineteen-year-old daughter Celia signed on with MGM for a promotional tour of Eastern cities since she was penniless and on the point of being deported without benefit of the studio's timely influence. "I am very happy," she said, as she signed the contract.[3]

One might logically suppose—if logic has any relevance here—that American studios would have felt more comfortable, and safer, vilifying Villa than weeping over his bier, even if he did have that endearing habit of constantly marrying which caused an outraged Teddy Roosevelt to brand him "a murderer and bigamist." Not only had Villa been a *foreign* brigand whose men had murdered American citizens less than twenty years before, but he also seemed to have gotten away with it and symbolically thumbed his nose at the gringos. Perhaps, in a way, this very escape from *Yanqui* justice endeared him to the romantic; or maybe it was his splendid cooperation with those old-time American cameramen that won Villa treatment generally reserved for our own domestic scum. But then again, perhaps making your pet cutthroat "sympathetic" was all that mattered, even if one had to walk over the bodies of one's murdered countrymen—figuratively speaking, of course—all the way to the bank. Anyway, hadn't Villa been from sunny, romantic Mexico? And hadn't he worn a big-brimmed hat, straddled a horse, and carried a six-shooter? That automatically put him in the same league as the rest of our Western killers, even if he flourished at a later date than most.[4]

Despite Celia's plugging of *Viva Villa!*, the Mexican public did not appear quite ready for it. The government initiated a newspaper campaign against the film and it was temporarily banned by the recently inaugurated President Cardenas. In one theater *Villa!* was literally booed off the screen, and firecrackers thrown into another injured three people.

Villa nevertheless remained a favored hero-butcher of the American filmmaker, although tradition dictated reinforcement by a Yankee intimate, preferably a hard-bitten adventurer such as Robert Mitchum, who flew his biplane into Buzz Kulik's 1968 *Villa Rides* (scripted by Robert Towne and Sam Peckinpah, no less) and found there Yul Brynner, complete with black fright wig. For *Pancho Villa* (1971), star Telly Savalas didn't even bother with a toupee, so to explain away his baldness the *Federales* shave his head for dark reasons of their own at the beginning. This made-in-Spain adventure, which would presumably find its most appreciative audience among fantasy-starved, gringo-hating Latins, had Telly aim his Columbus raid at some American heavies who'd done Pancho and the revolution a bad turn; instead of sneaking in by night to murder and loot, Villa's *bravos*, led by Pancho himself and his mandatory U.S. sidekick Scotty (Clint Walker, who wears a little yachtsman's cap and says things like "Belay that!" to remind us of his nautical origins), march boldly across the border with red flags flying and band playing, easily outwitting the pointedly stupid Americans led by Chuck Connors. Most distasteful.

The last Mexican celebrity that a sane person could expect to be whitewashed by Americans—there I go talking about normal mental processes again—is General Antonio Lopez de Santa Anna, self-styled "Napoleon of the West," dictator, forger, murderer, traitor, and perennial bogeyman of all good Texans. The vices and crimes of this dignitary were legion, but he is known in the United States chiefly for his conquest of the Alamo garrison. Prior to the storming of this mission fortress, Santa Anna, who hated Texans, ordered the playing of the *deguello,* signifying no quarter, and gave explicit and repeated orders that no prisoners be taken; following the battle the bodies of the slain were soaked with oil and burned like cordwood as a gesture of contempt.

In Frank Lloyd's 1955 *The Last Command,* Texas patriot Jim Bowie and Santa Anna (J. Carrol Naish) are good friends from the old days, and prior to the battle they have a civil little chat during which Santa Anna gently warns that if the *Tejanos* don't surrender he will be *forced* to sound the no-quarter signal. Doubtless the real Bowie, who was apparently killed while lying sick in bed if not without a struggle, would have been glad to know (as his reluctant friend's *soldados,* according to one witness, tossed his body about on their bayonets) that it was nothing personal. I guess pesos are as good as dollars at the box office.

Not a few loyal Texicans resented the nice-guy treatment given the Generalissimo by John Wayne in his own *The Alamo* (1960), a film made at great expense for reasons of patriotism rather than profit, but lousy anyway. It is clearly stated that no quarter shall be given, but Santa Anna partly makes up for this by chivalrously allowing an armistice so that noncombatants may depart safely. There was no such armistice, although the few women and children found in the mission after its capture *were* spared. Wayne, who starred as Davy Crockett, answered complaints by saying that Santa Anna really wasn't as bad as he'd been painted (he was) and that he'd started out well before seizing the opportunity for dictatorial power; a staunch conservative as well as a sincere friend of Mexico, the Duke chose an odd way of describing this process, saying that the Napoleon of the West had "pulled a Kennedy."

After the hordes of gringo miners began arriving in California during the great gold rush sparked off in 1848, they commenced straightaway to wear out their pants scrabbling among the rocks and dirt (thus necessitating the invention of Levi's) and, once they had achieved a safe numerical advantage and realized there was only so much gold-bearing country to go around, to trample on the rights of the Spanish-speaking inhabitants they found there ahead of them. While with unanswerable logic Germans, Frenchmen, and "Sydney Ducks" from Australia's penal colonies were classified as "Americans" for tax purposes, the native Mexican-Californians, along with Chinese and Chilean immigrants and others of unsuitable ethnic background, were lumped together as "foreigners" and subjected to heavy mining taxes, in addition to harassment, horsewhippings, and the occasional hanging.

As was the way with people brought together by such a Western economic boom, the population of the state at large—and, bearing in mind the frequent inadequacy of whatever law enforcement existed, "at large" seems an altogether expressive term—soon contained a distressingly high proportion of criminals. A good many of these came from the ranks of the downtrodden Californios, some of whom, on becoming bandits, could justify themselves on the grounds that they were preying off those who had dispossessed them and denied them the right to labor in the earth. The Anglo-Americans were, of course, more upset over being robbed and killed by Mexicans than by their own,* and it was soon agreed that something ought to be done.

By the early 1850s Californians had begun noticing that the most prominent of the bandits were all alleged to bear the common Mexican name of Joaquin; there were, apparently, five of them, surnamed Carrillo, Valenzuela, Ocomorenia, Botellier (or Botilleras), and Murieta (also spelled Murrieta and a few other ways as well). Uncertainty existed as to whether these were leaders of separate bands or belonged to the same group, but in either case their depredations seemed to extend over a considerable area. Finally a bill was proposed authorizing a reward for the elimination of "Joaquin," no last name given. But it was pointed out that putting a bounty on the head of a man unknown except by a first name, who had neither been examined nor convicted of any crime, was simply not proper, and the idea fell through. However, as the hubbub over all the banditry (whipped into a fine froth by bored journalists with nothing better to do) was becoming a political embarrassment, the legislature instead authorized a Texas hardcase named Harry S. Love to raise a company of twenty state rangers at excellent wages "for the purpose of capturing the party or gang of robbers commanded by the five Joaquins." The act was approved on May 11, 1853, by Governor Bigler, who on his own authority threw in a reward of $1,000 for any Joaquin killed or captured.

The California Rangers, who had been enlisted for a three-month period, rode around for two months or so and then had a fight with a party of Mexicans. They secured as trophies, and preserved in jars of alcohol, the head of a man alleged to have been the leader of the Mexicans, and a maimed hand from another corpse identified as that of Manuel "Three-Fingered Jack" Garcia.

---

*Not that the sob sisters wouldn't sometimes cry over a Mexican, provided he was sufficiently greedy and cruel, like Tiburcio Vasquez, to whom the good Anglo ladies of San Jose took "fresh flowers, delicate viands, [and] fine wines" as he languished in jail. Fortunately, almost everyone lost interest after Vasquez was hanged in 1875.

WILL BE EXHIBITED
FOR ONE DAY ONLY!

AT THE STOCKTON HOUSE!
THIS DAY, AUG. 12, FROM 9 A. M., UNTIL 6, P. M.

THE HEAD
Of the renowned Bandit!

JOAQUIN!
AND THE

HAND OF THREE FINGERED JACK!
THE NOTORIOUS ROBBER AND MURDERER.

"JOAQUIN" and "THREE-FINGERED JACK" were captured by the *State Rangers*, under the command of Capt. Harry Love, at the Arroyo Cantina, July 24th. No reasonable doubt can be entertained in regard to the identification of the head now on exhibition, as being that of the notorious robber, *Joaquin Muriatta*, as it has been recognised by hundreds of persons who have formerly seen him.

This contemporary poster insists that no "reasonable doubt can be entertained in regard to the identification of the head now on exhibition," since this relic of "Joaquin Muriatta" had supposedly "been recognized by hundreds of persons who have formerly seen him." (Wells, Fargo Bank, History Room)

Since the governor's reward had applied only to a Joaquin, the rangers quickly decided that the head had adorned the shoulders of such a one and rode triumphantly with their pickled relics into Sacramento. Accordingly, the press informed an anxious California that "the famous bandit, Joaquin, whose name is associated with a hundred deeds of blood," was no more.

Getting more specific, the rangers soon obtained affidavits purporting to prove that the head belonged to Joaquin Murieta, who seems actually to have existed in some form or another; they got their money, plus a bonus of $5,000 voted by an exceedingly grateful legislature, and the issue was laid temporarily to rest save for charges that the whole affair had been a gigantic humbug. The San Francisco *Alta California* claimed that the head bore no resemblance to that of Murieta and that the rangers had simply unloaded on some convenient Mexicans in order to collect themselves the reward; the conduct of governor and legislature, which had given such a scheme an excellent chance of success, was not regarded without suspicion. The *Alta*'s editor was also critical of the way in which some people had been blaming "every murder and robbery in the country" on *the* "Joaquin" rather than on any particular bandit, insisting that " 'Joaquin' is a fabulous character only, and this is widely known."

No matter. Spurious or no, hand and head were put on display by various owners until they vanished, allegedly in the great San Francisco earthquake of 1906. Joaquin himself soon found his chronicler in Yellow Bird, a part-Cherokee scribbler better known as William Rollin Ridge who produced his *The Life and Adventures of Joaquin Murieta, Celebrated California Bandit* in 1854. Ridge created the pattern for the standard Joaquin story: originally a fine, upstanding lad, Murieta takes to the road after repeated injustices at the hands of the gringos, in particular the rape of his wife, Rosita, the lynching of his innocent brother, and his own flogging. Subsequent authors picked up on this while adding whatever picturesque details (his wife was murdered as well as raped; her name was "Carmela" or the impossible "Belloro" rather than Rosita; he never *really* died) they thought appropriate, all to the distress of Ridge, who, however, died of "softening of the brain" before his new publisher—the old ones had absconded with the profits from the first printing—could bring out a second edition of the "genuine" *Life and Adventures* with a preface denouncing such piracies. Cincinnatus Heine Miller, a flamboyant if inferior bard who claimed whiskey as his inspiration and whose calling cards bore his self-imposed title of "Byron of the Rockies," wrote a bad poem about Joaquin and liked it so much that he finally changed his name to Joaquin Miller.[5] The bandit Murieta, or at least Yellow Bird's creation, was inevitably embalmed into reputable California histories, while memories of Joaquin began to crystallize in the brains of the old-timers and "likenesses" of the bandit to appear; he had become the necessary folk hero of a new and growing land. People were going to believe in him, or at least pretend to, come hell or high water, and by cracky, they were going to make others believe in him too; despite the apparently crushing blow to the myth delivered over thirty years ago by Joseph Henry Jackson, who diligently retraced Joaquin's treacherous trail back to Ridge himself, the fictionalized Murieta can still be found in such recent publications as the 1975 *Guns of the Gunfighters*, prepared by *Guns and Ammo* magazine.

After the legend had been allowed to jell for a few score years or so with little real disturbance, a 1919 *Saturday Evening Post* article touched off a renaissance of bad writing (he wore strings of human ears on his saddle horn;

his blood-mad lieutenant, Three-Fingered Jack, bit his victims' hearts and tore off their heads). In 1932 Walter Noble Burns struck yet again, with his magnificently worthless *Robin Hood of El Dorado: The Saga of Joaquin Murrieta*, weaving most of the previous lies into one breathless narrative tapestry and adorning it with that special Burnsian embroidery that made it as popular as it was imaginative and a natural vehicle for Warner Baxter, who'd won an Oscar for inventing the role of the Mexican Cisco Kid for *In Old Arizona* (1929); but in this instance Hollywood had jumped the gun and already begun making movies about Murieta before Burns could bring out his definitive version of the myth for the industry's inspiration. MGM's 1935 adaptation of *Robin Hood of El Dorado*, directed by William Wellman and differing, as Mr. Jackson has written, "from the Burns book in approximately the degree in which Hollywood stories usually do differ from their book sources," co-starred J. Carrol Naish as sidekick Jack and Margo as the unfortunate Rosita. Suffice it to say that, although its depiction of the persecution visited on Mexican-Californians was unusually bold for the time, it followed the well-worn outlaw trail, as did subsequent Joaquin efforts such as the 1966 *Murieta* and the 1969 *Desperate Mission*, a TV-movie starring Ricardo Montalban.

During the heyday of ethnic stereotyping, the ill-treatment of Mexicans was largely in the province of the Western since it was in that genre that they were depicted with the greatest frequency. Blacks received their heaviest punishment in other genres, though their treatment in the horse opera, when they did appear, usually did no more than mirror the current formula deemed acceptable to the public.

More often they were ignored. Blacks, in widely varying numbers, were present on all of America's frontiers during virtually all phases of Westward expansion, but their presence has traditionally been overlooked whether they were miners panning for gold in California, slaves toiling for the Five Civilized Tribes of Oklahoma, or homesteaders making their way in wagon trains to the plains of Nebraska. All black save for their officer corps, the Ninth and Tenth Cavalry, both established in 1866, were perhaps the finest of the army's ten mounted regiments and were known to their Indian opponents as "the buffalo soldiers," apparently because their kinky hair resembled the wool of the bison. (Besides being great fighters, they also had the lowest desertion rate in the army, of no small importance considering that roughly one out of three men recruited between 1867 and 1891 deserted.) Black infantrymen did their part during the same period, while a black scout and interpreter named Isaiah Dorman—known to the Sioux as a *wasicum sapa*, or black white man—died fighting with Reno's detachment at the Little Bighorn. There were many black cowboys, and some even bossed trail crews of both white and black drovers. Despite discrimination, such black frontiersmen often operating with a degree of freedom unusual in the nineteenth century, particularly in the less "civilized" regions: on occasion one was even allowed to shoot a white man or two if the circumstances were right.

Satan being an equal-opportunity employer, there were also black rustlers like Isom Dart, black con men like Dodge City's Ben Hodges, black gunmen like the fearsome Nigger Jim Kelly, and black all-around badmen like Crawford Goldsby, who was part Cherokee and who made quite a seamy name for himself under the alias of Cherokee Bill, rivaling the lowest of white Oklahoma badmen in his fondness for gratuitous slaughter. Finally betrayed (aha!) by an apparent friend for the reward, Bill was condemned by the implacable Judge Parker, killed a guard while trying to break prison, and was again sentenced to hang by Parker—who remarked this time around that he was sorry there was no higher penalty. The execution took place on May 19, 1896; by that time the famous Fort Smith hangings were no longer open to the public and only about a hundred invited guests were in the prison courtyard, although many others watched from walls or rooftops and one shed collapsed under its burden of bodies, injuring several onlookers.

Since Cherokee was a sadistic thief and murderer who killed people for the fun of it, I recommend his saga to any liberal-minded producer who yearns to make a film about a black-Indian Robin Hood, driven to his deeds of violence by white oppression. So far nothing's been done with it, which seems a pity.

Sheer ignorance may, of course, be partly blamed for the failure of blacks to assume their (ahem) proper place in the Western film; they were usually written out of popular history, and their role was rarely isolated and examined in any detail until the 1960s and such works as Leckie's *The Buffalo Soldiers*. But one should remember that the approach chosen by a writer or director was often more likely to be influenced by the fictional Western stories he'd already seen or read—the Western "tradition"—than on his own direct knowledge of the West. "Legend"—in this case that portion of Western history retained by the collective consciousness—also played its part, as Durham and Jones explained in their *The Negro Cowboys*: "When history became myth and legend, when the cowboys became folk heroes, the Negroes were . . . fenced out. They had ridden through the real West, but they found no place in the West of fiction."

But ignorance has never stopped Hollywood from doing what it wanted to do, and "legends," if it comes to that, can be whatever you say they are; most likely the real determinant was an uncertain mixture of contemporary racism and fear afflicting studio management and personnel. Prior to the postwar era, it was considered fairly daring to show blacks as *victims* of violence (or anything else), let alone show them inflicting it on others, a prerequisite for standard horse-opera heroism.[6] A Hollywood black possessing positive and self-assertive manly qualities was a rare find; more common was the occasional, negatively "uppity" nigra seen in Reconstruction movies such as *Gone with the Wind*, which seemed to hint that the abolition of slavery was just

Isom Dart, a well-known black stock thief of Wyoming, murdered at Brown's Park by hired gun Tom Horn. (Denver Public Library, Western History Department)

a sneaky Yankee trick aimed at inconveniencing Vivien Leigh. To give the moguls their due, it must be said that they occasionally did confirm the existence of black folk out on the wild frontier—as faithful retainers, happy-darky song and dance men, densely stupid comic characters, and so on.

Given such conditions, the job of dramatizing the Black West was at first left to a few hardy black independents in the 1910s, whose few attempts included Oscar Micheaux's 1918 *The Homesteader* ("a powerful drama . . . of the Great Northwest into which has been subtly woven the most subtle of America's problems—THE RACE QUESTION") and Noble Johnson's 1917 *The Trooper of Troop K*, which owed its success to a timely restaging of the Tenth Cavalry's (losing) fight at Carrizal the previous year—fought not against the Villistas they were out chasing, but against Carranzistas who had denied two companies of the Tenth a right of way through town.

The 1938 *Harlem on the Prairie*—that was the real title, folks—became the first in a series of independent Associated Features Westerns aimed at urban black audiences. The segregated casting sidestepped the taboo on having blacks shoot whites, but since this West was *wholly* Caucasian-free, the films could scarcely have had as their goal the realistic depiction of black Westerners even had the producers been aware of their existence; the real objective was the creation of black heroes.[7]

By the 1950s the old black stereotypes had pretty well passed from the Western film; but so had most black characters of any sort. Perhaps there was simply a lack of interest in nonstereotyped blacks, but in the case of pro-Indian pictures their absence did prevent the red man as safe, surrogate Negro from becoming too obvious. Two exceptions were Salkow's liberal-but-phony *Sitting Bull*, which gave Dale Robertson a runaway-slave sidekick who had joined the Sioux and was presumably inspired by the scout Dorman (though he doesn't die and is a rather servile type, despite Sitting Bull's addressing him as "my black brother") and Aldrich's *Apache*, in which black troopers guarded the Apache prisoners on board a train to Florida exile; any message to be drawn from the sight was left to the viewer. In *The Wonderful Country* (1959), not a pro-Indian film, the buffalo soldiers had a slightly larger but still marginal role, led, after their white officer is killed, by former "colored league" baseball star Satchel Paige in a brief running fight with the Apache.

Real "recognition" of nonservile Western blacks came only in the sixties. John Ford started the ball rolling with his *Sergeant Rutledge* (1960), the hero of which was played by Woody Strode even though white screen lovers Jeffrey Hunter and Constance Towers were given top billing; the film depicted the black troopers in the same heroic light as their white counterparts in Ford films such as *Rio Grande* but wasn't as good, though just a bit daring for the time since Strode is put on trial for raping and murdering a white girl and killing her father. (Warners played up the sexual angle with some distasteful, if vague, ads hinting at hard-breathing escapades that never materialized on screen.) By 1966, with films such as Richard Brooks's *The Professionals*

(Woody Strode the bow-and-arrow expert in Burt Lancaster's band of mercenaries) and *Duel at Diablo* (cynical horsebreaker Sidney Poitier killing some of Ralph Nelson's pre-*Soldier Blue* Indians), blacks had moved easily into action roles that were not only he-man but also essentially color-blind, leading many people to think that Hollywood was applying progressive present-day racial attitudes to the backward Old West just as the thirties and forties had imposed their own, unprogressive ones. (In some cases this was undoubtedly true.) Durham and Jones had anticipated such a reaction in 1965, expressing the view that blacks might have received their due at an earlier date had not filmmakers with knowledge of Old West conditions feared that "the accurate representation of the Negro's role in the opening of the West would paradoxically seem to be a falsification of history. . . . Americans have assumed that because Negroes have not been in Western fiction they were never in the West."

One should not lightly dismiss the importance of the historical information (or misinformation) communicated to the public through films or television; judging from the responses to ABC's dramatization (and, in some instances, distortion) of Alex Haley's *Roots*, one would think that black slavery and suffering had been some well-kept secret until allowed to light up the nation's living rooms. A cruder expression of ignorance was to be found in the words of a citizen possessing white-supremacist views, who complained to a *Newsweek* reporter in 1969 that nowadays you couldn't even turn on the dang TV set without seein' a nigger.

"Why," he gasped, as though revealing the ultimate sacrilege, "they're even playing cowboys!"

In the 1970s there appeared a crop of black Westerns as part of the "blaxploitation" craze—partly rooted in the same need for black heroes that had inspired *Harlem on the Prairie*, although the villains were now usually whites, their deaths often calculated to exploit the viewers' own pent-up hostility. *The Legend of Nigger Charley* (1971) starred Fred Williamson as the proud black who gets called "nigger" by the white heavies with incendiary results; in the sequel, *The Soul of Nigger Charley*, he seeks the forcible emancipation of Western slaves as well as the preservation of his own dignity. *Buck and the Preacher* (1972), Sidney Poitier's directorial debut, was dedicated to the memory of the black homesteaders and had them aided in their struggle against white heavies by nonreservation Indians, who remain a bit peeved at wagonmaster Buck (Poitier) for having served in the Union Army.

This at least gave the Indians something better to do than act as part of a hostile environment, and one should not imagine that black-Indian cooperation was unknown, although it usually took the form of blacks who abandoned white-style society to fight alongside "wild" Indians, like the black bugler (presumed to have been a cavalry deserter) who blew the Indian commands at Adobe Walls. But there were many more who at least in one sense remained

Sidney Poitier radiates machismo in *Buck and the Preacher*, aided by two custom-made shotgun-pistols. (Museum of Modern Art/Film Stills Archive)

"black white men" and helped subjugate the red men, a fact bound to be regarded with mixed feelings by contemporary blacks.

Which brings us to 1970's *Soul Soldier* (also known briefly as *The Red, White and Black*), doing a great disservice to the Tenth Cavalry with its low budget, poor direction, boring script, and distinctive anachronism (the regimental band prefers jazz). I must here admit with some shame that I failed in my duty by not seeing the second half, but during those appalling minutes which I actually spent viewing the film I did notice a bit of trendy blacks-and-Indians anxiety: while the cavalrymen are shown chasing down some Indian men, women, and children, an off-screen troubador sings, in a possibly guilt-stricken manner, "Who is ma enemy todayeee . . .?" When I ended my ordeal the soldiers were chasing some white horse thieves, which is one way of avoiding the problem. The black man's role in the Indian-fighting army may still receive less attention than it merits, but the reason is probably different.

The Chinese played no such violent role in the winning of the West—and that's part of their problem, if I may call it such. While making a major contribution to the civilization of the frontier as railway workers, gold miners, merchants, and toilers of all kinds, the Chinese, noted for their industrious and peaceable behavior ("A disorderly Chinaman," declared Mark Twain, "is rare and a lazy one does not exist"), figured scarcely at all in incidents of Western violence save as participants in some internecine tong wars—where hatchets and knives were often preferred to the more thoroughly "Western" sixgun—and as victims of innumerable white atrocities that gave the phrase "not a Chinaman's chance" its darkest connotation. It is violent conflict which attracts most people, and especially those of a romantic bent, to the mythic West, and the man with the gun who commands our attention. Save for an occasional curiosity such as the Far Eastern martial-arts expert in the 1972 pilot film and TV series *Kung Fu*—whose hero was half Anglo anyway and played by David Carradine in yellowface—the horse-opera Chinese has traditionally been a minor character possessed of an unenviable job and usually speaking broken English. He is likely to remain so.

At his sympathetic best he will probably be a victim, or a means by which the bigotry of the white characters may be laid bare.[8] In *McCabe and Mrs. Miller*, an English-accented gunman explains in detail how profitable it is to risk the lives of Chinese miners since you can dynamite out a ton of ore at a cost of only one dead Chinaman and a small fine for violating safety regulations. Earlier we have a conversation between Irish bartender Tim Sheehan (René Auberjonois) and John McCabe, who will later secure a so-called Chinese princess for the pioneer whorehouse he establishes in the town of Presbyterian Church.

MCCABE: You got many Chinks around here?
SHEEHAN: Just look under a rock.

Due to the lack of Chinese gunfighters (if not "hatchet men" equipped with firearms), cowboys, mountain men, and cavalry troopers, the courage of the Chinese in frontier America was not that melodramatic sort displayed by the usual Western hero: it was instead the heroism of enduring hardship, danger, and persecution, of backbreaking work, sweat, and boredom—the sort of courage displayed by the Western farmer, laborer, and miner.

And hardly anyone wants to make or see movies about farmers, laborers, and miners.

NOTES

1. As late as the 1960s the cartoon "Frito Bandito" peddled corn chips on TV until Chicano pressure groups succeeded in having him yanked; and a silver-skinned, Spanish-spouting space bandit even zoomed into one episode of Irwin Allen's typically moronic science-fiction series "Lost in Space"; as for the comic

dialect character, he found an animated berth in Hanna-Barbara's Quick-Draw McGraw cartoons, which supplied horse Quick-Draw with a sombreroed and accented jackass named Babalooie.

2. Burt subsequently redresses the balance by picking off the villains at half a mile with his big Sharps buffalo gun. According to George Fenin, *Valdez* dramatized "a message of peace and humanity," though the hero has to blow away six or eight bad guys to get that message across.

3. Villa's eighteen-year-old son, found driving a truck in San Diego, had earlier been signed to play Pancho as a youngster, but had shortly thereafter suffered a mental breakdown, necessitating his commitment to an appropriate institution. This condition was apparently not triggered by a reading of the script.

4. A film making a break with the Western-cliché format would be more likely to portray Mexican history with a degree of truth: Elia Kazan's 1952 *Viva Zapata!*, although an abstract film that distorted many facts, was termed "a distinguished achievement" by John Womack in his *Zapata and the Mexican Revolution*, though his seems the minority opinion. (I still don't like it much.) Warners' 1937 *Juarez*, a prestige picture with *Mr.* Paul Muni (as they insisted on billing him) playing that great Mexican patriot, was related to the usual Mexican-based oater only by its setting and a Colt Peacemaker used by a French officer to shoot a nationalist peon. In his biography of Muni, Jerome Lawrence suggests that *Juarez* might even have been a mite *too* accurate for its own dramatic good, and notes that, although it was well received when it became the first film shown at Mexico's National Theater in the Palace of Fine Arts, the Mexican Community Council had, "in these enlightened seventies," pressured Los Angeles TV stations not to show the film on the grounds that only Mexicans should play Mexicans. The results of such a policy being applied to every nationality are too hideous to think about.

5. A poet of greater reputation, the Chilean Nobel Prize winner Pablo Neruda, was moved to write a 1967 play about Joaquin which became an extensive exercise in *Yanqui*-baiting. Neruda claimed not only that the mythic Joaquin had really and truly existed but that he was Chilean by birth: "I have proof," he said, and offered none. Neruda was, however, not the most truthful of men, besides being an NKVD agent and pro-Soviet pimp who had helped David Alfaro Siqueiros make his getaway after that artist had attempted to murder Trotsky in Mexico. Neruda's proof probably consisted of the fact that after Ridge's story had been pirated by the California *Police Gazette*, this work was translated and pirated in turn and published in Mexico and Spain, so that Murieta became almost as big in those places as in the U.S.; from Spain the story traveled to France and thence to Chile where the bandit was renamed *El Bandido Chileño*. Many Chileans had participated in, and suffered persecution during, the California gold rush.

6. One exception was DeMille's *Plainsman*, in which Charles Bickford establishes his villainy by kicking a clumsy black docker—off camera, but with evident severity, judging by the expressions on the faces of the good guys to whom DeMille cuts.

7. Yet these films did, without at all intending to, reflect one *possible* face of the Black West, for there were several all-black communities formed by groups of settlers.

8. The most famous of all Judge Roy Bean anecdotes was conspicuously *not* laid bare in John Huston's film. It's the one about the Irish railway worker who was hailed before the court for killing a Chinese; realizing that the man's friends would likely start a race riot or take their frustration out on the court if justice did not err on the side of mercy, Roy solemnly leafed through a law book or two and declared that he could find no law against killing a Chinaman. In the film it is the murderer who brings up the argument, which Bean dismisses as irrelevant before dooming him to a terminal case of throat trouble.

9
Bisontennial
or Ambush at Credibility Gap

So much they scorn the crowd that if the throng
By chance go right, they purposely go wrong.
                                                    —POPE

Boy, if you don't watch it you'll grow up to be as big a liar as I
am.
                                          —MATT CLARK to Gary Grimes
                                          in *The Culpepper Cattle Company*

The "interpretations" of a certain Western celebrity filmed over the years help underline the degree to which buckets of hot tar have supplanted cans of whitewash in the old symbolic property chest. The career of this great Western figure deserves to be reviewed in some detail, in appreciation of his dual role as symbol of the adventurous West and commercial exploiter of its entertainment value.

Born in an authentic Iowa log cabin in 1846, William Frederick Cody, who claimed to have killed his first Indian at eleven or twelve and very likely did, became at age fifteen a rider for the Pony Express, a colorful and dangerous but short-lived advertising venture outmoded within the year by the more efficient, if less glamorous, transcontinental telegraph line. While thus employed, the young future hero rubbed elbows with such rough characters as Jack Slade, got chased by Indians, and participated along with newfound friend and idol Wild Bill Hickok and some other adventurers in an unimportant counterraid on a village of marauding red men. During the Civil

War young Cody first served his country by joining a band of Kansas Jayhawkers, and in after years was quite frank about his pro-Union activities during this period: "We were the biggest gang of thieves on record. . . . I thought I had a right to hound the Missourians, drive off their horses and cattle, and make life miserable for them." His widowed mother persuaded him to abandon these activities and Cody eventually saw service with several other military organizations, including the notorious Red Legs or Red Legged Scouts.

After the death of his mother Cody, now eighteen, "entered upon a dissolute and reckless life—to my shame be it said—and associated with gamblers, drunkards, and bad characters generally. I continued my dissipation about two months and was becoming a very 'hard case.'" Luckily his subconscious sense of duty saved him from himself: urged by friends to join the Seventh Kansas Cavalry, known as Jennison's Jayhawkers and including many former Red Legs, he "had no idea of doing anything of the kind; but one day, after having been under the influence of bad whiskey, I awoke to find myself a soldier in the Seventh Kansas."[1] Following his 1865 discharge, Cody married Louisa Frederici.

Trying his hand at Army scouting, hotel keeping, freighting, and real estate promotion, Cody then embarked on a brief but significant career as a buffalo hunter supplying meat to railway workers and earned his famous nickname of "Buffalo Bill." Despite Cody's toll of 4,280 kills over eight months (not really a very impressive number), he made no great contribution toward the near-extermination of the bison, since those animals killed for food or by sports shooters made only a small inroad into the vast herds decimated by hide-hunters, who sold the skins for lap robes, machine belts, and other leather goods.[2] Cody later played a large part in preserving the few remaining specimens, some of which he exhibited to the paying public.

His service with the railway ended, Cody signed on again as an Army scout; he was one of the best, and many notable Indian-fighting officers, including General Sheridan, were to sing his praises. In 1869, some time after playing a key role at the Battle of Summit Springs (in which he acted as chief of scouts and guide for the Fifth Cavalry, and apparently killed the Cheyenne Dog Soldier chief Tall Bull), Cody made the acquaintance of "Colonel" Edward Zane Carroll Judson, better known by his *nom de plume* of Ned Buntline. A thorough scoundrel and prolific author of dime novels, Buntline is universally conceded to have been a key figure in the national Buffalo Bill legend, but there is much confusion concerning his real role. A popular story which will undoubtedly endure forever has it that Ned, gone West to find a border hero he could write dime novels about, sought out Frank North of the Pawnee Scouts, who, being impatient of such foolishness, directed him to Cody, then asleep under a wagon. Dragging the recumbent hero from beneath his wooden canopy and brushing off the dirt, Buntline dubbed just plain Bill "Buffalo" and then puffed the legend into gigantic proportions with an endless stream of dime novels.

Buffalo Bill as a young scout. (Western History Collections, University of Oklahoma Library)

The truth was that Ned, rather than sallying West in search of heroes, was returning from California, where he'd staged an unsuccessful tour of temperance lectures sometimes delivered in a state of inebriation. The colonel did not invent the name "Buffalo Bill"—Cody already bore it and there were a number of other Buffalo Bills kicking around the frontier at much the same time—and wrote just one novel using Cody for 1869. Although this piece was entitled *Buffalo Bill, the King of Border Men*, its real hero was J. B. Hickok, even if Buntline did finally kill him off—and this at a time when the real Wild Bill was very much alive.[3] Serialized in the *New York Weekly*, the story did bring the flattered Cody a degree of national fame, but not enough to make his name a household word. For that he would need more exposure, soon forthcoming.

In 1871 Russia's Grand Duke Alexis went on a grand and well-publicized Western tour, and the American government resolved to make his stay an extremely pleasant one. Among his hosts were Generals Sheridan and Custer and Buffalo Bill, who helped arrange a glorious buffalo slaughter and other entertainment events that gave Cody his first experience in outdoor showmanship. Bill's services were such that he was invited by publisher James Gordon Bennett and some other Eastern notables to visit New York City at their expense; there he was guest of honor at a formal banquet, showed the dudes what a real scout and Injun fighter looked like, and sought out Ned Buntline, who had apparently lost interest in Cody but now realized his current potential as a moneymaker. A melodrama which had been adapted from Buntline's magazine serial was revived at the Bowery Theater; Cody, watching himself being portrayed by an actor, did not leap to his feet and denounce it as a pack of lies.

Ned decided to write two more Buffalo Bill stories and Cody went west again; on April 26, 1872, he participated in a small Indian fight during which he killed one or two braves and won a Congressional Medal of Honor, which wasn't always the distinction it is today since it was the only U.S. decoration available at the time. Concluding his report of the fight, the Third Cavalry captain in command wrote: "Mr. William Cody's reputation for bravery and skill as a guide is so well established that I need not say anything else but that he acted in his usual manner." After receiving some letters from Ned Buntline urging that he come to Chicago to play "himself" in a drama of Buntline's creation, Cody did.

He found on his arrival, according to his own account, that Buntline had neglected to write the play. But the gallant colonel soon rectified his error by retiring to a hotel room and emerging in four hours with something he called *The Scouts of the Prairie; or Red Deviltry As It Is*. Cody and scout "Texas Jack" Omohundro played themselves and Buntline the renegade trapper Cale Durg, who contributed to the production's moral tone by delivering a lecture on temperance while the Indians prepared to burn him at the stake. Despite some negative reviews, the play—which Don Russell has gone so far as to term the birth of the Western form—was a huge success and later went on tour; at Saint Louis Cody spotted his wife in the audience and yelled (to the crowd's delight), "Oh, mamma, I'm a bad actor," and after the show hit New York the *Herald* judged everything "so wonderfully bad it is almost good." The presence of the authentic heroes and the fresh subject matter were, of course, the main drawing cards. Soon Cody and Texas Jack decided to split with Buntline, and the great author's role in building a legend was ended save for a fourth and final Buffalo Bill novel.

Now an old hand at bad melodrama, Cody hired his old amigo Wild Bill Hickok—briefly—as a co-star, and carried on as usual after Texas Jack left to form his own show. However, he did do a brief stint of scouting between tours in 1874, and in 1876 cut his season short when his presence was requested with the Fifth Cavalry for the current campaign against the Sioux and Cheyenne. When, at Hat Creek near what is presently Montrose, Nebraska, two Army couriers attempting to reach the regiment were seen being pursued by a small band of scouting Cheyenne, Buffalo Bill and seven or eight other men dashed forth to save them. During the scrap Cody and a Cheyenne brave, who happened to be at the head of their respective parties, rode at each other in what would later be known as Buffalo Bill's Duel with Yellow Hand (although the somewhat obscure Cheyenne subchief, who had once scalped a blond woman, was actually named Hay-o-wei or Yellow Hair). This resulted in the highly publicized "first scalp for Custer." Eyewitness Chris Madsen recalled:

> They met by accident and fired the moment they faced each other. Cody's bullet went through the Indian's leg and killed his pinto pony. The Indian's bullet went wild. Cody's horse stepped into a prairie dog hole and stumbled but was up in a moment. Cody jumped clear of his mount. Kneeling, he took deliberate aim and fired the second shot. An instant before Cody fired the second shot, the Indian fired at him but missed. Cody's bullet went through the Indian's head and ended the battle.

"Jerking his warbonnet off," runs the account in Cody's memoirs, "I scientifically scalped him in about five seconds"; while Bill was doing this, the Fifth Cavalry charged and sent a main body of some 800 Cheyenne fleeing back to their agency. Despite its relative unimportance, this was Cody's most famous exploit, and in his 1879 autobiography he (or somebody) apparently felt the need to embellish it, adding a spoken challenge by the chief as he rode back and forth in front of his braves. The description may have been tailored simply to conform with a drama Bill staged soon after the killing called *The Red Right Hand; or, Buffalo Bill's First Scalp for Custer*; this featured an extended tomahawk and knife duel between Cody and the red man.

Following his Yellow Hand / Hair adventure, Cody was made chief of scouts with General Crook's Big Horn and Yellowstone expedition, quitting late in August on the grounds (not quite correct, as it turned out) that things were pretty well wrapped up as far as this particular campaign was concerned. However, he was persuaded to go on a risky mission as a dispatch bearer and subsequently spent some time serving Terry's Montana column. Except for a last, short interruption in 1890, when he was employed by General Miles during the Ghost Dance troubles on a mission to Sitting Bull (aborted by Indian agent James McLaughlin, who insisted that he could have his Indian police arrest Sitting Bull without bloodshed) and subsequently served as a brigadier of Nebraska state troops, this was his last active military service.

On returning to civilization from his duty with Terry's column, Cody commissioned and starred in *The Red Right Hand*, hanging Yellow Hand's scalp and warbonnet in store windows by way of advertisement; certain spoilsports denounced the display and Cody soon removed the trophies, forcing the curious to pay to see them at whatever theater Bill happened to be playing. In 1878 Bill found himself faced with another "Indian problem" when he was told that some Pawnees he had hired for his Dramatic Combination were held to be wards of the government, absent from their reservations without leave. Cody, however, had reasoned that "I was benefitting the Indians as well as the government, by taking them all over the United States, and giving them a correct idea of the customs, life, etc., of the pale faces, so that when they returned to their people they could make known all they had seen." Secretary of the Interior Carl Schurz and Commissioner of Indian Affairs E. A. Hayt accepted this argument and appointed Cody a special Indian agent.[4]

After some years of successfully treading the boards, Cody attempted to fulfill his hankering after something beyond—an outdoor exhibition which could give full play to the riding, roping, Indian attacks, and other open-air hijinks later to play such an important part in the Western film. (There had been a few earlier, undistinguished attempts at such an outdoor Western show, including Hickok's abortive effort and a mild Grand Buffalo Hunt arranged in Hoboken by P. T. Barnum in 1843.) For 1882 Cody was asked to set up a Fourth of July celebration in his home town of North Platte, Nebraska, and the subsequent "Old Glory Blow Out," with broncho-busting and other activities suited to its thousand cowboy contestants, marked the beginning of the true rodeo as well as that of the true "Wild West" show. The next year Cody, encouraged by the Blow Out's success, formed a brief partnership with bad-tempered exhibition shootist W. F. "Doc" Carver (so-called Evil Spirit of the Plains) in "The Wild West, W. F. Cody and Dr. W. F. Carver's Rocky Mountain and Prairie Exhibition"; when the partnership broke up, Bill continued his show in association with marksman Captain A. H. Bogardus and theatrical entrepeneur Nate Salsbury as "Buffalo Bill's Wild West—America's National Entertainment."

Already a pioneer in Western showmanship, Cody soon took another great leap forward by helping to create a cowboy hero acceptable to an Eastern public. Featuring real cowboys in his show, billing his sharpshooting adopted son Johnny Baker as "The Cowboy Kid," and forming a Cowboy Band, Cody also made William Levy "Buck" Taylor into America's first cowboy matinee idol; a 6-foot 5-inch Texas trailhand, he was proclaimed "King of the Cowboys," and in 1887 Colonel Prentiss Ingraham made him the first real dime-novel cowboy hero with Beadle's *Buck Taylor, King of the Cowboys*. Cody's publicists assured their readers that Buck was "amiable as a child," and one program sternly insisted that "The Cow Boys" in the show were "the genuine cattle herders of a reputable trade, and not the later misnomers of 'the road,' who, in assuming an honored title, have tarnished it in the East, while being in fact the cow-boy's greatest foe, the thieving, criminal 'rustler.'"[5]

Behind these comforting notices lay the fact that the cowboy had never

This unidentified, dressed-up cowboy undoubtedly had much pride in his profession. But could he also have been influenced by the romances of the nineteenth-century legend-makers who kept saying he was a hero? (Kansas State Historical Society)

really had much of a press until Buffalo Bill came along. If mentioned at all by some writer back East, it was likely to be as a troublesome ruffian who liked to shoot dudes' hats off, "hurrah" Kansas cowtowns by riding up and down the street firing a pistol, and occasionally kill someone. (Of course, he was usually judged by the brief time he spent in town blowing off steam after a long trail drive, rather than the months he might have spent eating dust on the job.) Sometimes the word "cowboy" could have even less desirable connotations; in Tombstone members of the rustling element were often referred to as "the cowboys" (since they were cowboys, or had been), and in 1881 President Arthur, addressing Congress on lawlessness in Arizona, made reference to a band of "armed desperadoes known as 'Cowboys.'" Public knowledge of the man and his activities tended to be sketchy.

Basically, he was a poorly paid manual laborer who tended cattle, mostly while mounted on the horse he found indispensable when dealing with long distances and the wild Texas longhorn (an animal rarely seen in Western films since it has been replaced by more docile and meatier breeds). His life consisted largely of hard, unpleasant work which, when not deadly dull, was likely to be very dangerous, though most of the danger was not presented by human foes. Possession of the qualities necessary to meet the perils and hardships, and his status as a horseman towering over the despised farmer and other no-accounts—few cowboys would walk anywhere if they could help it or do work they thought unworthy of a cowboy, such as milking cows—were what made the *vaquero* think of himself as something special.

But, of course, it was the noncowboy, with an appreciation of these manly virtues, who would make him a national folk figure, replacing the earlier scout and mountain man as the ideal Western hero. One such was Owen Wister, who in his introduction to *The Virginian*—a novel taking as its title character a laconic, noble drover—went so far as to call the cowboy "the last romantic figure upon our soil . . . a hero without wings," and deplore what he saw as the passing of the true, old-style trailhand.

Early motion pictures completed the work of making the cowboy the paramount symbol of the adventurous West begun by showmen, fiction writers, and artists such as Remington and Russell, the movies often refusing, in Wisterish fashion, to let him have much to do with cows. "Cowboy" became in the public mind, at home and abroad, merely a catchall term for any sort of Westerner, and "cowboy picture" has long been a common term for Westerns. We shall pass over that unhappy phenomenon of the thirties and forties, the cinematic "singing cowboy," in mournful silence.

Those films which profess to show the actual *working* cowboy almost inevitably emphasize the job's more dramatic aspects, such as stampedes and shoot-outs with Injuns or rustlers. But any "glory" attending the drover is likely to reside not in the falsification of his work as easy or enjoyable, but in his endurance of natural or man-made suffering; thus, while the sheer harshness is most likely to be stressed in antiromantic Westerns such as Tom Gries's 1968 *Will Penny* or Richards's *Culpepper Cattle Company*, it is also recognized in more traditionally "heroic" films. Conversely, even the most deliberately "realistic" cowboy films rely heavily on violence, and so might legitimately be accused of making cowboy life seem more eventful than it was. But given the demands of drama, which after all is made up of selected bits of reality, this hardly seems avoidable; to quote C. L. Sonnichsen concerning the violent West required by the romantic imagination: "It was real enough; it just wasn't real all the time." Of course, the other stuff can be interesting too, but it hardly fills the same need.

Better remembered today than the participation of any cowboy in the Wild West was that of the Sioux leader Sitting Bull, though his role was limited to displaying his person to large crowds and selling autographed photos of himself. Since he was technically supposed to be the "killer of Custer," Sitting Bull was sometimes booed, but, so the story goes, many of the catcallers were among those who later pressed him for his autograph and shook his hand. A photograph of Cody and Sitting Bull was widely distributed with the accurate if mawkish caption "Foes in '76—Friends in '85," but the chief went home after only one season and so missed the next big breakthrough in frontier entertainment.

In 1887 the Wild West, complete with buffalo, elk, deer, and Texas cattle, sailed away across the ocean blue, Cody having first secured an honorary colonelcy in the Nebraska militia so as to have a suitable title when presented to the nabobs of the Old World. Taking first England, then most of the Continent by storm, the Wild West played before Queen Victoria and just about every other European monarch worth naming. Although one London journalist questioned the propriety of high-ranking aristocrats honoring with their presence "a gentleman chiefly famed as an adroit scalper of Indians," Cody, one of those rare frontier scouts who could feel comfortable in a dress suit, was generally deemed fit to be received by crowned heads and to have his show blessed by the Pope.

Cody was in fact widely praised by his fellow Americans for giving those in the East and overseas a taste of the real, vanishing West, and he himself swore that the show was a "true receipt of life on the frontier, as I know it to be, and which no fictitious pen can describe," although said "receipt" was bound to show life at a considerably accelerated pace, one ad promising "A YEAR'S VISIT WEST IN THREE HOURS! NO TINSEL! NO GILDING! NO HUMBUG!" General Sherman gave him a pat on the back after his success in England: "You have caught one epoch of this country's history, and have illustrated it in the very heart of the modern world—London—and I want you to feel that on this side of the water we appreciate it". Elizabeth Custer likewise praised the Wild West; for many years her husband's death at the Little Bighorn was daily reenacted as one of the chief attractions. Stressing the educational value of the spectacle, Cody general manager and press agent extraordinaire John M. Burke, who for some reason called himself "Arizona John" and "Major," declined to refer to it as a show, much less a circus (the proper billing was "Buffalo Bill's Wild West," *never* "Buffalo Bill's Wild West Show") and, if pressed, would insist that it was an "exhibition."

The "epoch" of Western civilization which had produced the noble Cody was, of course, presented in highly positive (though reasonably authentic) terms; the day when so many Americans were seriously to question the ultimate cost and morality of their Manifest Destiny was yet to arrive. If the show could be said to have had an overriding message, it was that the winning of the West had been an exciting and glorious thing, and that Buffalo Bill himself, who did so much to glamorize it, was no slouch when it came to being a hero.

Had he never entered the show business, Cody would undoubtedly have enjoyed an impressive and well-earned niche in Western history as a prominent and heroic scout, but it is impossible to say how well today's public would have known his undeniably catchy nickname. As it was, he let neither his name nor his exploits nor any posthumous biographer do his work for him; although he had never deliberately set out to become a legend, Cody himself,

"Foes in '76, Friends in '85." (Kansas State Historical Society)

with the help of his associates, certainly did more than anyone else to impress his name on the national consciousness. In addition to the publicity from his theatrical ventures and Wild West, and the various versions of his autobiographical writings, one should consider the immense number of Buffalo Bill dime novels (about 1,700 including reprints) published during and after Cody's lifetime, some of them written by himself or carrying his signature—novels which no sane person was expected to believe in but which, like any good advertisement, kept the subject's name before the public and left many a reader with the vague impression that Bill Cody was a figure of Homeric dimensions.

But the Buffalo Bill mystique was so big and contained such an element of self-publicity that it inevitably aroused greater suspicion, and consequently more virulent debunking, than any other Western legend. Cody's cause was not helped by the extravagances of the writers connected with him (eventually including his sister, Mrs. Helen Cody Wetmore), although his own embroidery of the facts, sometimes at his own expense, was mostly confined to the type of humorous tall tale that was a tradition in the West.

Most of the "debunkers" writing after Cody's death did not attempt to put the mythic figure in perspective, but instead seemed determined only to portray, or at least believe in, Cody as a stumblebum who had never done anything more courageous than pot away at the foolish bison. Perhaps it simply seemed more natural, despite all the Western heroes and badmen willing to participate in exhibitions or early films at some point in their careers—Bob Ford, Frank North, Hickok, Tilghman, et al.—that a man who spent over half his life profiting from such Wild West antics should be a total phony. But this attitude led to some strange allegations by people dedicating to exposing frauds. Thus Eugene Cunningham, who did attempt to write with a sense of responsibility toward the facts,[6] stated in his introduction to *Triggernometry* that Cody, the old faker, could not have killed Yellow Hand at Hat Creek since he wasn't even at the scene on the day in qestion; but while Cunningham was willing to accept this tale, it simply had no basis in fact. More recent but equally disparaging statements about Cody from people who should have known better include those of Arthur K. More in his *The Frontier Mind*, Frank Waters in *The Earp Brothers of Tombstone*, and novelist Vardis Fisher in an essay on distortions in Western history; usually such writings give Ned Buntline all the credit for making him famous. It was a strange fate for a man with Cody's legitimate claim to the title of hero. But for the public his legend, and his personification of the frontier scout and adventurer, remained alive, if only as a set of romantic associations conjured up by the mention of a name.

The problems faced by Buffalo Bill in the early years of this century were not quite those which usually beset aging or outmoded heroes in elegiac Westerns. They included a messy divorce suit, bad investments, some poor seasons, and debts incurred through Cody's generously spendthrift ways. In 1913 a hard-pressed Cody signed an agreement with Messrs Bonfils and Tammen, the unscrupulous owners of the *Denver Post* and the Sells-Floto Circus, who, after an unprofitable season, gained control of the bankrupt Wild West and auctioned off its material assets; the heartbroken showman, who had been captured on film by Edison's primitive Kinetescope camera as early as 1894, then proposed to form an alliance with the Essanay Film Company.

"My object of desire," said Buffalo Bill, "has been to preserve history by the aid of the camera, with as many living participants in the closing Indian Wars of North America as could be procured." Such historic incidents as the scalping of Yellow Hair and Summit Springs would be restaged with, in some cases, members of the "original cast" playing themselves; novelist and former Indian fighter General Charles King wrote the scenario. The War Department helpfully supplied a full regiment of cavalry, rapid-firing Hotchkiss cannon, and such Old Army vets as General Miles, who was so set on realism that he insisted, over the objection of the Sioux extras (some of whom had been in the

Cody, now an old trouper, in show dress and whitened hair. (Western History Collections, University of Oklahoma Library)

original fight), that the Wounded Knee scenes be staged over the mass grave into which the frozen Indian dead had been hastily tossed twenty-three years earlier. Before the actual shooting began, Cody heard that some Indians were considering slipping real bullets into their Winchesters prior to this sequence, and urged them to drop any such notion; as it was the two sides were eerily reluctant to open fire on one another even with blanks.[7]

Cody then went back to work at the Sells-Floto Circus, and was distressed to find Bonfil and Tammen defrauding the public and using unsafe equipment. The old scout threatened to leave the show, but his partners claimed he still owed them money, so Cody stayed the rest of that season in exchange for the cancellation of all debts. He then joined the Miller Bros. and Arlington 101 Ranch Real Wild West, a concern whose personnel and accoutrements had been used by producer-director Thomas H. Ince in making Western films since 1911 and which was to produce a number of famed movie cowboys, such as Tom Mix. As the bleak 1916 season wore on, Cody wrote a pathetic letter to the Army adjutant general requesting a pension he felt he deserved as a Medal of Honor winner: "I need that ten dollars in my business as it rains all the time."[8]

Cody died in Denver on January 10, 1917, inspiring e. e. cummings to write his famous nonheroic poem ("Buffalo Bill's defunct . . ."). Although he had apparently desired burial in a grave overlooking the town of Cody, Wyoming, which he had helped develop, Buffalo Bill was instead interred at Lookout Mountain above Denver: Mrs. Cody had apparently been influenced in the choice of site by Bonfil and Tammen.

The first film to exploit the dead hero was rapidly glued together from footage in which Cody had himself acted in 1913, and released just nineteen days after he had breathed his last. Subsequent films, such as the 1922 *Buffalo Bill on the U.P. Trail*, would seem rather less opportunistic, if only because of the decent interval that had elapsed since Cody's death; but nearly all honored the legendary hero with adventures which, if no more accurate historically, were at least more credible than the stilted paper romances of a Buntline or Ingraham. Perhaps the first faint antiromantic note was sounded in George Stevens's 1935 *Annie Oakley*, which restricted him to Wild West show affairs and consequently made him seem less a hero than a simple nice guy not above participating in some mild fakery; "Ned, you're a genius," he tells Buntline, after the latter has concocted a fictitious blood-and-thunder background for troupe markswoman Annie Oakley.*

Some Buffalo Bill films have Cody boldly and bloodily adventuring stirrup to stirrup with his pard Wild Bill, although their offstage exploits scouting for the Army and hunting deserters and other malefactors together for the government were free of any major violence. Such a movie team had, of course, been anticipated in their theatrical efforts and such stories as that (published first in a Hickok "biography" and later used by Cody publicists) which placed them at the Washita, carving their way with knives through a wall of Indians prior to Hickok's personally killing Black Kettle.

The first *Plainsman*, like its 1966 remake, celebrated the Cody-Hickok

---

*The film itself (like Cody's publicists in real life) resisted the temptation to furnish one, though it did feature an amusingly outrageous climax, with Sitting Bull rampaging about the gaslit streets of New York to reunite Annie (Barbara Stanwyck) with the fictitious love interest (Preston Foster). The Irving Berlin musical *Annie Get Your Gun*, filmed in 1950, also spurned Western-style heroics, but Annie did inspire a successful TV show of the fifties with Gail Davis shooting to wound in preserving law and order.

team, but it was an unequal partnership glory-wise. Mr. De Mille theorized later that the "character" of Hickok had dominated James Ellison's Cody against the director's will, although he did give some credit to Gary Cooper's portrayal. But those historical facts on which De Mille chose to draw didn't help. Perhaps the ideal mythic hero of the Wild West is the unfettered free spirit and adventurer whose he-man world has little place for civilized frippery. But De Mille's Cody actually plans to settle down in the *hotel business*, no less, with a wife and, we learn, expectant mother who wants to keep him at home instead of out fighting the redskins. Such a tied-down scout couldn't help but play second fiddle to Cooper's Hickok, a "noble anarch" (as Henry Nash Smith would have put it) fated to be civilization's champion even though he feels ill at ease with the order it brings. Of the two men, Cody actually had a far more impressive record as Indian fighter and trailer, but it was Hickok who played chief civilizer here—*The* Plainsman, epitomizing his class.

Cody got his own full-scale "epic," complete with Technicolor and minus Hickok, in 1944; *Buffalo Bill* was produced by Darryl Zanuck, who'd seen the real Cody in action "when I was a kid in Omaha." The film had a rather curious origin, being one of two movies (the other was the 1942 *Thunderbirds*) that William A. "Wild Bill" Wellman had agreed to direct for Zanuck "sight unseen" for the privilege of making *The Ox-Bow Incident* (1943), a resolutely downbeat Western without heroes which, as expected, was a box-office dud.[9] But the version of the Cody story finally set forth by Wellman in no way conformed to his original notion of how such material should have been handled. As the director recalled it, newspaperman and author Gene Fowler had called him over to his house one day and opened up a drawer-from which he had extracted a sheaf of papers, announcing that he wanted to write a screenplay about "the fakiest guy who ever lived," namely, Buffalo Bill: "And boy, I'm telling you, when we got into that thing, it was true." (One would like to know just what their source material was.) But after almost three months, with the script half completed, an intoxicated Fowler telephoned Wellman and asked him to come over.

> And I walked up to that place and said, "What's wrong?" . . . He said, "Bill, you know, you can't stab Babe Ruth, you couldn't kill Dempsey, you can't kill any of these wonderful heroes that our kids, my kids, your kids, my grandchildren, your gandchildren, everyone else worships and likes. Buffalo Bill is a great figure, and we cannot do it. What do you say, what do we do?" "Let's burn the goddamned thing." So early in the morning we got drunk and we put it in, page after page. And burned up three months of the most wonderful work I've ever done with a writer in my whole life. And he was right.

Probably the noblest motive for whitewashing you can think of; one wonders how far the screenplay would have echoed the false charges of Cody's debunkers. But perhaps Fowler's motives weren't quite so simple as they appeared to the idealistic Wellman. Buffalo Bill had been his childhood hero (in spite of his grandmother's inexplicably telling him that Yellow Hand had been suffering from tuberculosis and already had "one moccasin in the grave" when Cody killed him), and Fowler later met the man himself while a brash, suitably cynical reporter for the *Denver Post*. Although their relationship got off to an unpromising start, they later became drinking pals of sorts, and after Cody's death Mr. Tammen had Fowler put in charge of the funeral arrangements, telling him it would be a fine thing for the Sells-Floto Circus if Bill were planted in Colorado. Of the entombment Fowler would later write disparagingly: "There was a circus atmosphere about the whole thing. A lot of us drank straight rye from bottles while speeches were being made by expert liars." But referring to Cody by his Indian name of Pahaska or Long Hair in writing up the funeral for the *Post*, Fowler waxed eloquent and gave him a noble send-off:

> The 25,000 citizens who saw them press the earth over the sleeping form of Pahaska, the trail blazer, this afternoon were touched by the romance, the thrill of it all. . . .
> To Nature and to God this afternoon we Americans of the West surrendered Pahaska to his final slumber.
> Pahaska, Farewell!

Perhaps Fowler was also hesitant about condemning Cody for Wild West fakery because he himself had been guilty of writing Miller's *Billy the Kid* and had bragged of having left his conscience behind upon going to Hollywood.

But Wellman's film was no mere idealization of Cody, no purified biography with the sadder facts (or debunking fictions) left out. That would have been too easy, child's play for such writers as Aeneas MacKenzie, Clements Ripley, and Cecile Kramer, who based their screenplay on a story by Frank Wink. (Blamed if I know why it took all those writers. I'm sure that given a week or so I could have come up with something equally bad all by myself.) Plagiarism from history was kept to a minimum, and imagination given free rein just so long as no cliché was disturbed from its resting place. But despite its wide popular appeal and enshrinement of Cody (Joel McCrea) as the perfect buckskin hero, the film seems too heavy on sentiment and too light on the type of myth craved by the discriminating Western fan.

The chief battle fought by McCrea's Cody is that against the white Eastern shyster rather than against the Indians, who, though threatened by the railroad and civilization, manage to secure a temporary truce, only to be goaded into war again by the slaughter of the buffalo—which, of course, originates with the machinations of a single profiteer named Schuyler Vanderveer. Oddly enough, however, Cody, originally hired to help out in the hide business, worries more about the thing "getting out of hand" when sportsmen start shooting them from trains and otherwise gratuitously.

Cody finally has to kill his old friend Chief Yellow Hand (Anthony Quinn, back in the Cheyenne tribe) in a fierce knife fight which buys time for the Fifth Cavalry to arrive and engage the redskins in the exciting, expensive battle Bosley Crowther found so beautiful and terrible. Needless to say, Bill does not scalp his former buddy: "They were all friends of mine," says he sadly, after we've been permitted to enjoy the slaughter. Unfortunately, Bill's wife, Louisa (Maureen O'Hara), doesn't understand that a man's gotta do what a man's gotta do and, in a huff at Bill's running off to save the settlers from the Horrors of Indian Warfare, heads for the big city with her infant son, Kit Carson Cody, who soon falls ill. When Bill, in town to receive the Medal of Honor, gets word of this, he rushes to her side only to learn that Kit has already passed on. The doctor informs him that the disease was diphtheria spread by contaminated water, gratuitously adding that it is "a disease of civilization." This must have pleased all haters of civilization in the theater, but the six-year-old Kit actually died of scarlet fever. "The West wasn't good enough for him," snarls Bill, prior to walking out on Louisa. "If you'd left him alone he'd still be alive."

At a testimonial dinner hosted by the evil Vanderveer, Bill surprisingly denies that the only good Indian is a dead Indian, adds that the red man is a free American fighting for his homeland, and concludes that the only Indian Vanderveer cares about is the one on the penny. Cody follows this little social gaffe with demands for a congressional inquiry into shady business dealings in Indian country, so Vanderveer and the other capitalists spur their controlled press into publishing a montage of fake newspaper headlines, abusing Cody and casting doubt upon his slaying of Yellow Hand. Soon the public has accepted wholeheartedly this revamped version of their idol. Bill responds hero-style by punching out an editor, but Ned Buntline (Thomas Mitchell), who had broadcast Cody's name in the East with his dime novels, favors a conciliatory approach and urges Cody to apologize: "I built you up and I don't want to see him tear you down," he says altruistically.

Instead, a now impoverished Bill finds himself in a penny arcade, performing a humiliating shooting act on a pulley-drawn wooden horse; Buntline discovers him in the midst of his degradation and tells Mrs. Cody, who shows up and lets Bill shoot a penny from betwixt her fingers prior to their instant reconciliation. Bill keeps working at the arcade, however, and in between shows talks to the cluster of children who hang on his every word concerning the West's glories. "Why," says Bill, "if you could see three hundred Indians charging in full war paint . . ." "Not a bad idea," interjects Ned Buntline, just arrived. But Bill doesn't want to revisit his old haunts because of racial guilt: "I'll never go west—until I can look an Indian in the face."

"By the Lord Harry," thunders Buntline, "if the East won't go to the West, we'll bring the West to the East!"

So is the famous Wild West born, though where the money came from is anyone's guess. No further mention of the Indian problem is made and we are left to assume that Cody can look 'em in the eye only if they're on his payroll. The show itself is seen in a brief montage sequence, the climax coming when Buffalo Bill, now white-haired from decades of faithful service (that's his loyal wife there in the box seat), rides out into the spotlight and in a voice tinged with sadness speaks of his loyal audience, and of the fact that he must now leave them. "Goodbye," he says. "God bless you all."

Clearly illuminated in the darkened tent, a small boy on crutches has risen from his seat. "And God bless you too, Buffalo Bill!" Cody rides off into the exit to the tune of "Auld Lang Syne" and we dissolve to The End, superimposed over the same picture of a discouraged Indian slumped on his pony (based on the heroic James Earle Fraser statue *End of the Trail*) that had appeared under the main titles.[10]

The public liked it, but Wellman couldn't; after his work with Fowler the whole thing seemed as "fakey" as that final scene, and with the passing of years even Zanuck, as quoted by Mel Gussow, seems to have regretted the film's might-have-beens.

> I'm flirting very much with Buffalo Bill. I think it is the kind of subject . . . if I can handle it myself, that might be an Epic. I made pictures about all of them, Belle Starr, Wyatt Earp, Jesse James. I even made a picture called *Buffalo Bill*. . . . But if I did it today it would be far different. . . . I got this bug on, a colorful, honest panorama, not a glamorization, a *Grapes of Wrath* Indian picture.

Joel McCrea's Cody enjoys neither civilization nor the fame created for him by Thomas Mitchell's Ned Buntline (on McCrea's left). (Museum of Modern Art/Film Stills Archive)

Nobody, I suppose, will ever make that picture, and I can't imagine anyone really doing it back in 1944; aside from some worried producer wondering whether the public would accept it, this was an era in which two men would apparently destroy their own work rather than shatter an idol of American youth. A truly "honest" panorama might have rubbed just a bit too much gloss off the deathless hero.

Although Wellman might have worried about preserving Cody's image, his film contrived to be false to the myth of the Western adventurer even as it avoided history: there were lies in it, but not the right kind. The ideal mythic Cody would be a descendant of Cooper's Leatherstocking, a heroic scout and Noble Savage who stands in opposition to decadent Eastern and European ways, and to the restrictions or corruption of the civilizaton he serves. (The "good woman" is often linked with Eastern values and may serve as a domesticating threat.) Wellman's film emerged as a decidedly bland and uninspiring piece of work because it ignored most of the elements of myth without providing a satisfactory substitute, like mature drama. McCrea's Cody gets hitched early on to a stupid Eastern woman who doesn't understand the way things are, then gets involved in a frontier soap opera—and despite all his fine talk about the evils of civilization and calling for the wild, he finally resolves the tension by bugging out of the West entirely and becoming an Eastern showman who goes to Europe.

The real killer, though, was all that Lo-the-poor-Indian treacle; Cody spends so much time letting his heart bleed that he has scarce any time to be dashing. What was objectionable was not, of course, the pro-Indian posturing itself, but its wholesale cramming into a film where it was actually harmful; the Indians' own tragic end of trail required a somewhat serious film, which *Buffalo Bill*—where the only excitement comes during the big Indian-killing scene—failed to become despite its sentiment and solemnity.

Ironically, Paramount's 1953 *Pony Express*, financially far less ambitious, did a much better job of making Bill into a dream hero. This adequately preposterous effort portrayed the two Bills as twin gods who save California from subversive elements, but Charlton Heston's supervirile Cody, who, given the time of the story, must have been around fifteen years old, easily outclassed the comparatively homely Forrest Tucker's Hickok—killing Indians without regret, stabbing Yellow Hand to death in a formal knife duel, and finally rejecting the reformed bad woman (the good woman, a Calamity Jane–type tomboy, having just been killed off) to mount up and gallop away over the boundless prairie, free as the wind. And nobody mentions show biz; the Wild West "exhibition" was great as a way of making Cody a legend, but where movie myth was concerned it just gets in the way of things.

Apparently ignoring the Western authors who chose to regard Buffalo Bill only as a prince among armchair Indian fighters, the movies posed no serious threat to his legend until the 1970s. In an age not particularly concerned with maintaining the romantic delusions of children (or anybody else) and often rough on Indian fighters as a class, Cody was liable to get burned either way. If he *was* perceived as a great white warrior, he was evil because he slew the Noble Red Man, then enjoying a vogue; if not, he was bad because he was a phony. Either way, he should have been ashamed of himself for killing bison, a pastime which has rarely been portrayed as a glorious one on film.[11]

In 1970 Arthur Penn had Dustin Hoffman, badly in need of funds, refuse to become a hide-hunter in *Little Big Man* (he *had* become one in the novel) at the entreaty of Martin Balsam, who keeps losing bits of his anatomy throughout the film and was intended, I presume, to symbolize the essential rottenness of the white society that had made Penn wealthy; "There's old Buffalo Bill himself," says Balsam, referring to a buckskinned horseman seen from the back. (Sadly, Berger himself had dismissed Cody as a "long-haired blowhard.") In 1973 Marco Ferreri's *Touche Pas la Femme Blanche* (Touch Not the White Woman) took naughty fun in burlesquing the exploits of both Buffalo Bill (Michel Piccoli) and General Custer (Marcello Mastroianni); the West comes East with a vengeance here, with Indian combats and other dramatic high points shot in the streets of modern Paris and some left-wing jokes about such things as Indians and Algerians.

The lamentable *This Is the West That Was* made—I guess—more of an attempt at credibility than Ferreri's film and was widely seen by the tolerant, hence more important from a "legendary" viewpoint. Since the carefully chosen photos under the credits were followed by an opening montage "exposing" some Western myths by such clever techniques as showing Geronimo bumping his head against a tree and a number of famous outlaws falling off their horses, it was obvious that the writer-director (whose name is not worth mentioning here; anyway, I've forgotten it) wanted to finish off as many legends as possible.[12] So we have to have an updated version of the Hickok-Cody partnership with Buffalo Bill (who again should have been a young boy, this being 1861) an unshaven lout played by Matt Clark.

Such films were not terribly significant. The big moment, the major revisionist addition to Buffalo Billyana, came in the summer of '76, just in time for the Bicentennial, with Robert Altman's *Buffalo Bill and the Indians; or Sitting Bull's History Lesson*. That's what he called it, although the screenplay, which he co-wrote with Alan Rudolph, was, in his own words, an attempt to "create our own history." The movie was inspired by an extremely bad play called *Indians*, written by Arthur Kopit in a didactic, self-indulgent style and attempting with breezy incompetence to make Buffalo Bill's Wild West into a microcosm of red-white intercourse. Altman very properly dropped nearly everything he found in this unpromising piece of source material, the better to create his own work of art—the theme of which seems to have escaped many critics. They thought it had something to do with the concept of the hero as star, or the relationship between myth and reality. But that was all so much crap. The real message was this: Buffalo Bill was bad.

The film opens in 1885 with a fake Indian raid during which one of the show Indians is accidentally killed in a fall. Employer Cody (Paul Newman, who had bought the rights to *Indians* years before and plays the thirty-nine-year-old Bill as a gray-bearded, burned-out old wreck) shows absolutely no concern, thereby revealing himself as an evil person and probably a supporter of genocide as well; on learning that the dead brave was a Shoshone, he merely takes the opportunity to brag of how he won the Medal of Honor fighting that nonhostile tribe. (The generally peaceful demeanor of the Shoshones toward whites is, however, not pointed out. Perhaps Altman was just being ignorant.) Debunking, if one may call it that, soon degenerates into overkill, although Altman does manage to avoid having Cody rape a child or steal from a blind beggar. Buffalo Bill becomes not only an egomaniac, but also a physical coward, an idiot, a crude racist, and an inept scout who, as *Newsweek*'s Jack Kroll put it, "couldn't track an Indian across a sandbox." He is also a drunkard who quaffs whiskey from huge schooners because his contract with Salsbury allows him only so many drinks a day; this bit was inspired by a legend long discredited. (Cody had no need for such an agreement since he wisely arranged his sprees so as not to interfere with the show schedule.)

Altman uses an occasional factoid to bolster his case: that Newman uses shot-loaded revolver shells to shoot thrown glass balls proves him still more vile. But the chief reason behind Cody's use of shotted shells in his rifle or pistol was the danger which solid slugs presented to his audience. Firing them at small thrown objects while galloping at full speed inside a crammed arena (a difficult task even when using a shotgun) had its risks, and even the great Annie Oakley appears to have used shot in her rifle on occasion—though Cody was probably more receptive to the idea than most since in 1878, while riding off the stage of a Baltimore theater, he had wounded a young boy in the gallery with a careless shot in the air from his Winchester, loaded for exhibition shooting with ball and a reduced powder charge.

Just in case you *still* don't get the message, Altman periodically cuts away from the action on the show grounds—what there is of it—to bring us Ned Buntline (a horribly miscast Burt Lancaster who looks and behaves like an unemployed mortician) infesting a nearby saloon and muttering into his beer about how he made Cody into Buffalo Bill and invented all his deeds of daring; the film's credits bill Lancaster only as "The Legend Maker," while Newman is "The Star." There is dramatic improbability as well as inaccuracy here, since Altman never tells us why *Buntline*, of all people, should sit brooding over such matters; instead Fraud no. 1 (Altman) uses Fraud no. 2 (Lancaster) to "expose" Fraud no. 3 (Newman). It would be charitable to assume that Altman's apparent hypocrisy was the result of victimization by hack historians, but internal evidence indicates that Altman knew the basic facts of the Cody story and just wasn't interested in them.

Not content with demolishing Cody in what must be among the most hate-obsessed Westerns ever made, the director must put every other (white) character through the wringer. Annie Oakley (Geraldine Chaplin) accidentally shoots husband Frank Butler through the shoulder at a range of about five feet, while Butler himself is told by a female cast member that she is pregnant by him, a revelation of misbehavior so casually and irrelevantly tossed in that it seems motivated less by a desire for comedy than by a vindictive determination not to let anyone escape. Indian Agent James McLaughlin becomes, just for the hell of it, an ever cruder racist than Cody, referring to his charges as "dog eaters." Minor troupe members, allotted no dialogue with which to reveal their subhuman depravity, amuse themselves by hoisting a small boy up on a pulley and poking hot branding irons against his rear.

A marginal plot is provided with the struggle of Noble Red Men against pre-Hollywood commercialism. The diminutive Frank Kaquitts, an honest-to-goodness Native American (to be specific, Canadian), plays Sitting Bull with all the depth and eloquence of a cigar-store Indian, remaining silent throughout while his interpreter (Will Sampson) mysteriously translates his thoughts into words of wisdom. The well-known friendship between Cody and Sitting Bull naturally becomes a fierce hatred on the part of Bill, who attempts unsuccessfully to humiliate "The Indian" and, after Sitting Bull has returned to the reservation and been killed offscreen by McLaughlin's Indian police, is sufficiently low-down to "reenact" the chief's death by fighting a fake knife duel with the now white-corrupted Sampson, flourishing "Sitting Bull's" warbonnet and flashing a desperate-glory grin as the camera pulls back for the final fade.

The reviews were, on the whole, favorable, Altman having enjoyed the benefits of critical ignorance (which would have done no harm had it not been coupled with a wholly unwarranted credulity) and, perhaps, those books to which the odd doubter could fly to be assured that Cody was a con man beyond all redemption. Cynicism about the reputation of Western heroes is usually justified. But perhaps this critical willingness (eagerness?) to accept the depressing, anti-American version of history set forth by "our Bicentennial gift to America," as Altman called the film, betokened a more serious American malady, although we cannot properly regard *Buffalo Bill and the Indians* as a "popular entertainment" reflecting some need of the mass audience since few people went to see it.

The film itself is so silly that it is impossible to account for its creation in rational terms. But, of course, there is often little that is rational in the "Wild West," which breeds a highly infectious form of dementia forcing seemingly normal people—whether they are "romantics" or cynics seems to make no difference—to do, say, and write strange things. No wonder that in his flippant book on gun control Robert Sherrill casually refers to the American people making a folk hero out of Jesse James "for absolutely no reason relating to sanity," or that Professor Leslie Fiedler, in his *The Return of the Vanishing American*, was driven to speak of "that peculiar form of madness which dreams, and achieves, and *is* the true West," and to suggest the use of hallucinogens for those sincerely intent on exploring that disputed artistic territory.

Between the pulp-adventure fantasy of a Wellman and the hatchet-swinging comic fantasy of an Altman there may seem little to choose. But in this case I must confess myself feeling a shade less unfriendly toward the Joe McCrea version. Reckon it's just the romantic in me.

Or something.

NOTES

1. Cody recalled such flavorful fragments of biography in the first (1879) version of his memoirs, which, judging by this sort of unprofessional frankness, he must actually have written, though it was presumably tied up grammatically and stylistically by other hands. This tome was subsesquently reworked a number of times by ghosts and publicists, Cody possessing a fine indifference to whatever fables were written about him by associates or published under his name.

2. The slaughter of the buffalo was met with widespread indifference or even approval, the two great alleged benefits of extermination being the clearing of rangeland for the white man's cattle and the destruction of the "wild" Indians' food supply, which would force the red man to rely on the government for (often inadequate) provisions. Very nearly anticipating the design of that noble coin, the buffalo nickel (which really should be revived, despite its somewhat ironic overtones), Phil Sheridan, in urging that the Texas legislature *not* pass a bill protecting the bison, suggested that hide-hunters be rewarded with medals bearing a dead buffalo on one side and a "discouraged" Indian on the other.

3. Hickok's reaction to this particular novel, if he ever saw it, is unknown. In 1849 the famous mountain man and guide Kit Carson, an early Western hero who had gained a national reputation through the writings of explorer John C. Frémont and preceded Cody as a symbol of the frontier scout, had an odd experience when he sought to free a white woman held captive by some Apaches, who, however, killed her and escaped: in their camp Carson found a paperback novel, its cover showing him rescuing a fair maiden from fiendish red men. In one possibly apocryphal tale, Carson, shown a journal cover that had him protecting a terrified female while dead Indians littered the surrounding countryside, is quoted as remarking: "That there might be true but I hain't got no reckerlection of it." While we're on the subject, a number of films have been made about Carson—the latest being a 1977 Disney TV movie called *Kit Carson and the Mountain Men*—and none of them are worth a pinch of dried owl dung, although in 1939 James Cagney had planned a serious treatment for Warners which finally became a good-badman film, *The Oklahoma Kid*: "When I got the final script," wrote Cagney, "it had as much to do with actual history as the Katzenjammer Kids."

4. Others viewed Cody's activities with less approving eyes, and he would later be accused by Eastern-based reformers of encouraging "savage" behavior (such as painting up for war and chasing stagecoaches) among the untutored show Indians even as said reformers were trying to civilize them out of their native culture. Some educated Indians, on the other hand, were to charge that the red men themselves were simply being "exploited" while the public had its barbaric stereotype of the first Americans reinforced by the exhibit. There were even charges that Cody's Indians were mistreated, though these proved to be nonsense; Cody was always greatly respected by the Indian players themselves.

5. A note on terminology seems in order here: the word "rustler" originally applied to a herder who was trying to gather in some cattle, only later being applied exclusively to stock thieves. "Cowboy" was not quite as popular a term for cattle drover as it is now and in some places never caught on.

6. Writing angrily to one friend concerning another friend who wrote what was supposed to be Western history, Cunningham wondered: "Did he ever know what a *lie* is? I have asked myself many times. Or just Common Decency? Or was he (simply) incapable of seeing anything but material to be twisted and distorted *at his fancy* to make a story?"

7. Sioux witnesses disagreed as to how accurately this now-vanished film portrayed the Wounded Knee tragedy, but since the pompous Miles had been the one to press charges against the Seventh's commander following the slaughter, it seems likely that it was unflattering to the army. What with so many veterans on hand, Cody's footage *may* have been as accurate as any ever shot for a Western. (It has been suggested that the footage was deliberately destroyed while awaiting possible use as an army recruiting aid.)

8. There was actually no such pension and Cody couldn't have received one anyway; the regulations dictated that only members of the armed forces were eligible for the medal and civilian scout Cody was stricken from the noll of recipients at about this time by a board of review examining abuses of the award, though it is doubtful that he was made aware of this action.

9. Wellman claimed that he had previously received an offer to direct from an unnamed producer who wanted to film the Walter Van Tilburg novel with Mae West singing to the cowboys around a large barbeque pit, but had declined the offer and later bought the property himself. Although commonly referred to as an antilynching story, *The Ox-bow Incident* actually seems more concerned with mob psychology than the basic issue of taking the law into one's own hands (which is what most heroes in standard Westerns do anyway, though with "Judge Colt and his jury of six" rather than Judge Lynch), especially as the victims are innocent of a crime belatedly discovered never to have taken place. Michael Wood has mischievously suggested that it argued not so much against lynching per se as against not getting your facts straight before you do. In many cases the Western strangulation bee, unlike the Southern-style lynching, was simply a form of do-it-yourself justice resorted to in the absence of effective, legally constituted authorities; in the 1929 *Virginian*, Gary Cooper could plausibly claim to be serving justice (and the plot line of Wister's book) by hanging his best friend for cattle theft, though William S. Hart protested that a true-blue Westerner would be unlikely to treat a comrade that way.

10. Wellman tried his best to get out of directing this soppy frosting on the *Kitsch*, even asking Zanuck himself to do it. But that hardhearted producer refused. "I had to do it, and when I did it, honestly and truly, I turned around and damn near vomited because I think that's the fakiest thing I ever saw in my—Poor little crippled kid—'God bless you, Buffalo Bill.'"

11. Besides Wellman's *Buffalo Bill*, with its hide hunter/sports hunter mixup, other films condemning it in whole or in part include Richard Brooks's 1956 *The Last Hunt* and even Stanley Kramer's 1971 film of Glendon Swarthout's *Bless the Beasts and Children*, which disapproved of modern "sportsmen" blowing away penned-up bison to reduce the herd surplus. Sometimes love of nature or the legitimate ecological concern of the day could give way to dangerous fantasy: the 1970s saw a plague of low-budget "wilderness" Westerns (such as the 1974 *The Life and Times of Grizzly Adams*, a Winnie-the-Pooh treatment of hunter and trapper James Capen Adams which inspired a TV show of the same name) designed for people who liked their steak but didn't like to think where it came from and enjoyed imagining that the mountain men were all veggies who spent their time petting furry critters. (Eating fish was usually okay since they weren't as cute and don't suffer as loudly.)

12. The only historical figure in the film to escape is Nat Love, a black cowboy who claimed the name "Deadwood Dick" (a popular dime-novel character) and published his unlikely memoirs in 1907. He is present in the movie just long enough to introduce himself, presumably just to prove that there were blacks out West or that the writer knew something about the frontier even if he never made any worthwhile use of that knowledge.

Bibliography

In this work I have commented several times on the stacks of bad books available to the unwary reader; having done so, it would be churlish of me to take my leave without offering at least some suggestions for those who would read more in this field. Accordingly, I have indicated with an asterisk certain works on the West, or on Westerns, which I consider scholarly, illuminating, or simply interesting; the absence of such a mark does not in itself imply disparagement of any other work listed. Also arbitrarily included in this bibliography are brief but, I trust, not entirely valueless comments on certain listed items, reliable and otherwise.

*Adams, Ramon F. *Burs under the Saddle*. Norman: University of Oklahoma Press, 1964.
   This mammoth work is devoted solely to pointing out errors in previous works on the lawless West and should be consulted by every cautious student of its sanguinary characters and events.

*———. *A Fitting Death for Billy the Kid*. Norman: University of Oklahoma Press, 1965.
   Mr. Adams traces the fanciful embroideries of the Kid legend back to their earliest sources, painting a bleak portrait of Western badman literature.

*———. *Six-Guns and Saddle Leather: A Bibliography of Books and Pamphlets on Western Outlaws and Gunman*. Norman: University of Oklahoma Press, 1954.
   More discouraging words on the literature of the violent West, Mr. Adams finding few pearls in the refuse heap.

*———. *Western Words: A Dictionary of the American West*. Norman: University of Oklahoma Press, 1968.

*Ambrose, Stephen E. *Crazy Horse and Custer: The Parallel Lives of Two American Warriors*. Garden City, N.Y.: Doubleday, 1975.
   The author attempts to compare and contrast U.S. cavalryman and Sioux chief and examine them in relation to their respective cultures. A number of inaccuracies might have been avoided, but the book remains well worth reading.

Anderson, Charles D., ed. *Outlaws of the Old West*. Los Angeles, Calif.: Mankind Publishing Co., 1973.

Anobile, Richard J. *John Ford's Stagecoach*. New York: Universe Books, 1975.

*Athearn, Robert G. *William Tecumseh Sherman and the Settlement of the West*. Norman: University of Oklahoma Press, 1956.

*Axtell, James. "Who Invented Scalping?" *American Heritage*, April 1977.

Baker, Pearl. *The Wild Bunch at Robbers Roost*. Rev. ed. New York: Abelard-Schuman, 1971.

Baldick, Robert. *The Duel: A History of Duelling*. New York: Clarkson N. Potter, 1965.

Bartholemew, Ed. *Wyatt Earp*. 2 vols. Fort Davis,.Tex.: Frontier Book Co., 1964 and 1967.
An adequately researched but badly written (and even more badly *printed*) biography that debunks Wyatt neither wisely nor too well.

*Bazin, André. *What Is Cinema?* Vol. 2. Edited by Hugh Gray. Berkeley and Los Angeles: University of California Press, 1971.

*Berger, Thomas. *Little Big Man*. New York: Dial Press, 1964.

Betenson, Lula Parker (as told to Dora Flack). *Butch Cassidy, My Brother*. Provo, Utah: Brigham Young University Press, 1975.

*Betzinez, Jason, with Wilbur Sturtevant Nye. *I Fought with Geronimo*. Harrisburg, Pa.: Stackpole Books, 1959.

"Billy the Kid." *Life*. August 4, 1941.

Blake, Michael. *American Civil War Cavalry*. London: Almark Publishing Co., 1973.

———. *American Civil War Infantry*. London: Almark Publishing Co., 1973.

Bogdanovich, Peter. *Alan Dwan: The Last Pioneer*. New York: Praeger Publishers, 1970.

———. *John Ford*. Berkeley and Los Angeles: University of California Press, 1968.

———. *Pieces of Time: Peter Bogdanovich on the Movies*. New York: Arbor House, 1974.

*Bourke, John G. (Captain, Third Cavalry, U.S.A.). *On the Border with Crook*. Lincoln: University of Nebraska Press, 1971.
A classic frontier memoir by an aide to General Crook which should be read by anyone interested in the Indian wars of the post–Civil War period.

Brown, Dee. *Bury My Heart at Wounded Knee: An Indian History of the American West*. New York: Holt, Rinehart and Winston, 1971.

*——— (D. Alexander Brown). *Fort Phil Kearny: An American Saga*. New York: G. P. Putnam's Sons, 1962.

*——— (D. Alexander Brown). *The Galvanized Yankees*. Urbana: University of Illinois Press, 1963.

——— (D. Alexander Brown), with Martin F. Schmitt. *Fighting Indians of the West*. New York: Scribner's Sons, 1948.

Breihan, Carl W., with Charles A. Rosamond. *The Bandit Belle*. Seattle, Wash.: Hangman Press, Superior Publishing Co., 1970.

*Brownlow, Kevin. *The War, the West, and the Wilderness*. New York: Alfred A. Knopf, 1979.
Fascinating accounts of the interaction between the "real thing" and the world of the filmmaker during the era of silent war films, Westerns, and "wilderness" films, the section on Westerns being particularly striking.

Burke, John. *Buffalo Bill: The Noblest Whiteskin*. New York: G. P. Putnam's Sons, 1973.

Burns, Walter Noble. *The Robin Hood of El Dorado: The Saga of Joaquin Murrieta*. New York: Coward-McCann, 1932.

————. *The Saga of Billy the Kid*. New York: Doubleday, Page and Co., 1926.

————. *Tombstone: An Iliad of the Southwest*. New York: Doubleday, Doran and Co., 1927.

Burt, Olive Woolley. *American Murder Ballads*. New York: Oxford Univerity Press, 1958.

Cagney, James. *Cagney by Cagney*. Garden City, N.Y.: Doubleday, 1976.

*Calder, Jenni. *There Must Be a Lone Ranger*. New York: Taplinger, 1975.

Camp, Walter Mason. *Custer in '76: Walter Camp's Notes on the Custer Fight*. Edited by Kenneth Hammer. Provo, Utah: Brigham Young University Press, 1976.
Interviews with participants, red and white.

Carpenter, Edmund. *Oh! What a Blow That Phantom Gave Me!* New York: Holt, Rinehart and Winston, 1974.

Carroll, John M., ed. *The Black Military Experience in the American West*. Liveright, 1971.

————. *Custer in Texas*. Liveright, 1975.

Cary, Lucian. *The Colt Gun Book*. New York: Arco, 1961.

Casey, Robert J. *The Texas Border and Some Borderliners: A Chronicle and a Guide*. Indianapolis, Ind.: Bobbs-Merrill, 1950.

*Cawelti, John. *The Six-Gun Mystique*. Bowling Green, Ohio: Bowling Green University Popular Press, 1971.

Crisman, Harry E. (from an original manuscript by Jim Herron). *Fifty Years on the Owl Hoot Trail*. New York: Sage Books, 1969.

*Clemens, Samuel L. *Roughing It*. Madison, Wis.: American Publishing Company, 1871.
Mark Twain meets the Wild West. You are not, of course, obliged to believe quite all of it.

*Clendenen, Clarence C. *Blood on the Border: The United States Army and the Mexican Irregulars*. New York: Macmillan, 1969.
Covers not only military action against Mexican bandits and/or revolutionaries up until and including the Pancho Villa era, but also Indian troubles complicated by the U.S.-Mexican border.

Coolidge, Dane. *Fighting Men of the West*. New York: E. P. Dutton, 1932.

Cunningham, Eugene. *Triggernometry: A Gallery of Gunfighters*. Caldwell, Idaho: Caxton Printers, 1941.

Custer, Elizabeth B. *"Boots and Saddles"; or, Life in Dakota with General Custer.* New York: Harper and Brothers, 1885.
Idealized reminiscences of the general by one who knew him best, or at any rate thought she did.

————. *Following the Guidon.* New York: Harper and Brothers, 1890.

*Custer, General George Armstrong. *My Life on the Plains; or, Personal Experiences with Indians.* Norman: University of Oklahoma Press, 1962.
A vivid narrative which tells us even more about the man who wrote it than about the events in which he participated. Complete with extensive musings on the "Indian problem."

———— (uncredited, with others). *Wild Life on the Plains and Horrors of Indian Warfare.* New York: Arno Press and The New York Times, 1969.
A facsimile reprint of a pirated 1891 edition of Custer's memoirs, to which are added various pieces of quaint Victorian writing (most of negligible reliability) on Indians, white heroes, and Wild West personalities. Includes the famous Nichols–Wild Bill interview sans byline and a magazine article by Custer on fighting the Sioux during the Yellowstone campaign of 1873.

"Custer's Last Stand." *Life*, December 8, 1941.

*Davis, Britton. *The Truth about Geronimo.* Edited by M. M. Quaife. New Haven, Conn.: Yale University Press, 1963.
A colorful first-hand narrative of the Apache wars by an officer who led Indian scouts during the 1880s and who concludes his book with a denunciation of General Miles's conduct toward the Apaches following their surrender.

Dalton, Emmett, and Jack Jungmeyer. *When the Daltons Rode.* New York: Doubleday, Doran and Co., 1931.

De Arment, Robert K. *Bat Masterson, The Man and the Legend.* Norman: University of Oklahoma Press, 1979.

De Mille, Cecil B. *Autobiography.* Edited by Donald Hayne. Englewood Cliffs, N.J.: Prentice-Hall, 1959.

*De Voto, Bernard. *Across the Wide Missouri: With an Account of the Discovery of the Miller Collection by Mae Reed Porter.* Boston: Houghton Mifflin, 1947.
The harsh romance of the mountain men and the Western fur trade in the first half of the nineteenth century.

————. "The Easy Chair." *Harper's*, December 8, 1955.

Dobie, J. Frank. *Cow People.* Boston: Little, Brown and Co., 1964.

————. *A Vaquero of the Brush Country.* Boston: Little, Brown and Co., 1929.

Downey, Fairfax, and Jacques Noel Jacobsen, Jr. *The Red-Bluecoats: The Indian Scouts.* Fort Collins, Colo.: Old Army Press, 1973.

Drago, Harry Sinclair. *Great American Cattle Trails: The Story of the Old Cow Paths of the East and the Longhorn Highways of the Plains.* New York: Dodd, Mead and Co., 1965.

Dunne, John Gregory. *The Studio.* New York: Farrar, Straus and Giroux, 1969.

Durham, Philip, and Everett L. Jones. *The Negro Cowboys.* New York: Dodd, Mead and Co., 1965.

Eyles, Allan. *The Western: An Illustrated Guide.* South Brunswick, N.J.: A. S. Barnes. 1967.

Fairchild, Hoxie Neale. *The Noble Savage: A Study in Romantic Naturalism*. New York: Columbia University Press, 1928.
Early depictions of the New World's aborigines and other idealized primitives as virtuous foils to civilized vice.

*Faulk, Odie B. *Dodge City: The Most Western Town of All*. New York: Oxford University Press, 1977.

*———. *The Geronimo Campaign*. New York: Oxford University Press, 1969.

*———. *Tombstone: Myth and Reality*. New York: Oxford University Press, 1972.
Faulk naturally devotes some time to the Earp myth and other violence, but is more interested in the everyday life of the mining town.

Fenin, George N., and William K. Everson. *The Western: From Silents to the Seventies*. New York: Grossman Publishers, 1973.
Perhaps the best general history of the Western, despite certain errors and a last chapter (by Mr. Fenin) that flies into spasms of trendy bleeding-art liberalism in discussing films such as *Little Big Man* and *Soldier Blue*.

Fiedler, Leslie A. *The Return of the Vanishing American*. Stein and Day, Briarcliff Manor N.Y.: 1968.
Concerned with Western literature rather than film, the author heralds a "New Western" breaking down all conventions of the form and calls for a spirit of "madness" in approaching the West; the author's definition of the "Western" is quite broad, encompassing any story containing an "Indian" or suitable nonwhite substitute. Fiedler's most notorious theory is undoubtedly that which proposes that the real love interest is between white hero and "colored" companion.

Fire, John/Lame Deer, and Richard Erdoes. *Lame Deer: Seeker of Visions*. New York: Simon and Schuster, 1972.

*Foster-Harris. *The Look of the Old West*. Illustrated by Evelyn Curro. New York: Bonanza Books, 1955.
An informal guide covering weapons, clothes civilian and military, and such oddments as chewing tobacco and watch fobs.

*Frantz, Joe B., and Julian E. Choate. *The American Cowboy: The Myth and the Reality*. Norman: University of Oklahoma Press, 1955.

Fraser, John. *Violence in The Arts*. London: Cambridge University Press, 1974.

*French, Philip. *Westerns: Aspects of a Movie Genre*. New York: Viking Press, 1974.
Looks at the Western's post–World War II maturity and its role as social and political allegory.

Friar, Ralph E. and Natasha A. *The Old Good Indian . . . The Hollywood Gospel*. New York: Drama Book Specialists/Publishers, 1972.

*Frost, Lawrence A. *The Court-Martial of General George Armstrong Custer*. Norman: University of Oklahoma Press, 1968.
An account of Custer's 1867 forced march and subsequent trial, by a leading Custer authority and fan. Should be supplemented by the less complimentary account in Hoig's *Battle of the Washita*.

Gelmis, Joseph. *The Film Director as Superstar*. Garden City, N.Y.: Doubleday, 1970.

Georgakas, Dan. "They Have Not Spoken: American Indians in Film." *Film Quarterly*, Spring 1972.

Gillett, James B. *Six Years with the Texas Rangers*. Edited by Milo Milton Quaife. Chicago: the Lakeside Press, 1943.

Glass, Major E. L. N., 10th Cavalry, ed. *The Tenth Cavalry 1866–1921*. Fort Collins, Colo.: Old Army Press, 1972.

*Graham, Colonel W. A. *The Custer Myth: A Sourcebook of Custeriana*. Harrisburg, Pa.: Stackpole Company, 1953.

———. *The Story of the Little Big Horn*. Harrisburg, Pa.: Stackpole, 1945.

Gregory, Dick. *No More Lies: The Myth and Reality of American History*. Edited by James R. McGraw. New York: Harper and Row, 1971.

*Grinnell, George Bird. *The Fighting Cheyennes*. Norman: University of Oklahoma Press, 1956.

Guns of the Gunfighters. Los Angeles: Peterson Publishing Co., 1975.

Gussow, Mel. *Don't Say Yes Until I Finish Talking: A Biography of Darryl F. Zanuck*. Garden City, N.Y.: Doubleday, 1971.

*Haley, James L. *The Buffalo War: The History of the Red River Indian Uprising of 1874*. Garden City, N.Y.: Doubleday, 1976.

Haley, J. Evetts. *Jeff Milton: A Good Man with a Gun*. Norman: University of Oklahoma Press, 1948.

Hardin, John Wesley. *The Life of John Wesley Hardin, as written by himself*. Norman: University of Oklahoma Press, 1961.
He never killed a man who didn't need it; or so he says here.

*Heizer, Robert F. *The Destruction of California Indians*. Layton, Utah: Peregrine Smith, 1974.

Hibbert, Christopher. *The Roots of Evil: A Social History of Crime and Punishment*. Boston: Little, Brown and Co., 1963.

*Hoig, Stan. *The Battle of the Washita: The Sheridan-Custer Indian Campaign of 1867–69*. Garden City, N.Y.: Doubleday, 1976.
Unfortunately marred by its presuppositions and anti-Custer bias, the book nevertheless contains much valuable information on the Washita campaign and Custer's irresponsible conduct on his 1867 forced march.

*Hollon, W. Eugene. *Frontier Violence: Another Look*. New York: Oxford University Press, 1974.
Devotes much time to the less romantic forms of mayhem (the persecution of Chinese, etc.) and the reasons for same, as well as to the more familiar violence which has become the standard material of the Western film.

*Horan, James D. *The Authentic Wild West: The Gunfighters*. New York: Crown Publishers, 1976.
With emphasis on period documents, this volume concentrates on notorious gunmen and killers such as Billy the Kid or Hickok; the author's *Outlaws* volume does the same for the more notorious bandits such as Jesse James and Butch Cassidy.

*———. *The Authentic Wild West: The Outlaws*. New York: Crown Publishers, 1977.

*———. *Desperate Men*. New York: G. P. Putnam's Sons, 1949.
The James-Youngers and the Wild Bunch well covered, with "only a few minor errors," according to Mr. Adams.

————, and Paul Sann. *Pictorial History of the Wild West*. New York: Crown Publishers, 1954.
Still in print, this history is appropriately skeptical of Western myths, but requires some updating in view of what is now generally known about certain individuals, especially Wyatt Earp.

Horowitz, James. *They Went Thataway*. New York: E. P. Dutton, 1976.
Asking where all the Saturday-matinee heroes of his youth have gone, the "Front Row Kid" embarks on a quest with stops at Dodge City and Tombstone, a tour of Roy Rogers's museum erected in honor of himself, and interviews with several venerable stars such as Joel McCrea.

Hunt, Frazier and Robert. *I Fought with Custer: The Story of Sergeant Windolph, Last Survivor of the Battle of the Little Bighorn*. New York: Scribner's, 1947.

Hyde, George E. *A Life of George Bent, Written from His Letters*. Edited by Savoie Lottinville. Norman: University of Oklahoma Press, 1968.

————. *The Pawnee Indians*. Norman: University of Oklahoma Press, 1973.

*Innes, Ben. *Bloody Knife! Custer's Favorite Scout*. Fort Collins, Colo.: Old Army Press, 1973.
The gory life of Custer's Arikara scout and comrade Bloody Knife, who died with Reno's detachment at the Little Bighorn. In one or two spots perhaps a bit too trusting of seemingly garbled or confused Indian accounts, but an excellent and unconventional book.

"It Was Only 75 Years Ago." *Life*, July 9, 1951.

*Jackson, Joseph Henry, *Bad Company*. New York: Harcourt, Brace and Co., 1949.
This carefully researched and entertaining history of early California bandits includes the author's important detective work on the "Joaquin" legend.

Jones, Douglas C. *The Court-Martial of George Armstrong Custer*. New York: Charles Scribner's Sons, 1976.

Kael, Pauline. *Deeper into Movies*. Boston: Little, Brown and Co., 1973.

————. *Kiss Kiss Bang Bang*. Boston: Little, Brown and Co., 1968.

Katz, William Loren. *The Black West: A Documentary and Pictorial History*. Garden City, N.Y.: Doubleday, 1971.

King, General Charles. *Campaigning with Crook*. Norman: University of Oklahoma Press, 1966.
Includes an eyewitness account of Buffalo Bill's duel with "Yellow Hand."

Kinsley, D. A. *Favor the Bold*. 2 vols. New York: Holt, Rinehart and Winston, 1967, 1968.

Kitses, Jim. *Horizons West*. Bloomington: Indiana University Press, 1969.

————. "The Rise and Fall of the American West." *Film Comment*, Winter 1970–71.
An interview with Borden Chase.

*Kuhlman, Charles. *Legend into History: The Custer Mystery. An Analytical Study of the Battle of the Little Big Horn*. Harrisburg, Pa.: Stackpole Company, Telegraph Press, 1951.

La Farge, Oliver. *A Pictorial History of the American Indian*. New York: Crown Publishers, 1959.

Lake, Stuart N. *Wyatt Earp, Frontier Marshal*. Boston: Houghton Mifflin, 1931.

Lasky, Jesse L., Jr. *Whatever Happened to Hollywood?* New York: Funk and Wagnalls, 1975.

Lawrence, D. H. *Studies in Classic American Literature*. New York: Viking, 1964.

Leab, Daniel J. *From Sambo to Superspade: The Black Experience in Motion Pictures*. Boston: Houghton Mifflin, 1975.

Leckie, William H. *The Buffalo Soldiers: A Narrative of the Negro Cavalry in the West*. Norman: University of Oklahoma Press, 1967.

*Leonard, Thomas C. "The Reluctant Conquerors: How the Generals Viewed the Indians." *American Heritage*, August 1976 (from an article originally published in the *American Quarterly*).

Lord, Walter. *A Time to Stand*. New York: Harper and Brothers, 1961.
    The story of the Alamo.

Lyon, Peter. *The Wild, Wild West*. New York: Funk and Wagnalls, 1969.
    An expansion of two articles published in *American Heritage* for August 1960. The author seems to take an unusually hostile stance against Westerns themselves and our all too human interest in the violence of the frontier as he debunks various "heroes."

*Mails, Thomas E. *The Mystic Warriors of the Plains*. Garden City, N.Y.: Doubleday, 1972.
    A beautifully illustrated book on the dress, customs, and warfare of the Plains Indians at the height of their power, between the introduction of European horses and the destruction of the Indians' life-style by the whites.

*Marshall, Brigadier General S.L.A., USAR. *Crimsoned Prairie: The Wars between the United States and the Plains Indians during the Winning of the West*.
    A respected military historian's narrative and analysis of major Indian campaigns and battles from the 1860s onward. Includes a "revisionist" theory on the Wounded Knee slaughter.

————. Edited by Cote Marshall. *Bringing Up the Rear: A Memoir*. San Rafael, Calif.: Presidio Press, 1979.

*Marquis, Thomas B. *Keep the Last Bullet for Yourself: The True Story of Custer's Last Stand*. New York: Two Continents Publishing Group, Reference Publications, 1976.

*———— (interpreter). *Wooden Leg: A Warrior Who Fought Custer*. Lincoln: University of Nebraska Press, n.d.
    Originally published in 1931 as *A Warrior Who Fought Custer*.

Marx, Samuel. *Mayer and Thalberg: The Make-Believe Saints*. New York: Random House, 1975.

McBride, Joseph, ed. *Focus on Howard Hawks*. Englewood Cliffs, N.J.: Prentice-Hall, 1972.

————, and Gerald Peary. "Hawks Talks." *Film Comment*, May–June 1974.

McCracken, Harold, ed. *Frederic Remington's Own West*. New York: Dial Press, 1960.

McEvoy, Henry K. *Knife Throwing: A Practical Guide*. Rutland, Vt.: Charles E. Tuttle Company, 1973.

Members of the Potomic Corral of the Westerners. *Great Western Indian Fights*. Lincoln: University of Nebraska Press, 1966.

*Merington, Marguerite, ed. *The Custer Story: The Life and Intimate Letters of General George Armstrong Custer and His Wife Elizabeth*. Old Greenwich, Conn.: Devin-Adair, 1950.

Miller, Floyd. *The Last Frontier Marshal*. Garden City, N.Y.: Doubleday, 1968.

*Miller, Nyle H., and Joseph W. Snell. *Great Gunfighters of the Kansas Cowtowns 1867–1886*. Lincoln: University of Nebraska Press, 1967.
A collection of contemporary newspaper accounts, condensed somewhat from the same team's *Why the West Was Wild*. Most of the twenty-one personalities covered were not particularly "great," but the book is no less interesting for all that.

Moley, Raymond. *The Hays Office*. Englewood, N.J.: Jerome S. Ozer, 1971.
A facsimile of the 1945 edition.

*Monoghan, Jay, ed. *The Book of the American West*. New York: Bonanza Books, 1960.
A heavily illustrated introduction to the subject, covering in separate sections various subjects such as guns, wildlife, Indian wars, cowboys, and law and order.

*———. *Custer: The Life of General George Armstrong Custer*. Boston: Little, Brown and Co., 1959.
Despite a tendency to add the occasional dramatic flourish and dialogue of somewhat mysterious origin, and rather too much pro-Custer bias, this has remained the best full-length biography of the Boy General, with a willingness to acknowledge some of Custer's faults lacking in the works of earlier devotees. The book actually covers his part in the Civil War better than his subsequent Indian campaigns, concerning which some controversies tend to be skimmed over rather lightly. (For a guide to Custer literature, see Tal Luther's *Custer High Spots*, published by the Old Army Press).

Mooney, James. *The Ghost-Dance Religion and the Sioux Outbreak of 1890*. Abridged, with an introduction by Anthony F. C. Wallace. Chicago: University of Chicago Press, 1965.
Chiefly an ethnological report, first published in 1896.

*Mullin, Robert N., ed. *Maurice Garland Fulton's History of the Lincoln County War*. Tucson: University of Arizona Press, 1968.

*Nachbar, Jack, ed. *Focus on the Western*. Englewood Cliffs, N.J.: Prentice-Hall, 1974.
An important collection of essays on the Western, which the editor considers "the single most important story form of the twentieth century."

Nash, Jay Robert. *Bloodletters and Badmen: A Narrative Encyclopedia of American Criminals from the Pilgrims to the Present*. New York: M. Evans and Co., Inc. Distributed by J. B. Lippincott, 1973.

O'Connor, Richard. *Bat Masterson*. Garden City, N.Y.: Doubleday, 1957.

———. *Pat Garrett*. Garden City, N.Y.: Doubleday, 1960.

Olsen, Theodore V. *Soldier Blue* (original title: *Arrow in the Sun*). New York: Dell, 1970.

Packer, James S. "It Don't Hurt Much, Ma'am." *American Heritage*, February 1971.
The effects of gunshot wounds on real Westerners.

Pointer, Larry. *In Search of Butch Cassidy*. Norman: University of Oklahoma Press, 1977.
The author's theory of Cassidy's survival puts forward a gory, allegedly autobiographical sketch by one William T. Philips, who died in Spokane, Washington, in 1937, as the work of the notorious Butch.

Raine, William MacLeod. *Famous Sheriffs and Western Outlaws*. New York: Doubleday, 1929.

Rascoe, Burton. *Belle Starr: "The Bandit Queen."* New York: Random House, 1941.

Richards, Jeffrey. *Visions of Yesterday*. London: Routledge and Kegan Paul, 1973.
Discourses on the cinema of American populism, British imperialism, and the Third Reich.

*Rickey, Don. *Forty Miles a Day on Beans and Hay: The Enlisted Soldier Fighting the Indian Wars*. Norman: University of Oklahoma Press, 1963.
Largely based on interviews with hundreds of aged Indian Wars veterans, the book re-creates in great detail the conditions under which the soldiers of the tiny Regular Army helped win the West.

Ringgold, Gene, and DeWitt Bodeen. *The Films of Cecil B. DeMille*. Secaucus, N.J.: Citadel Press, 1969.

*Roberts, Gary L. "The West's Gunmen," parts I and II. In *The American West*, January and March 1971.
Observations on both legend-making and legend-breaking writings.

*Rosa, Joseph G. *The Gunfighter: Man or Myth?* Norman: University of Oklahoma. Press, 1969.

*———. *They Called Him Wild Bill: The Life and Adventures of James Butler Hickok*. Norman: University of Oklahoma Press, 1974.
The best biography of Hickok, meticulously researched. A revision of the 1964 edition. The author might have gone into somewhat greater detail in responding to criticisms of Hickok as lawman.

Rosenberg, Bruce A. *Custer and the Epic of Defeat*. University Park: Pennsylvania State University Press, 1974.
The psychological and historical factors which molded the raw fact of Custer's defeat into the classic myth of the Last Stand. (Incidentally, Mr. Rosenberg is mistaken in saying that the famous photograph of the Iwo Jim flag-raising was posed. Just shows how well *anti*-heroic myths may survive.)

Russell, Don. "How Many Indians Were Killed? White Man versus Red Man: The Facts and the Legend." *The American West*, July 1973.

*———. *The Lives and Legends of Buffalo Bill*. Norman: University of Oklahoma Press, 1960.
The essential life of Cody, which, unfortunately, appears to have escaped the notice of many subsequent debunkers.

Sandoz, Mari. *Cheyenne Autumn*. New York: Hastings House, 1953.

Schaefer, Jack. *Heroes without Glory: Some Goodmen of the Old West*. Boston: Houghton-Mifflin, 1965.
The author of *Shane* attempts to honor some individual unsung heroes of the West, from bear hunters to Indian agents. However, listing Chisum as a "goodman" may seem questionable to some, as might Schaefer's uncritical acceptance of some tales about the well-known Elfago Baca.

Schickel, Richard. *The Men Who Made the Movies: Interviews with Frank Capra, George Cukor, Howard Hawks, Alfred Hitchcock, Vincente Minnelli, King Vidor, Raoul Walsh, and William A. Wellman*. New York: Atheneum, 1975.

Sell, Henry Blackman, and Victor Weybright. *Buffalo Bill and the Wild West*. New York: Oxford University Press, 1955.

*Settle, William A. *Jesse James Was His Name; or Fact and Fiction Concerning the Careers of the Notorious James Brothers of Missouri*. Columbia: University of Missouri Press, 1966.
This study devotes considerable attention to the creation, sustenance, and growth of the James myth as well as to the gang's actual exploits.

Sherman, Eric, and Martin Rubin. *The Directors' Event: Interviews with Five American Film-Makers*. New York: Atheneum, 1970.

*Shirley, Glenn. *Henry Starr, Last of the Real Badmen*. New York: David McKay, 1965.

Smith, Gene and Jane Barry. *The Police Gazette*. New York: Simon and Schuster, 1972.

Smith, Helena Huntington. "Sam Bass and the Myth Machine." *The American West*, January 1970.

*Smith, Henry Nash. *Virgin Land: The American West as Symbol and Myth*. Cambridge, Mass.: Harvard University Press, 1950.

Sonnichsen, C. L. *Roy Bean, Law West of the Pecos*. New York: Macmillan, 1943.

———. "The West That Wasn't." *The American West*, November–December 1977.

———. "The Wyatt Earp Syndrome." *The American West*, May 1970.

———, and William V. Morrison. *Alias Billy the Kid*. Albuquerque: University of New Mexico Press, 1955.

*Stands in Timber, John, and Margot Liberty, with the Assistance of Robert M. Utley. *Cheyenne Memories*. New Haven, Conn.: Yale University Press, 1967.

*Steckmesser, Kent Ladd. *The Western Hero in History and Legend*. Norman: University of Oklahoma Press, 1965.
A major work setting forth in concise form the lives and mythic development of Kit Carson, Hickok, Billy the Kid, and George Armstrong Custer, and attempting to explain the whys and wherefores of their deification.

Steiner, Stan. *The New Indians*. New York: Harper and Row, 1968.

*Stewart, Edgar I. *Custer's Luck*. Norman: University of Oklahoma Press, 1955.
A leading account of the Little Bighorn fight.

Terrell, John Upton, and Colonel George Walton. *Faint the Trumpet Sounds: The Life and Trial of Major Reno*. New York: David McKay, 1966.
A biography and attempted defense of Reno. Pretty bad on both counts.

Thomas, Bob. *Thalberg: Life and Legend*. Garden City, N.Y.: Doubleday, 1969.

Thomas, Tony, Rudy Behlmer and Clifford McCarty. *The Films of Errol Flynn*. Secaucus, N.J.: Citadel, 1969.

Thompson, Richard. "Stoked." *Film Comment*, July–August 1976.
John Milius interviewed.

*Thrapp, Daniel L. *The Conquest of Apacheria*. Norman: University of Oklahoma Press, 1967.
A blood-soaked, comprehensive history of the Apache wars.

Tilghman, Zoe A. *Marshal of the Last Frontier*. Arthur H. Clark, 1949.

*Tuska, Jon. *The Filming of the West*. Garden City, N.Y.: Doubleday, 1976.
A big, fascinating book combining a history of the Western film and its stars with interviews and a few vignettes of life on Western film sets.

*Utley, Robert M. *Frontier Regulars: The United States Army and The Indian 1865–1891*. New York: Macmillan, 1973.

*————. *Frontiersmen in Blue: The United States Army and the Indian 1848–1865*. New York: Macmillan, 1967.
This book and its sequel make up an invaluable study of the "Indian problem" as encountered by the military establishment.

————. *The Last Days of the Sioux Nation*. New Haven, Conn.: Yale University Press, 1963.

————, ed. *Life in Custer's Cavalry: Diaries and Letters of Albert and Jennie Barnitz 1867–68*. New Haven, Conn.: Yale University Press, 1977.
An officer's-eye view of Custer as military tyrant, together with other observations on Army life.

*Van de Water, Frederic F. *Glory-Hunter: A Life of General Custer*. Indianapolis, Ind.: Bobbs-Merrill, 1934.

Vidor, King. *King Vidor on Film Making*. New York: David McKay, 1972.

Wagner, Geoffrey. *Parade of Pleasure: A Study of Popular Iconography in the USA*. Library Publishers, 1955.

Walsh, Richard J., in collaboration with Milton S. Salsbury. *The Making of Buffalo Bill: A Study in Heroics*. Indianapolis, Ind.: Bobbs-Merrill, 1928.
Attempts to provide the necessary alternative to the ridiculous myths then surrounding Cody, but lacks adequate probing into Cody's early days as a scout.

Walsh, Raoul. *Each Man In His Time: The Life Story of a Director*. New York: Farrar, Straus and Giroux, 1974.

Warshow, Robert. *The Immediate Experience: Comics, Theatre, and Other Aspects of Popular Culture*. New York: Atheneum, 1970.

*Waters, Frank. *The Earp Brothers of Tombstone: The Story of Mrs. Virgil Earp*. New York: Clarkson N. Potter, 1960.

*Webb, Walter Prescott. *The Great Plains*. Lexington, Mass.: Ginn and Co., 1931.

*————. *The Texas Rangers: A Century of Frontier Defense*. Boston: Houghton Mifflin, 1935.

Wellman, Paul I. *A Dynasty of Western Outlaws*. Garden City, N.Y.: Doubleday, 1961.

————. *The Indian Wars of the West*. Garden City, N.Y.: Doubleday, 1954.
Previously published as *Death on Horseback* in 1947, combining books on the Plains and Apache wars, *Death on the Prairie*, 1934, and *Death in the Desert*, 1935.

Wilk, Max. *The Wit and Wisdom of Hollywood—From the Squaw Man to the Hatchet Man*. New York: Atheneum, 1971.

Wilstach, Frank J. *Wild Bill Hickok, Prince of Pistoleers*. New York: Doubleday and Page, 1926.

Wister, Owen. *The Virginian: A Horseman of the Plains*. New York: Macmillan, 1925.

Womack, John. *Zapata and the Mexican Revolution*. New York: Alfred A. Knopf, 1969.

Wood, Michael. *America in the Movies; or "Santa Maria, It Had Slipped My Mind."* New York: Basic Books, 1975.

Zolotow, Maurice. *Shooting Star: A Biography of John Wayne*. New York: Simon and Schuster, 1974.

Index

Italicized page numbers denote illustrations.